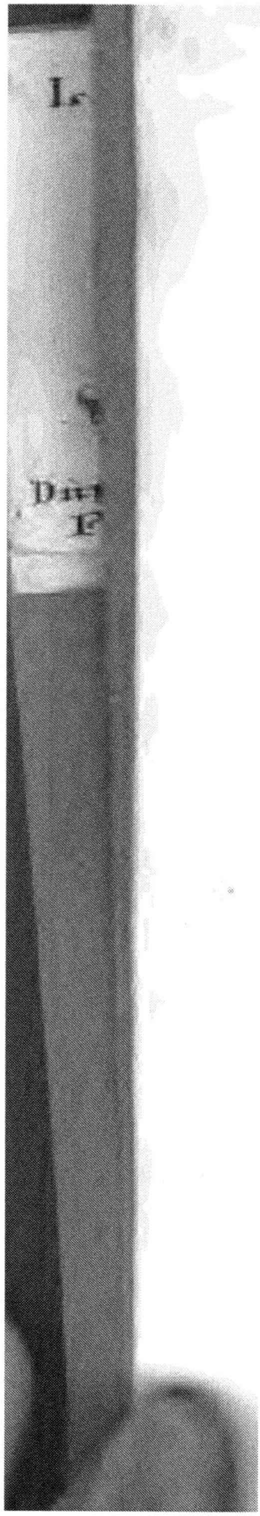

Library of Old Authors.

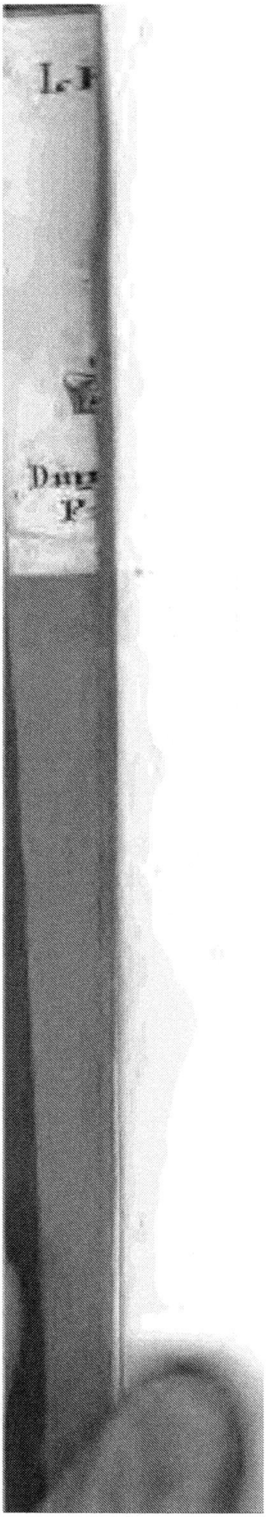

THE COMPLETE WORKS OF RICHARD CRASHAW,

CANON OF LORETTO.

EDITED BY

WILLIAM B. TURNBULL, ESQ.

OF LINCOLN'S INN, BARRISTER AT LAW.

LONDON:

JOHN RUSSELL SMITH,

SOHO SQUARE.

1858.

TO THE

VERY REV. MARK ALOYSIUS TIERNEY,

CANON OF ST. GEORGE'S, SOUTHWARK,

F.R.S., F.S.A.,

ETC.

THIS SMALL VOLUME

IS AFFECTIONATELY INSCRIBED BY ITS EDITOR, IN ACKNOWLEDGEMENT OF THE VIRTUES, THE TALENTS, AND THE INDEPENDENCE WHICH DISTINGUISH HIM AS A PRIEST, A SCHOLAR, AND A GENTLEMAN.

PRELIMINARY OBSERVATIONS.

OF Richard Crashaw, whose works are comprised in the ensuing pages, little is known; and for that little we are mainly beholden to the industry of Wood, upon whose curt notice in the *Fasti Oxonienses* was founded the more elabórate memoir by Hayley in Kippis' edition of the *Biographia Britannica*, which served as the sole unvaried authority until the subject was treated by the Rev. Robert Aris Willmott in the first series of *Lives of the English Sacred Poets*. Both in the records of those educational establishments where, in his youth, he was trained, and of that holy retreat in which he closed his maturer years, have searches been fruitlessly made, in the hope that some additional fact, however minute, might be discovered. I am, therefore, obliged to recapitulate in few words what is already familiar to every one; referring the reader to the elegant and more copious sketch by Mr. Willmott.

According to the scanty sources of information, Crashaw was the son of William Crashaw, B. D., a divine of some eminence in his time,* and preacher at the Temple. The date of his birth has not been ascertained, but it may have been about 1616; since, the first steps of his education having been taken at the Charter-house, on the foundation of which he was placed by Sir Randolph Crew and Sir Henry Yelverton, he was elected a scholar of Pembroke Hall, Cambridge, March 26, 1632, and became a Fellow of Peterhouse in the same University, in 1637; having removed to that College on the 20th of March previous. His Bachelor's degree was taken in 1633. In 1641 he is recorded by Wood as one of the persons incorporated that year at Oxford; but to what degree admitted is not stated, as his name does not appear in the public register, and Wood's authority was "the private observation of a certain Master of Arts, that was, this year, living in the University." Wood, however, adds:—"Afterwards, he was Master of Arts, in which degree it is probable he was incorporated." Beyond these features of his academical career, we are certain of nothing save of its termination; which happened during the Great Rebellion in 1644, when the Earl of Manchester, under the authority of Parliament, "reformed" (as they were pleased to style it) the University, by expelling such members as refused to subscribe the Covenant. On this occasion Crashaw was one of the sixty-five Fellows ejected. After the loss of his fellowship, having embraced the

* The tone of his religious sentiments, very different from those of his son, may be gathered from the titles of his printed discourses; *e. g.* "The Bespotted Jesuite: whose Gospell is full of blasphemy against the Blood of Christ," &c., 1641, 4to.

Catholic religion, he repaired to Paris: and in this city he was found by Cowley in a state of destitution, about 1646. To the friendship of this amiable brother-poet he was indebted for sympathy and relief, and an introduction to the exiled queen, Henrietta Maria, from whom he also received what small aid her own limited finances would allow, with recommendatory letters to persons of influence at Rome. There he is said to have become secretary to Cardinal Palotta, and soon thereafter to have been appointed one of the Canons of the Church of Loretto. This preferment he only held for a very short space; dying and being interred at Loretto about 1650. Such is the faint outline of his life.

Among the patrons of Crashaw, in his altered circumstances, the Countess of Denbigh appears to have been prominent. His gratitude is expressed by his dedication to her of the *Carmen Deo Nostro*, " in hearty acknowledgement of his immortal obligation to her goodness and charity," and by his efforts to bring her within the pale of the Catholic Church. Whether they were successful or not I cannot ascertain. This lady was Elizabeth, daughter and coheir of Edward Bourchier, Earl of Bath, and third of the four wives of Basil, second Earl of Denbigh, whom she predeceased in 1670. I had hoped to have found some traces of Crashaw among the archives at Newnham Paddox; but Viscount Fielding, having kindly directed a search to be made, informs me that no document relating to him exists there.

Our ideas of the personal character of Crashaw must be formed from his writings, the enthusiastic affection of Cowley, and the friendship of Selden. To the fo of such sources the editor of the edition of 1649 j points, while referring to the last line of his verse Bishop Andrews' portrait:—

"Look on the following leaves, and see him breathe.

The qualities which recommended him to the estee two such men as those now named, can have been c common order, and make the absence of materials his biography the more truly to be deplored.

As a poet, his works have ever been appreciated those most qualified to decide upon their sterling be ties,* and have suggested to others (too frequently wi out acknowledgment) some of their finest imageries. every volume of any pretensions to taste, designed offer specimens of English poetry, extracts are to found; yet, with the exception of being partially, a by no means accurately, printed in the bulky and i convenient collections of Chalmers and Anderson, it somewhat remarkable that, in an age when familiar with our Old English Authors is so eagerly sought, full reprint should have been deferred till now. (those which have preceded it, the following is a list:-

Epigrammata Sacra, published anonymously at Cam bridge, 1634, 8vo.

Steps to the Temple, London, 1646, 12mo.

The same, with additions and a frontispiece, Londo 1648, 12mo.

Carmen Deo Nostro, Paris, 1652, 8vo. with beautifu plates.

* Among such I would particularly name the Rev. Robert Aris Willmott, above mentioned.

Lines to Lady Denbigh (p. 146 of the present edition), London, Sept. 23, 1653, 4to. pp. 4.

Steps to the Temple, London, 1649, 8vo. with frontispiece. To this second edition, in its text the most inaccurate of all, a fresh title-page, bearing the date of 1670, was afterwards affixed.

Poetry, by Peregrine Phillips, London, 1785, 12mo.

All these are very scarce, that of Paris extremely so. I have already commended its illustrations, and, as it would seem, from the epigram at p. 145 *seq.*, that they had been designed by Crashaw, a list of them may not be deemed superfluous, in order as they appear in the elegant little volume from the press of "Peter Targa, printer to the Archbishope of Paris, in S. Victor's streete at the golden sunne." A copy of this produced £4 14*s*. 6*d*. at Sir Mark Sykes' sale in 1824, and would, if in fair condition, command a much higher price now. That in the Grenville Library is, perhaps, the finest in existence.

1. "To the noblest and best of ladies." A heart with padlock inscribed "*Non Vi.*" Beneath, these lines:—

> 'Tis not the work of force but skill
> To find the way into man's will;
> 'Tis love alone can hearts unlock:
> Who knows the word, he needs not knock.

2. "To the name above every name,"—"*Numisma Urbani* 6." A dove under the tiara, surrounded by a glory: legend, "*In unitate Deus est.*"

3. "To the Holy Nativity." The Holy Family at Bethlehem. Beneath, these lines:—

> Ton Créateur te faict voir sa naissance,
> Deignant souffrir pour toy des son enfance.
> Quem vidistis Pastores, &c.
> Natum vidimus, &c.

4. " To the glorious Epiphany." The adoration the Magi.

5. " The Office of the Holy Cross." The crucifi Redeemer. Beneath :—

> Tradidit semetipsum pro nobis oblationem et hostiam Deo in odorem suavitatis.—*Ad Ephe.* 5.

6. " The Recommendation." The Ascended Saviou Above it :—

> Expostulatio Jesu Christi cum mundo ingrato.

Beneath :—

> Sum pulcher : at nemo tamen me diligit.
> Sum nobilis : nemo est mihi qui serviat.
> Sum dives : a me nemo quicquam postulat.
> Et cuncta possum : nemo me tamen timet.
> Æternus exsto : quæror a paucissimis.
> Prudensque sum : sed me qui est qui consulit ?
> Et sum Via : at per me quotusquisque ambulet ?
> Sum Veritas : quare mihi non creditur.
> Sum Vita : verum rarus est qui me petit.
> Sum Vera Lux : videre me nemo cupit.
> Sum misericors : nullus fidem in me collocat.
> Tu, si peris, non id mihi imputes, Homo :
> Salus tibi est a me parata : hac utere.
>
> *I. Messager excud.*

7. " Sancta Maria Dolorum." The Blessed Virgin seated on a sepulchre under the Cross with instruments of the passion, the chalice, &c., holding the dead Saviour on her lap. *Messager excud.*

8. " Hymn of St. Thomas." A Remonstrance. " *Ecce panis Angelorum.*"

9. " Dies Iræ." The last Judgment. " *Dies Iræ, Dies Illa.*"

10. "O Gloriosa Domina." Our Lady and Infant. Angels holding a crown over her head, surmounted by the Holy Dove. Beneath:—

> S. Maria Major.
> Dilectus meus mihi et ego illi,
> Qui pascitur inter lilia. Cant.
> *I. Messager excud.*

11. "The Weeper." A weeping female resting upon a bleeding and inflamed heart, surrounded by a glory. Beneath:—

> Lo, where a wounded heart with bleeding eyes conspire!
> Is she a flaming fountain or a weeping fire?

12. "Hymn to St. Teresa." Portrait, scroll over her head inscribed: "*Misericors Domini in æternum cantabo.*" Beneath:—

> La Vray Portraict de Ste. Terese Fondatrice des Religieuses, et Religieux réformez de l'ordre de N. Dame de mont Carmel: Decedée le 4e: Octo. 1582. Canonisée le 12e. Mars 1622.—*I. Messager excud.*

The volume concludes with "Hope" by Cowley, and "M. Crashaw's Answer for Hope," separately, and not combined, as usual, in form of dialogue.

After the sheets containing them had been printed off, a correspondent of the "Notes and Queries" (the Rev. J. L. B. Major, in 2nd series, vol. IV. p. 286) pointed out, on the authority of Banks' Life of Dr. Rainbow, Bishop of Carlisle, that the first of the two poems, "On the Frontispiece of Isaacson's Chronology explained," beginning, "If with distinctive eye and mind you look," was written, not by Crashaw, but by

Rainbow. Upon referring to this very scarce little volume, I find the following:—

"In his youth he had a rich vein in poesy, in which appeared somewhat of Ovid's air and fancy, tempered with the judgment of Virgil; but none of his poetical exercises and diversions have been published, but a paper of verses upon the Frontispiece of Mr. Henry Isaacson's Chronology, which accurate Chronologer was our Bishop's particular friend, and had formerly been amanuensis to that living library while he was alive, the reverend and learned Bishop Andrews; and another short paper on Mr. Skelton's Art of Short-writing.

"Of the honour of the former of these poems, printed without the addition of any name in 1633, he was robbed by the publisher of Mr. Richard Crashaw's poems, entituled *Steps to the Temple,* and ascribed by him to that ingenious epigrammatist. But he having no title to it, but what the modest silence of Mr. Rainbow gave him, I have recovered it to the true owner by a *melius inquirendum,* and subjoined it here."—*P.* 84.

This is sufficiently distinct; yet it is somewhat singular that the lines should neither have been claimed by the Bishop, nor disowned by Crashaw, who must have seen, if he did not superintend, at least one of the editions of his own poems containing them; and that no one during the life of either party should have detected and denounced the misappropriation. Isaacson died in 1656, four years after Crashaw; and Dr. Rainbow in 1684, his biography by Banks being published in 1688. If Banks is correct as regards the first of these complimentary effusions, the second may, perhaps, have as little right to be attributed to Crashaw, both being printed without name or initials. The latter alone, it may be observed, has been printed by Phillips in his volume of selections in 1785.*

In preparing the present edition, the first that contains the whole of Crashaw's writings known, I have carefully examined and collated all the earlier ones. To their proper places in the *Epigrammata* I have restored those portions which had erratically entered into the different editions of the *Delights of the Muses;* and I have added to that division of the present volume the verses "Upon two green apricocks;" printing by themselves the Latin poems which follow them in the edition of 1648. While refraining from the practice of cumbering the pages with various readings, I have endeavoured to render the text with due accuracy; and if in this I shall anywise be found to have failed, at all events I have prepared the ground for some future more competent editor.

These brief observations cannot be concluded more appropriately than by the beautiful monody of Cowley upon his friend and fellow-poet.

ON THE DEATH OF MR. CRASHAW.

Poet and Saint! to thee alone are given
The two most sacred names of earth and heaven;
The hardest, rarest, union which can be,†
Next that of Godhead and humanity.

---

* Among the other commendatory verses prefixed to Isaacson's work are some by Mr. Staninough, upon whose death the lines at p. 104 were composed by Crashaw.

† As judiciously amended by Mr. Willmott, instead of "The *hard and* rarest."

Long did the Muses banish'd slaves abide,
And built vain pyramids to mortal pride:
Like Moses thou (tho' spells and charms withstand)
Hast brought them nobly home, back to their holy la

Ah, wretched we, Poets of earth! but thou
Wert living the same Poet which thou'rt now;
Whilst angels sing to thee their airs divine,
And joy in an applause so great as thine.
Equal society with them to hold,
Thou need'st not make new songs, but say the old;
And they (kind spirits!) shall all rejoice to see,
How little less than they, exalted man may be.

Still the old heathen gods in numbers dwell,
The heavenliest thing on earth still keeps up hell:
Nor have we yet quite purg'd the Christian land;
Still idols here, like calves at Bethel stand.
And tho' Pan's death long since all or'cles broke,
Yet still in rhyme the fiend Apollo spoke;
Nay, with the worst of heathen dotage, we
(Vain men!) the monster woman deifie;
Find stars, and tie our fates there in a face,
And Paradise in them, by whom we lost it, place.
What diff'rent faults corrupt our muses thus?
Wanton as girls, as old wives fabulous.

Thy spotless muse, like Mary, did contain
The boundless Godhead; she did well disdain
That her eternal verse employed should be
On a less subject than eternity;
And for a sacred mistress scorn'd to take
But her whom God himself scorn'd not his spouse to make:
It (in a kind) her miracle did do,
A fruitful mother was, and virgin too.

How well (blest Swan) did fate contrive thy death,
And made thee render up thy tuneful breath
In thy great mistress' arms? Thou most divine,
And richest offering of Loretto's shrine!
Where, like some holy sacrifice t' expire,
A fever burns thee and love lights the fire.

Angels (they say) brought the fam'd chapel there,
And bore the sacred load in triumph thro' the air:
'Tis surer much they brought thee there; and they,
And thou, their charge, went singing all the way.

Pardon, my mother Church, if I consent
That angels led him, when from thee he went;
For ev'n in error, sure no danger is,
When join'd with so much piety as his.
Ah! mighty God, with shame I speak't, and grief;
Ah! that our greatest faults were in belief!
And our weak reason were ev'n weaker yet,
Rather than thus, our will's too strong for it!
His faith, perhaps, in some nice tenets might
Be wrong; his life, I'm sure, was in the right:
And I, myself, a Catholic will be;
So far at least, great Saint! to pray to thee.

Hail, Bard triumphant! and some care bestow
On us, the Poets militant below:
Oppos'd by our old enemy, adverse Chance,
Attack'd by Envy and by Ignorance;
Enchain'd by Beauty, tortured by desires,
Expos'd by Tyrant-love, to savage beasts and fires.
Thou from low earth in nobler flames didst rise,
And like Elijah mount alive the skies.
Elisha like (but with a wish much less,
More fit thy greatness and my littleness;)
Lo here I beg (I whom thou once didst prove
So humble to esteem, so good to love)
Not that thy spirit might on me doubled be,
I ask but half thy mighty spirit for me:
And when my muse soars with so strong a wing,
'Twill learn of things divine, and first of thee to sing.*

W. B. Turnbull.

Lincoln's-Inn.
Feb. 1858.

---

* In these verses, says Johnson, "there are beauties which common authors may justly think not only above their attainment, but above their ambition."

NOTE.

Since the completion of the text, I have been annoy by discovering that the lines " On a Treatise of Charity at page 77, were originally prefixed to the " Five Poen and Learned Discourses " of Robert Shelford, Rector Ringsfield, Suffolk, 4to. Cambridge, 1635; and th the following lines have been left out in the editions Crashaw's Poems. The reason for such omission i obvious. Should a second impression of this volume b required, they shall be inserted in their proper place but it must be admitted that, however just the sentimen expressed in them, the subtraction of these lines doe not impair the beauty of the poem.

Nor shall our zealous ones still have a fling
At that most horrible and horned thing,
Forsooth the Pope: by which black name they call
The Turk, the Devil, Fairies, Hell and all,
And something more. O he is Antichrist:
Doubt this, and doubt (say they) that Christ is Christ.
Why, 'tis a point of faith. Whate'er it be,
I'm sure it is no point of charity.
In sum, no longer shall our people hope,
To be a true Protestant, 's but to hate the Pope.

PREFACE TO THE ORIGINAL EDITION.

LEARNED READER,

THE author's friend will not usurp much upon thy eye; this is only for those whom the name of our divine poet hath not yet seized into admiration; I dare undertake that what Jamblichus (*in vita Pythagoræ*) affirmeth of his master at his contemplations—these poems can; viz. they shall lift thee, reader, some yards above the ground; and as in Pythagoras' school every temper was first tuned into a height by several portions of music, and spiritualized for one of his weighty lectures, so mayest thou take a poem hence, and tune thy soul by it into a heavenly pitch; and thus refined and borne up upon the wings of meditation, in these poems thou mayest talk freely of God, and of that other state.

Here's Herbert's second, but equal, who hath retrieved poetry of late, and returned it up to its primitive use; let it bound back to Heaven's gates whence it came. Think ye St. Augustine would have stained his graver learning with a book of poetry, had he fancied their dearest end to be the vanity of love-sonnets and epithalamiums? No, no! he thought, with this our poet, that every foot in a high-born verse might help to measure the soul into that better world. Divine poetry; I dare hold it, in position against Suarez on the subject, to be the language of the angels; it is the quintessence of phantasy and discourse centred in Heaven; 'tis the very outgoings of the soul; 'tis what alone our author is able to tell you, and that in his own verse.

It were profane but to mention here in the preface those under-headed poets, retainers to seven shares and a half; madrigal fellows, whose only business in verse is to rhyme a poor sixpenny soul, a suburb sinner, into hell. May such arrogant pretenders to poetry vanish with their prodigious issue of tumorous heats and flashes of their adulterate brains; and for ever after may this our poet fill up the better room of man! Oh! when the general arraignment of poets shall be to give an account of their higher souls, with what a triumphant brow shall our divine poet sit above and look down upon poor Homer, Virgil, Horace, Claudian, &c. who had amongst them the ill luck to talk out a great part of their gallant genius upon bees, dung, frogs, and gnats, &c. and not as himself here, upon Scriptures, divine graces, martyrs, and angels!

Reader, we style his Sacred Poems, "Steps to the Temple," and aptly, for in the Temple of God, under His wing, he led his life in St. Mary's Church, near St. Peter's college; there he lodged under Tertullian's roof of angels; there he made his nest more gladly than David's swallow near the house of God: where, like a primitive saint, he offered more prayers in the night than others usually offer in the day. There he penned these poems,—steps for happy souls to climb Heaven by.

And those other of his pieces, entitled, "The Delights of the Muses," though of a more human mixture, are as sweet as they are innocent.

The praises that follow are but few of many that might be conferred on him: he was excellent in five languages (besides his mother-tongue), viz. Hebrew, Greek, Latin, Italian, Spanish, the two last whereof he had little help in; they were of his own acquisition.

Amongst his other accomplishments in academic (as well pious as harmless) arts, he made his skill in poetry, music, drawing, limning, graving, (exercises of his curious invention and sudden fancy,) to be but his subservient recreations for vacant hours, not the grand business of his soul.

To the former qualifications I might add that which would crown them all: his rare moderation in diet—almost Lessian temperance; he never created a Muse out of distempers, nor, with our Canary scribblers, cast any strange mists of surfeits before the intellectual beams of his mind or memory; the latter of which he was so much a master of, that he had there, under lock and key in readiness, the richest treasures of the best Greek and Latin poets, some of which authors he had more at his command by heart than others that only read their works to retain little and understand less.

Enough, reader; I intend not a volume of praises larger than this book, nor need I longer transport thee to think over his vast perfections. I will conclud that I have impartially writ of this learned young gei man, now dead to us, as he himself doth, with the line of his poem upon Bishop Andrews' picture be his sermons:—

Verte paginas.

Look on the following leaves, and see him breathe.

The Author's Motto.

Live, Jesus, live, and let it be
My life to die for love of Thee.

CONTENTS.

STEPS TO THE TEMPLE.

THE DELIGHTS OF THE MUSES.

SACRED POEMS.

POEMATA LATINA.

EPIGRAMMATA SACRA.

THE WEEPER.

HAIL sister springs,
Parents of silver-footed rills!
Ever bubbling things!
Thawing crystal! Snowy hills!
Still spending, never spent; I mean
Thy fair eyes, sweet Magdalene.

Heavens thy fair eyes be;
Heavens of ever-falling stars;
'Tis seed-time still with thee,
And stars thou sow'st, whose harvest dares
Promise the earth to countershine
Whatever makes Heaven's forehead fine.

But we're deceived all:
Stars indeed they are too true,
For they but seem to fall
As Heaven's other spangles do:
It is not for our earth and us,
To shine in things so precious.

Upwards thou dost weep;
Heaven's bosom drinks the gentle stream.
Where the milky rivers creep,
Thine floats above and is the cream.
Waters above the heavens, what they be,
We are taught best by thy tears and thee.

Every morn from hence,
A brisk cherub something sips,
Whose soft influence
Adds sweetness to his sweetest lips;
Then to his music: and his song
Tastes of this breakfast all day long.

Not in the evening's eyes,
When they red with weeping are
For the Sun that dies,
Sits Sorrow with a face so fair.
Nowhere but here did ever meet
Sweetness so sad, sadness so sweet.

When Sorrow would be seen
In her brightest majesty,
For she is a queen,
Then is she drest by none but thee.
Then, and only then, she wears
Her richest pearls, I mean thy tears.

The dew no more will weep,
The primrose's pale cheek to deck;
The dew no more will sleep,

Nuzzled in the lily's neck.
Much rather would it tremble here,
And leave them both to be thy tear.

There is no need at all,
That the balsam-sweating bough
So coyly should let fall
His med'cinable tears; for now
Nature hath learnt t'extract a dew,
More sovereign and sweet from you.

Yet let the poor drops weep,
Weeping is the case of woe;
Softly let them creep,
Sad that they are vanquish'd so;
They, though to others no relief,
May balsam be for their own grief.

Such the maiden gem
By the wanton spring put on,
Peeps from her parent stem,
And blushes on the watery sun:
This watery blossom of thy eyne
Ripe, will make the richer wine.

When some new bright guest
Takes up among the stars a room,
And Heaven will make a feast,
Angels with crystal vials come;
And draw from these full eyes of thine
Their Master's water, their own wine.

Golden though he be,
Golden Tagus murmurs; though
Were his way by thee,
Content and quiet he would go;
So much more rich would he esteem
Thy silver, than his golden stream.

Well does the May that lies
Smiling in thy cheeks, confess
The April in thine eyes;
Mutual sweetness they express.
No April e'er lent kinder showers,
Nor May return'd more faithful flowers.

O cheeks! Beds of chaste loves,
By your own showers seasonably dash'd.
Eyes! nests of milky doves,
In your own wells decently wash'd.
O wit of love! that thus could place
Fountain and garden in one face.

O sweet contest; of woes
With loves, of tears with smiles disporting!
O fair and friendly foes,
Each other kissing and comforting!
While rain and sunshine, cheeks and eyes,
Close in kind contrarieties.

But can these fair floods be
Friends with the bosom fires that fill ye!
Can so great flames agree

Eternal tears should thus distil thee!
O floods, O fires, O suns, O showers!
Mix'd and made friends by love's sweet pow'rs.

'Twas his well-pointed dart
That digg'd these wells, and dress'd this vine;
And taught that wounded heart
The way into these weeping eyne.
Vain loves avaunt! bold hands forbear!
The lamb hath dipped his white foot here.

And now where'er he strays
Among the Galilean mountains,
Or more unwelcome ways,
He's follow'd by two faithful fountains;
Two walking baths, two weeping motions,
Portable and compendious oceans.

O thou, thy Lord's fair store,
In thy so rich and large expenses,
Even when he show'd most poor,
He might provoke the wealth of princes.
What prince's wanton'st pride e'er could
Wash with silver, wipe with gold?

Who is that King, but he
Who call'st his crown to be call'd thine,
That thus can boast to be
Waited on by a wand'ring mine,—
A voluntary mint, that strews
Warm silver show'rs where'er he goes?

O precious prodigal!
Fair spendthrift of thyself! thy measure,
Merciless love! is all
Even to the last pearl in thy treasure.
All places, times, and objects be
Thy tear's sweet opportunity.

Does the day-star rise?
Still thy stars do fall, and fall;
Does day close his eyes?
Still the fountain weeps for all.
Let night or day do what they will,
Thou hast thy task, thou weepest still.

Does thy song lull the air?
Thy falling tears keep faithful time.
Does thy sweet-breath'd pray'r
Up in clouds of incense climb?
Still at each sigh, that is, each stop,
A bead, that is, a tear, does drop.

At these thy weeping gates,
Watching their wat'ry motion,
Each winged moment waits,
Takes his tear, and gets him gone.
By thine eye's tinct ennobled thus,
Time lays him up: he's precious.

Not, *so long she lived*,
Shall thy tomb report of thee;
But, *so long she grieved*,

Thus must we date thy memory.
Others by moments, months, and years,
Measure their ages; thou, by tears.

So do perfumes expire;
So sigh tormented sweets, oppress'd
With proud unpitying fires;
Such tears the suff'ring rose that's vex'd
With ungentle flames does shed,
Sweating in a too warm bed.

Say, ye bright brothers,
The fugitive sons of those fair eyes
Your fruitful mothers,
What make you here? what hopes can 'tice
You to be born? what cause can borrow
You from those nests of noble sorrow?

Whither away so fast?
For sure the sordid earth
Your sweetness cannot taste,
Nor does the dust deserve their birth.
Sweet, whither haste you then? O, say
Why you trip so fast away?

We go not to seek
The darlings of Aurora's bed,
The rose's modest cheek,
Nor the violet's humble head.
Though the field's eyes, too, weepers be,
Because they want such tears as we.

Much less mean we to trace
The fortune of inferior gems,
Preferr'd to some proud face,
Or perch'd upon fear'd diadems.
Crowned heads are toys. We go to meet
A worthy object, our Lord's feet.

THE WEEPER.

[*In the edition of* 1670, *the volume by Mr. Phillips in* 1785, *in Chalmers' collection, and others, the previous Poem is printed with numerous alterations and omissions, in manner following.*]

HAIL sister springs,
Parents of silver-forded rills!
Ever bubbling things!
Thawing crystal! Snowy hills!
Still spending, never spent; I mean
Thy fair eyes, sweet Magdalene.

Heavens thy fair eyes be;
Heavens of ever-falling stars;
'Tis seed-time still with thee,
And stars thou sow'st, whose harvest dares
Promise the earth to countershine
Whatever makes Heaven's forehead fine.

But we're deceived all:
Stars they're indeed too true,
For they but seem to fall
As Heaven's other spangles do:
It is not for our earth and us,
To shine in things so precious.

Upwards thou dost weep;
Heaven's bosom drinks the gentle stream.
Where the milky rivers meet,
Thine crawls above and is the cream.
Heaven, of such fair floods as this,
Heaven the crystal ocean is.

Every morn from hence,
A brisk cherub something sips,
Whose soft influence
Adds sweetness to his sweetest lips;
Then to his music: and his song
Tastes of this breakfast all day long.

When some new bright guest
Takes up among the stars a room,
And Heaven will make a feast,
Angels with their bottles come;
And draw from these full eyes of thine
Their Master's water, their own wine.

The dew no more will weep,
The primrose's pale cheek to deck;
The dew no more will sleep,

Nuzzled in the lily's neck.
Much rather would it tremble here,
And leave them both to be thy tear.

Not the soft gold which
Steals from the amber-weeping tree,
Makes sorrow half so rich,
As the drops distill'd from thee.
Sorrow's best jewels lie in these
Caskets of which Heaven keeps the keys.

When Sorrow would be seen
In her brightest majesty,
For she is a queen,
Then is she drest by none but thee.
Then, and only then, she wears
Her richest pearls, I mean thy tears.

Not in the evening's eyes,
When they red with weeping are
For the Sun that dies,
Sits Sorrow with a face so fair.
Nowhere but here did ever meet
Sweetness so sad, sadness so sweet.

Sadness, all the while
She sits in such a throne as this,
Can do nought but smile,
Nor believe she sadness is:
Gladness itself would be more glad
To be made so sweetly sad.

There is no need at all,
That the balsam-sweating bough
So coyly should let fall
His med'cinable tears; for now
Nature hath learn'd t' extract a dew,
More sovereign and sweet from you.

Yet let the poor drops weep,
Weeping is the case of woe;
Softly let them creep,
Sad that they are vanquish'd so;
They, though to others no relief,
May balsam be for their own grief.

Golden though he be,
Golden Tagus murmurs; though
Might he flow from thee,
Content and quiet would he go;
Richer far does he esteem
Thy silver, than his golden stream.

Well does the May that lies
Smiling in thy cheeks, confess
The April in thine eyes;
Mutual sweetness they express.
No April e'er lent softer showers,
Nor May returnèd fairer flowers.

Thus dost thou melt the year
Into a weeping motion;
Each minute waiteth here,

Takes his tear and gets him gone;
By thine eye's tinct ennobled thus,
Time lays him up: he's precious.

Time, as by thee he passes,
Makes thy ever-watery eyes
His hour-glasses;
By them his steps he rectifies.
The sands he used no longer please,
For his own sands he'll use thy seas.

Does thy song lull the air?
Thy tear's just cadence still keeps time.
Does thy sweet-breath'd prayer
Up in clouds of incense climb?
Still at each sigh, that is, each stop,
A bead, that is, a tear, doth drop.

Does the night arise?
Still thy tears do fall, and fall.
Does night lose her eyes?
Still the fountain weeps for all.
Let night or day do what they will,
Thou hast thy task, thou weepest still.

Not, *so long she lived,*
Will thy tomb report of thee;
But, *so long she grieved,*
Thus must we date thy memory.
Others by days, by months, by years,
Measure their ages, thou by tears.

Say, watery brothers,
Ye simpering sons of those fair eyes
Your fertile mothers,
What hath our world that can entice
You to be born? what is't can borrow
You from her eyes swoll'n wombs of sorrow?

Whither away so fast?
O whither? for the sluttish earth
Your sweetness cannot taste,
Nor does the dust deserve your birth.
Whither haste ye then? O, say
Why ye trip so fast away?

We go not to seek
The darlings of Aurora's bed,
The rose's modest cheek,
Nor the violet's humble head.
No such thing; we go to meet
A worthier object, our Lord's feet.

THE TEAR.

WHAT bright soft thing is this,
Sweet Mary, thy fair eyes' expense?
A moist spark it is,
A watery diamond; from whence
The very term, I think, was found
The water of a diamond.

O, 'tis not a tear,
'Tis a star about to drop
From thine eye its sphere;
The sun will stoop and take it up.
Proud will his sister be to wear
This thine eye's jewel in her ear.

O, 'tis a tear,
Too true a tear: for no sad eyne,
How sad soe'er,
Rain so true a tear as thine;
Each drop leaving a place so dear,
Weeps for itself, is its own tear.

Such a pearl as this is,
Slipt from Aurora's dewy breast,
The rose-bud's sweet lip kisses;
And such the rose itself, when vext
With ungentle flames, does shed,
Sweating in too warm a bed.*

Such the maiden gem
By the wanton spring put on,
Peeps from her parent stem,
And blushes on the watery sun:
This watery blossom of thy eyne,
Ripe, will make the richer wine.

* See these latter lines and the following verse in "The Weeper," as printed in the editions of 1646, 1648, and 1652.

Fair drop, why quak'st thou so?
'Cause thou straight must lay thy head
In the dust? O no;
The dust shall never be thy bed:
A pillow for thee will I bring,
Stuffed with down of angel's wing.

Thus carried up on high,
For to Heaven thou must go,
Sweetly shalt thou lie,
And in soft slumbers bathe thy woe;
Till the singing orbs awake thee,
And one of their bright chorus make thee.

There thyself shalt be
An eye, but not a weeping one;
Yet I doubt of thee,
Whither th' hadst rather there have shone
An eye of Heaven; or still shine here,
In th' heaven of Mary's eye, a tear.

DIVINE EPIGRAMS.

On the Water of our Lord's Baptism.

EACH blest drop on each blest limb,
Is wash'd itself, in washing Him:
'Tis a gem while it stays here;
While it falls hence 'tis a tear.

ACTS VIII.

On the Baptized Ethiopian.

LET it no longer be a forlorn hope
To wash an Ethiop:
He's wash'd, his gloomy skin a peaceful shade
For his white soul is made:
And now, I doubt not, the Eternal Dove
A black-faced house will love.

On the Miracle of multiplied Loaves.

SEE here an easy feast that knows no wound,
That under hunger's teeth will needs be found:
A subtle harvest of unbounded bread.
What would ye more? Here food itself is fed.

Upon the Sepulchre of our Lord.

HERE, where our Lord once laid his Head,
Now the grave lies buried.

The Widow's Mites.

TWO mites, two drops, yet all her house and land,
Fall from a steady heart, though trembling hand:
The other's wanton wealth foams high, and brave;
The other cast away, she only gave.

LUKE XV.

On the Prodigal.

TELL me, bright boy, tell me, my golden lad,
Whither away so frolic? why so glad?
What all thy wealth in council? all thy state?
Are husks so dear? troth 'tis a mighty rate.

On the still surviving Marks of our Saviour's Wounds.

WHATEVER story of their cruelty,
Or nail, or thorn, or spear have writ in Thee,
Are in another sense
Still legible;
Sweet is the difference:
Once I did spell
Every red letter
A wound of Thine;
Now, what is better,
Balsam for mine.

ACTS V.

The Sick implore St. Peter's Shadow.

UNDER thy shadow may I lurk awhile,
Death's busy search I'll easily beguile:
Thy shadow, Peter, must show me the sun,
My light's thy shadow's shadow, or 'tis done.

Mark vii.

The Dumb healed, and the People enjoined silence.

CHRIST bids the dumb tongue speak; it
speaks: the sound
He charges to be quiet; it runs round.
If in the first He us'd His finger's touch:
His hand's whole strength here could not be too much.

Matthew xxviii.

Come, see the place where the Lord lay.

SHOW me Himself, Himself, bright Sir, O show
Which way my poor tears to Himself may go.
Were it enough to show the place, and say,
Look, Mary, here see where thy Lord once lay;
Then could I show these arms of mine and say,
Look, Mary, here see where thy Lord once lay.

To Pontius washing his Hands.

THY hands are wash'd, but O, the water's spilt
That labour'd to have wash'd thy guilt:
The flood, if any can, that can suffice,
Must have its fountain in thine eyes.

To the Infant Martyrs.

GO, smiling souls, your new-built cages break,
In Heav'n you'll learn to sing ere here to speak;
Nor let the milky fonts that bathe your thirst
Be your delay;
The place that calls you hence is, at the worst,
Milk all the way.

On the Miracle of Loaves.

NOW, Lord, or never, they'll believe on Thee;
Thou to their teeth hast proved Thy deity.

MARK IV.

Why are ye afraid, O ye of little faith?

AS if the storm meant Him;
Or, 'cause Heaven's face is dim,
His needs a cloud.
Was ever froward wind
That could be so unkind,
Or wave so proud?
The wind had need be angry, and the water black,
That to the mighty Neptune's self dare threaten wrack.

There is no storm but this
Of your own cowardice
That braves you out;
You are the storm that mocks
Yourselves; you are the rocks
Of your own doubt:
Besides this fear of danger there's no danger here,
And he that here fears danger does deserve his fear.

On the Blessed Virgin's bashfulness.

THAT on her lap she casts her humble eye,
'Tis the sweet pride of her humility.
The fair star is well fixt, for where, O where,
Could she have fixt it on a fairer sphere?

'Tis Heav'n, 'tis Heav'n she sees, Heav'n's God there lies;
She can see Heaven, and ne'er lift up her eyes:
This new guest to her eyes new laws hath given,
'Twas once look up, 'tis now look down to Heaven.

Upon Lazarus's Tears.

RICH Lazarus! richer in those gems, thy tears,
Than Dives in the robes he wears:
He scorns them now, but O, they'll suit full well
With th' purple he must wear in hell.

Two went up into the Temple to pray.

TWO went to pray? O rather say,
One went to brag, th' other to pray.

One stands up close, and treads on high,
Where th' other dares not lend his eye.

One nearer to God's altar trod,
The other to the altar's God.

Upon the Ass that bore our Saviour.

HATH only anger an omnipotence
In eloquence?
Within the lips of love and joy doth dwell
No miracle?
Why else had Balaam's ass a tongue to chide
His master's pride?
And thou, Heaven-burthen'd beast, hast ne'er a word
To praise thy Lord?

That he should find a tongue and vocal thunder,
Was a great wonder;
But O, methinks 'tis a far greater one,
That thou find'st none.

Matthew viii.

I am not worthy that Thou shouldst come under my Roof.

THY God was making haste into thy roof,
Thy humble faith and fear keeps Him aloof:
He'll be thy guest; because He may not be,
He'll come—into thy house? No, into thee.

Upon the Powder-day.

HOW fit our well-rank'd Feasts do follow,
All mischief comes after All-Hallow.

I am the Door.

AND now th' art set wide ope, the spear's sad art,
Lo! hath unlock'd Thee at the very heart.
He to himself, I fear the worst,
And his own hope,
Hath shut these doors of heaven, that durst
Thus set them ope.

Matthew x.

The Blind cured by the Word of our Saviour.

THOU speak'st the word, Thy word's a law;
Thou spak'st, and straight the blind man saw.
To speak and make the blind man see,
Was never man, Lord, spake like Thee.

To speak thus was to speak, say I,
Not to his ear, but to his eye.

MATTHEW XXVII.

And He answered them nothing.

O MIGHTY Nothing! unto thee,
Nothing, we owe all things that be.
God spake once when He all things made,
He saved all when He Nothing said.
The world was made of Nothing then;
'Tis made by Nothing now again.

To our Lord, upon the Water made Wine.

THOU water turn'st to wine, fair friend of life;
Thy foe, to cross the sweet arts of Thy reign,
Distils from thence the tears of wrath and strife,
And so turns wine to water back again.

MATTHEW XXII.

Neither durst any Man from that day ask Him any more Questions.

MIDST all the dark and knotty snares,
Black wit or malice can or dares,
Thy glorious wisdom breaks the nets,
And treads with uncontrolled steps.
Thy quell'd foes are not only now
Thy triumphs, but Thy trophies too:
They, both at once Thy conquests be,
And Thy conquest's memory.
Stony amazement makes them stand

Waiting on Thy victorious hand,
Like statues fixèd to the fame
Of Thy renown, and their own shame:
As if they only meant to breathe,
To be the life of their own death.
'Twas time to hold their peace when they
Had ne'er another word to say:
Yet is their silence unto Thee,
The full sound of Thy victory:
Their silence speaks aloud, and is
Thy well pronounced panegyris.
While they speak nothing, they speak all
Their share in Thy memorial.
While they speak nothing, they proclaim
Thee with the shrillest trump of fame.
To hold their peace is all the ways
These wretches have to speak Thy praise.

Upon our Saviour's Tomb, wherein never man was laid.

HOW life and death in Thee
Agree!
Thou hadst a virgin womb
And tomb.
A Joseph did betroth
Them both.

It is better to go into Heaven with one Eye, &c.

ONE Eye? a thousand rather, and a thousand more,
To fix those full-faced glories. O, he's poor
Of eyes that has but Argus' store;
Yet, if thou'lt fill one poor eye with Thy Heaven an
Thee,

O grant, sweet Goodness, that one eye may be
All, and every whit of me.

Luke xi.

Upon the dumb Devil cast out, and the slanderous Jews put to silence.

TWO devils at one blow Thou hast laid flat,
A speaking devil this, a dumb one that;
Was't Thy full victory's fairer increase
That th' one spake, or that th' other held his peace?

Luke x.

And a certain Priest coming that way, looked on him, and passed by.

WHY dost thou wound my wounds, O thou that passest by,
Handling and turning them with an unwounded eye?
The calm that cools thine eye does shipwreck mine, for O,
Unmoved to see one wretched is to make him so!

Luke xi.

Blessed be the Paps which Thou hast sucked.

SUPPOSE He had been tabled at thy teats,
Thy hunger feels not what He eats:
He'll have His teat ere long, a bloody one,—
The mother then must suck the Son.

To Pontius washing his blood-stained Hands.

IS murder no sin? or a sin so cheap,
That thou need'st heap
A rape upon't? till thy adult'rous touch
Taught her these sullied cheeks, this blubber'd face.
She was a nymph, the meadows knew none such,
Of honest parentage, of unstain'd race,
The daughter of a fair and well-famed fountain,
As ever silver-tipp'd the side of shady mountain.
See how she weeps, and weeps, that she appears
Nothing but tears;
Each drop's a tear that weeps for her own waste.
Hark, how at every touch she does complain her!
Hark, how she bids her frighted drops make haste,
And with sad murmurs chides the hands that stain her!
Leave, leave for shame, or else, good judge, decree,
What water shall wash this, when this hath washèd thee.

MATTHEW XXIII.

Ye build the Sepulchres of the Prophets.

THOU trimm'st a Prophet's tomb, and dost
bequeath
The life thou took'st from him unto his death.
Vain man! the stones that on his tomb do lie
Keep but the score of them that made him die.

Upon the Infant Martyrs.

TO see both blended in one flood,
The mothers' milk, the children's blood,
Makes me doubt if Heaven will gather
Roses hence, or lilies rather.

John xvi.

Verily I say unto you, Ye shall weep and lament

WELCOME, my grief, my joy; how dear's
To me my legacy of tears!
I'll weep, and weep, and will therefore
Weep, 'cause I can weep no more.
Thou, Thou, dear Lord, even Thou alone,
Giv'st joy, even when Thou givest none.

John xv.

Upon our Lord's last comfortable Discourse with His Disciples.

ALL Hybla's honey, all that sweetness can,
Flows in thy song, O fair, O dying swan!
Yet is the joy I take in't small or none;
It is too sweet to be a long-lived one.

Luke xvi.

Dives asking a Drop.

A DROP, one drop, how sweetly one fair drop
Would tremble on my pearl-tipp'd finger's top!
My wealth is gone, O, go it where it will,
Spare this one jewel, I'll be Dives still!

Mark xii.

Give to Cæsar——
And to God——

ALL we have is God's, and yet
Cæsar challenges a debt;
Nor hath God a thinner share,
Whatever Cæsar's payments are;

All is God's; and yet, 'tis true,
All we have is Cæsar's too.
All is Cæsar's; and what odds,
So long as Cæsar's self is God's?

But now they have seen and hated.

SEEN? and yet hated Thee? they did not see,
They saw Thee not, that saw and hated Thee:
No, no, they saw Thee not, O Life! O Love!
Who saw aught in Thee that their hate could move?

Upon the Crown of Thorns, taken from our Blessed Lord's Head, all bloody.

KNOW'ST thou this, soldier? 'tis a much
changed plant, which yet
Thyself didst set.
'Tis changed indeed; did Autumn e'er such beauties bring
To shame his Spring?*
O! who so hard an husbandman did ever find
A soil so kind?
Is not the soil a kind one which returns
Roses for thorns?

She began to wash His Feet with Tears and wipe them with the Hairs of her Head.

HER eyes' flood licks His feet's fair stain,
Her hair's flame licks up that again.
This flame thus quench'd hath brighter beams,
This flood thus stainèd fairer streams.

* These two lines are not in the version of the Paris edition of 1652.

On St. Peter cutting off Malchus's Ear.

WELL, Peter, dost thou wield thy active sword;
Well for thyself, I mean, not for thy Lord.
To strike at ears is to take heed there be
No witness, Peter, of thy perjury.

John iii.

But Men loved Darkness rather than Light.

THE world's Light shines: shine as it will,
The world will love its darkness still;
I doubt though, when the world's in hell,
It will not love its darkness half so well.

Acts xxi.

I am ready not only to be bound but to die.

COME death, come bands, nor do you shrink, my ears,
At those hard words man's cowardice calls fears.
Save those of fear, no other bands fear I;
Nor other death than this; the fear to die.

On St. Peter casting away his Nets at our Saviour's Call.

THOU hast the art on't, Peter, and canst tell
To cast thy nets on all occasions well.
When Christ calls, and thy nets would have thee stay,
To cast them well's to cast them quite away.

Our Lord in His Circumcision to His Father.

TO Thee these first-fruits of my growing death,
For what else is my life? lo! I bequeath.
Taste this, and as Thou lik'st this lesser flood,
Expect a sea, my heart shall make it good.
Thy wrath that wades here now ere long shall swim,
The flood-gate shall be set wide ope for him.
Then let him drink, and drink, and do his worst,
To drown the wantonness of his wild thirst.
Now's but the nonage of my pains, my fears
Are yet both in their hopes, not come to years.
The day of my dark woes is yet but morn,
My tears but tender, and my death new-born.
Yet may these unfledged griefs give fate some guess,
These cradle-torments have their towardness;
These purple buds of blooming death may be
Erst the full stature of a fatal tree;
And, till my riper woes to age are come,
This knife may be the spear's *prœludium.*

On the Wounds of our crucified Lord.

O THESE wakeful wounds of Thine!
Are they mouths? or are they eyes?
Be they mouths, or be they eyne,
Each bleeding part some one supplies.

Lo, a mouth! whose full-bloom'd lips
At too dear a rate are roses.
Lo, a blood-shot eye! that weeps
And many a cruel tear discloses.

O thou that on this foot hast laid
  Many a kiss and many a tear,
Now thou shalt have all repaid,
  Whatsoe'er thy charges were.

This foot hath got a mouth and lips,
  To pay the sweet sum of thy kisses;
To pay thy tears, an eye that weeps,
  Instead of tears, such gems as this is.

The difference only this appears,
  Nor can the change offend,
The debt is paid in ruby tears,
  Which thou in pearls didst lend.

On our crucified Lord, naked and bloody.

THEY have left Thee naked, Lord; O that they had!
  This garment, too, I would they had denied.
  Thee with Thyself they have too richly clad,
Opening the purple wardrobe of Thy side.
  O never could there garment be too good
  For Thee to wear, but this of Thine own blood!

Easter-day.

RISE, Heir of fresh Eternity,
  From thy virgin-tomb:
  Rise, mighty Man of wonders, and Thy world
with Thee;
  Thy tomb, the universal East,
    Nature's new womb,
Thy tomb, fair Immortality's perfumèd nest.

Of all the glories make noon gay
  This is the morn;
This rock buds forth the fountain of the streams of day;
  In joy's white annals lives this hour,
    When life was born,
No cloud-scowl on his radiant lids, no tempest-lower.

Life, by this light's nativity,
  All creatures have;
Death only by this day's just doom is forced to die.
  Nor is death forced; for may he lie
    Throned in thy grave,
Death will on this condition be content to die.

On the bleeding Wounds of our crucified Lord.

JESU, no more, it is full tide;
  From Thy head and from Thy feet,
From Thy hands and from Thy side,
  All Thy purple rivers meet.

What need Thy fair head bear a part
  In showers? as if Thine eyes had none;
What need they help to drown Thine heart,
  That strives in torrents of its own?

Thy restless feet now cannot go,
  For us and our eternal good,
As they were ever wont! What though
  They swim, alas! in their own flood?

Thy hands to give, Thou canst not lift;
Yet will Thy hand still giving be;
It gives, but O, itself's the gift:
It gives though bound, though bound 'tis free.

But O, Thy side; Thy deep digg'd side
That hath a double Nilus going,
Nor ever was the Pharian tide
Half so fruitful, half so flowing.

Water'd by the showers they bring,
The thorns that Thy blest brows encloses,
A cruel and a costly spring,
Conceive proud hopes of proving roses.*

No hair so small but pays his river
To this Red Sea of Thy blood,
Their little channels can deliver
Something to the general flood.

But, while I speak, whither are run
All the rivers named before?
I counted wrong; there is but one:
But O, that one is one all o'er.

Rain-swoll'n rivers may rise proud,
Bent all to drown and overflow;
But when indeed all's overflow'd,
They themselves are drownèd too.

* This verse is not in the version of the Paris edition of 1652.

This Thy blood's deluge, a dire chance,
  Dear Lord, to Thee, to us is found
A deluge of deliverance,
  A deluge lest we should be drown'd.

Ne'er wast Thou, in a sense so sadly true,
The well of living waters, Lord, till now!

Samson to his Delilah.

CRUEL, could not once blinding me suffice?
  When first I look'd on thee I lost mine eyes.

Psalm xxiii.

HAPPY me! O happy sheep!
  Whom my God vouchsafes to keep;
  Even my God, even He it is
That points me to these ways of bliss;
On whose pastures cheerful Spring
All the year doth sit and sing,
And, rejoicing, smiles to see
Their green backs wear his livery.
Pleasure sings my soul to rest,
Plenty wears me at her breast,
Whose sweet temper teaches me
Nor wanton nor in want to be.
At my feet the blubb'ring mountain,
Weeping, melts into a fountain,
Whose soft silver-sweating streams
Make high noon forget his beams.
When my wayward breath is flying
He calls home my soul from dying,

Strokes and tames my rabid grief,
And does woo me into life:
When my simple weakness strays,
Tangled in forbidden ways,
He, my Shepherd, is my guide,
He's before me, on my side,
And behind me, He beguiles
Craft in all her knotty wiles:
He expounds the giddy wonder
Of my weary steps, and under
Spreads a path clear as the day,
Where no churlish rub says nay
To my joy-conducted feet,
Whilst they gladly go to meet
Grace and Peace, to meet new lays
Tuned to my great Shepherd's praise.
Come now all ye terrors, sally,
Muster forth into the valley,
Where triumphant darkness hovers
With a sable wing, that covers
Brooding horror. Come thou, Death,
Let the damps of thy dull breath
Overshadow even the shade,
And make darkness' self afraid;
There my feet, even there shall find
Way for a resolvèd mind.
Still my Shepherd, still my God,
Thou art with me; still Thy rod,
And Thy staff, whose influence
Gives direction, gives defence.
At the whisper of Thy word

Crown'd abundance spreads my board:
While I feast, my foes do feed
Their rank malice, not their need;
So that with the selfsame bread
They are starved, and I am fed.
How my head in ointment swims!
How my cup o'erlooks her brims!
So, even so still may I move
By the line of Thy dear love;
Still may Thy sweet mercy spread
A shady arm above my head,
About my paths; so shall I find
The fair centre of my mind,
Thy temple, and those lovely walls
Bright ever with a beam that falls
Fresh from the pure glance of Thine eye,
Lighting to Eternity.
There I'll dwell for ever, there
Will I find a purer air.
To feed my life with, there I'll sup
Balm and nectar in my cup,
And thence my ripe soul will I breathe
Warm into the arms of death.

Psalm cxxxvii.

ON the proud banks of great Euphrates' flood
There we sat, and there we wept:
Our harps, that now no music understood,
Nodding on the willows slept,
While unhappy captives we,
Lovely Sion, thought on thee.

They, they that snatch'd us from our country's breast
Would have a song carved to their ears
In Hebrew numbers, then, O cruel jest!
When harps and hearts were drown'd in tears:
Come, they cried, come, sing and play
One of Sion's songs to day.

Sing? play? to whom shall we sing or play
If not, Jerusalem, to thee?
Ah! thee, Jerusalem; ah! sooner may
This hand forget the mastery
Of music's dainty touch, than I
The music of thy memory.

Which when I lose, O may at once my tongue
Lose this same busy speaking art,
Unperch'd, her vocal arteries unstrung,
No more acquainted with my heart,
On my dry palate's roof to rest
A wither'd leaf, an idle guest!

No, no, thy good, Sion, alone must crown
The head of all my hope-nursed joys.
But, Edom, cruel thou! thou criedst, Down, down
Sink Sion, down, and never rise!
Her falling thou didst urge and thrust,
And haste to dash her into dust!

Dost laugh? proud Babel's daughter! Do, laugh on,
Till thy ruin teach thee tears;
Even such as these, laugh, till a 'venging throng

Of woes too late do rouse thy fears;
  Laugh, till thy children's bleeding bones
  Weep precious tears upon the stones!

QUEM VIDISTIS PASTORES, ETC.

A Hymn of the Nativity, sung by the Shepherds.

CHORUS.

COME, we shepherds whose blest sight
  Hath met Love's noon in Nature's night;
  Come, lift we up our loftier song,
And wake the sun that lies too long.

To all our world of well-stol'n joy
  He slept, and dreamt of no such thing,
While we found out Heaven's fairer eye,
  And kiss'd the cradle of our King;
Tell him he rises now too late
To show us aught worth looking at.

Tell him we now can show him more
  Than he e'er show'd to mortal sight,
Than he himself e'er saw before,
  Which to be seen needs not his light:
Tell him, Tityrus, where th' hast been,
Tell him, Thyrsis, what th' hast seen.

TITYRUS.

Gloomy night embraced the place
  Where the noble infant lay:
The babe look'd up, and show'd His face;

In spite of darkness it was day.
It was Thy day, sweet, and did rise,
Not from the East, but from Thy eyes.
Chorus. It was Thy day, sweet, &c.

THYRSIS.

Winter chid aloud, and sent
The angry North to wage his wars:
The North forgot his fierce intent,
And left perfumes instead of scars.
By those sweet eyes' persuasive powers,
Where he meant frosts he scatter'd flowers.
Chorus. By those sweet eyes', &c.

BOTH.

We saw Thee in Thy balmy nest,
Young dawn of our eternal day;
We saw Thine eyes break from the East,
And chase the trembling shades away:
We saw Thee, and we blest the sight,
We saw Thee by Thine own sweet light.

TITYRUS.

Poor world, said I, what wilt thou do
To entertain this starry stranger?
Is this the best thou canst bestow—
A cold and not too cleanly manger?
Contend, the powers of heaven and earth,
To fit a bed for this huge birth.
Chorus. Contend, the powers, &c.

THYRSIS.

Proud world, said I, cease your contest,
  And let the mighty babe alone,
The phœnix builds the phœnix' nest,
  Love's architecture is His own.
The babe, whose birth embraves this morn,
Made His own bed ere He was born.
    Chorus. The babe whose birth, &c.

TITYRUS.

I saw the curl'd drops, soft and slow,
  Come hovering o'er the place's head,
Off'ring their whitest sheets of snow,
  To furnish the fair infant's bed.
Forbear, said I, be not too bold,
Your fleece is white, but 'tis too cold.

THYRSIS.

I saw th' obsequious seraphim
  Their rosy fleece of fire bestow,
For well they now can spare their wings,
  Since Heaven itself lies here below.
Well done, said I; but are you sure
Your down, so warm, will pass for pure?
    Chorus. Well done, said I, &c.

BOTH.

No, no, your King's not yet to seek
  Where to repose His royal head;
See, see how soon His new-bloom'd cheek
  'Twixt mother's breasts is gone to bed.

Sweet choice, said we, no way but so,
Not to lie cold, yet sleep in snow!
Chorus. Sweet choice, said we, &c.

FULL CHORUS.

Welcome all wonders in one sight!
Eternity shut in a span!
Summer in winter! day in night!

CHORUS.

Heaven in earth! and God in man!
Great little one, whose all-embracing birth
Lifts earth to Heaven, stoops Heaven to earth!

Welcome, tho' nor to gold, nor silk,
To more than Cæsar's birthright is:
Two sister seas of virgin's milk,
With many a rarely-temper'd kiss,
That breathes at once both maid and mother,
Warms in the one, cools in the other.

She sings Thy tears asleep, and dips
Her kisses in Thy weeping eye;
She spreads the red leaves of Thy lips,
That in their buds yet blushing lie.
She 'gainst those mother diamonds tries
The points of her young eagle's eyes.*

Welcome—tho' not to those gay flies,
Gilded i' th' beams of earthly kings,
Slippery souls in smiling eyes—

* This verse is not in the version of the Paris edition of 1652.

But to poor shepherds, homespun things,
Whose wealth's their flocks, whose wit's to be
Well read in their simplicity.

Yet, when young April's husband show'rs
Shall bless the fruitful Maia's bed,
We'll bring the first-born of her flowers,
To kiss Thy feet, and crown Thy head.
To Thee, dread Lamb! whose love must keep
The shepherds while they feed their sheep.

To Thee, meek Majesty, soft King
Of simple graces and sweet loves!
Each of us his lamb will bring,
Each his pair of silver doves!
At last, in fire of Thy fair eyes,
Ourselves become our own best sacrifice!

SOSPETTO D'HERODE.

LIBRO PRIMO.

ARGOMENTO.

CASTING the times with their strong signs,
Death's master His own death divines;
Struggling for help, His best hope is
Herod's suspicion may heal His:
Therefore He sends a friend to wake
The sleeping tyrant's fond mistake,
Who fears, in vain, that He whose birth
Means heav'n should meddle with his earth.

MUSE, now the servant of soft loves no mo
Hate is thy theme, and Herod; whose unbl
Hand—so what dares not jealous greatness?—tore
A thousand sweet babes from their mothers' breast,
The blooms of martyrdom. O, be a door
Of language to my infant lips, ye best
Of confessors! whose throats, answering his swords
Gave forth your blood for breath, spoke souls for word

Great Anthony! Spain's well-beseeming pride,
Thou mighty branch of emperors and kings;
The beauties of whose dawn what eye may bide,
Which with the sun himself weighs equal wings!

Map of heroic worth! whom far and wide
To the believing world Fame boldly sings:
   Deign thou to wear this humble wreath that bows,
   To be the sacred honour of thy brows.

Nor needs my Muse a blush, or these bright flow'rs,
Other than what their own blest beauties bring;
They were the smiling sons of those sweet bow'rs
That drink the dew of life, whose deathless spring
Nor Syrian flame, nor Borean frost deflow'rs:
From whence heav'n-labouring bees, with busy wing,
   Suck hidden sweets, which well-digested proves
   Immortal honey for the hive of loves.

Thou, whose strong hand, with so transcendent worth,
Holds high the reign of fair Parthenope,
That neither Rome nor Athens can bring forth
A name in noble deeds rival to thee!
Thy fame's full noise makes proud the patient earth,
Far more than matter for my Muse and me.
   The Tyrrhene seas and shores sound all the same,
   And in their murmurs keep thy mighty name!

Below the bottom of the great abyss,
There, where one centre reconciles all things,
The world's profound heart pants; there placèd is
Mischief's old master: close about him clings
A curl'd knot of embracing snakes, that kiss
His correspondent cheeks: these loathsome strings
   Hold the perverse prince in eternal ties,
   Fast bound, since first he forfeited the skies.

The judge of torments, and the king of tears,
He fills a burnish'd throne of quenchless fire:
And, for his old fair robes of light, he wears
A gloomy mantle of dark flames; the tire
That crowns his hated head, on high appears,
Where seven tall horns, his empire's pride, aspire:
And, to make up hell's majesty, each horn
Seven crested Hydras horribly adorn.

His eyes, the sullen dens of death and night,
Startle the dull air with a dismal red:
Such his fell glances as the fatal light
Of staring comets, that look kingdoms dead:
From his black nostrils and blue lips, in spite
Of hell's own stink, a worser stench is spread:
His breath hell's lightning is: and each deep groan
Disdains to think that heav'n thunders alone.

His flaming eyes' dire exhalation
Unto a dreadful pile gives fiery breath;
Whose unconsumed consumption preys upon
The never-dying life of a long death.
In this sad house of slow destruction,
His shop of flames, he fries himself, beneath
A mass of woes; his teeth for torment gnash,
While his steel sides sound with his tail's strong lash.

Three rigorous virgins, waiting still behind,
Assist the throne of th' iron-sceptred king:
With whips of thorns and knotty vipers twined
They rouse him, when his rank thoughts need a sting:

Their locks are beds of uncomb'd snakes, that wind
About their shady brows in wanton rings:
  Thus reigns the wrathful king, and while he reigns,
  His sceptre and himself both he disdains.

Disdainful wretch! how hath one bold sin cost
Thee all the beauties of thy once bright eyes!
How hath one black eclipse cancell'd and crost
The glories that did gild thee in thy rise!
Proud morning of a perverse day! how lost
Art thou unto thyself, thou too self-wise
  Narcissus! foolish Phaeton! who, for all
  Thy high-aim'd hopes, gain'dst but a flaming fall.

From death's sad shades to the life-breathing air,
This mortal enemy to mankind's good
Lifts his malignant eyes, wasted with care,
To become beautiful in human blood:
Where Jordan melts his crystal, to make fair
The fields of Palestine, with so pure a flood,
  There does he fix his eyes: and there detect
  New matter, to make good his great suspect.

He calls to mind th' old quarrel, and what spark
Set the contending sons of heav'n on fire:
Oft in his deep thought he revolves the dark
Sibyl's divining leaves: he does enquire
Into th' old prophecies, trembling to mark
How many present prodigies conspire
  To crown their past predictions; both
  Together, in his pond'rous mind both

Heaven's golden-wingèd herald late he saw
To a poor Galilean virgin sent;
How low the bright youth bow'd, and with what awe
Immortal flow'rs to her fair hand present.
He saw th' old Hebrew's womb neglect the law
Of age and barrenness, and her babe prevent
His birth, by his devotion, who began
Betimes to be a saint, before a man.

He saw rich nectar-thaws release the rigour
Of th' icy North; from frost-bound Atlas' hands
His adamantine fetters fall; green vigour
Gladding the Scythian rocks and Libyan sands;
He saw a vernal smile sweetly disfigure
Winter's sad face, and through the flow'ry lands
Of fair Engaddi, honey-sweating fountains
With manna, milk, and balm, new broach the mountains.

He saw how, in that blest day-bearing night,
The heav'n-rebukèd shades made haste away;
How bright a dawn of angels with new light
Amazed the midnight world, and made a day
Of which the morning knew not; mad with spite,
He mark'd how the poor shepherds ran to pay
Their simple tribute to the babe, whose birth
Was the great business both of heav'n and earth.

He saw a threefold sun, with rich increase,
Make proud the ruby portals of the East;
He saw the temple sacred to sweet Peace,
Adore her Prince's birth, flat on her breast;

He saw the falling idols all confess
A coming Deity; he saw the nest
  Of pois'nous and unnatural loves, earth-nurst,
  Touch'd with the world's true antidote, to burst.

He saw heav'n blossom with a new-born light,
On which, as on a glorious stranger, gazed
The golden eyes of night; whose beam made bright
The way to Bethle'm, and as boldly blazed,
Nor ask'd leave of the sun, by day as night;
By whom, as heav'n's illustrious handmaid, raised,
  Three kings, or, what is more, three wise men went
  Westward to find the world's true orient.

Struck with these great concurrences of things,
Symptoms so deadly unto death and him,
Fain would he have forgot what fatal strings
Eternally bind each rebellious limb.
He shook himself, and spread his spacious wings:
Which, like two bosom'd sails, embrace the dim
  Air with a dismal shade; but all in vain,
  Of sturdy adamant is his strong chain.

While thus heav'n's highest counsels, by the low
Footsteps of their effects, he traced too well,
He toss'd his troubled eyes, embers that glow
Now with new rage, and wax too hot for hell.
With his foul claws he fenced his furrow'd bro
And gave a ghastly shriek, whose horrid yel
  Ran trembling through the hollow vaults
  The while his twisted tail he gnaw'd for

Yet on the other side fain would he start
Above his fears, and think it cannot be:
He studies Scripture, strives to sound the heart,
And feel the pulse of every prophecy;
He knows, but knows not how, or by what art,
The heav'n-expecting ages hope to see
  A mighty babe, whose pure, unspotted birth
  From a chaste virgin womb should bless the earth.

But these vast mysteries his senses smother,
And reason—for what's faith to him?—devour:
How she that is a maid should prove a mother,
Yet keep inviolate her virgin flow'r;
How God's Eternal Son should be man's brother,
Poseth his proudest intellectual pow'r;
  How a pure spirit should incarnate be,
  And life itself wear death's frail livery.

That the great angel-blinding light should shrink
His blaze, to shine in a poor shepherd's eye;
That the unmeasured God so low should sink,
As pris'ner in a few poor rags to lie;
That from His mother's breast He milk should drink
Who feeds with nectar heav'n's fair family;
  That a vile manger His low bed should prove
  Who thunders on a throne of stars above;

That He whom the sun serves should faintly peep
Through clouds of infant flesh; that He, the old
Eternal Word, should be a child, and weep;
That He who made the fire should fear the cold;

That heav'n's high majesty His court should keep
In a clay-cottage, by each blast controll'd;
That glory's self should serve our griefs and fears;
And free eternity submit to years:

And further, that the law's eternal giver
Should bleed in His own law's obedience;
And to the circumcising knife deliver
Himself, the forfeit of his slaves' offence;
That the unblemish'd Lamb, blessed for ever,
Should take the mark of sin, and pain of sense;
These are the knotty riddles, whose dark doubt
Entangles his lost thoughts, past finding out.

While new thoughts boil'd in his enragèd breast,
His gloomy bosom's darkest character
Was in his shady forehead seen express'd.
The forehead's shade, in grief's expression there,
Is what in sign of joy among the blest
The face's light'ning, or a smile is here.
Those stings of care that his strong heart oppress'd,
A desperate *O me!* drew from his deep breast.

O me! thus bellow'd he; *O me!* what great
Portents before mine eyes their pow'rs advance?
And serve my purer sight, only to beat
Down my proud thought, and leave it in a trance?
Frown I; and can great nature keep her seat?
And the gay stars lead on their golden dance?
Can His attempts above still prosp'rous be,
Auspicious still, in spite of hell and me?

He has my heaven—what would He more?—whose bright
And radiant sceptre this bold hand should bear;
And for the never-fading fields of light,
My fair inheritance, he confines me here,
To this dark house of shades, horror, and night,
To draw a long-lived death, where all my cheer
Is the solemnity my sorrow wears,
That mankind's torment waits upon my tears.

Dark, dusky man, He needs would single forth,
To make the partner of His own pure ray:
And should we pow'rs of Heav'n, spirits of worth,
Bow our bright heads before a king of clay?
It shall not be, said I, and clomb the North,
Where never wing of angel yet made way:
What though I miss'd my blow? yet I stroke high,
And to dare something is some victory.

Is He not satisfied? Means He to wrest
Hell from me too, and sack my territories?
Vile human nature means He not t' invest,—
O my despite!—with His divinest glories?
And rising with rich spoils upon His breast,
With His fair triumphs fill all future stories?
Must the bright arms of heaven rebuke these eyes?
Mock me, and dazzle my dark mysteries?

Art thou not Lucifer? he to whom the droves
Of stars that gild the morn in charge were given?
The nimblest of the lightning-wingèd loves?
The fairest, and the first-born smile of heaven?

Look in what pomp the mistress planet moves,
Rev'rently circled by the lesser seven;
Such, and so rich, the flames that from thine eyes
Oppress'd the common people of the skies.

Ah, wretch! what boots thee to cast back thy eyes
Where dawning hope no beam of comfort shows?
While the reflection of thy forepast joys
Renders thee double to thy present woes;
Rather make up to thy new miseries,
And meet the mischief that upon thee grows.
If hell must mourn, heav'n sure shall sympathise;
What force cannot effect, fraud shall devise.

And yet whose force fear I? Have I so lost
Myself? my strength, too, with my innocence?
Come, try who dares, heav'n, earth, whate'er dost boast
A borrow'd being, make thy bold defence:
Come, thy Creator, too; what though it cost
Me yet a second fall? we'd try our strengths.
Heaven saw us struggle once, as brave a fight
Earth now should see, and tremble at the sight.

Thus spoke th' impatient prince, and made a pause;
His foul hags raised their heads, and clapp'd their hands;
And all the powers of hell, in full applause,
Flourish'd their snakes, and toss'd their flar
We, said the horrid sisters, wait thy laws,
Th' obsequious handmaids of thy high co
Be it thy part, hell's mighty lord, to l
On us thy dread commands, ours to ol

What thy Alecto, what these hands can do,
Thou mad'st bold proof upon the brow of heav'n;
Nor should'st thou bate in pride, because that now
To these thy sooty kingdoms thou art driven:
Let heav'ns Lord chide above, louder than thou,
In language of His thunder, thou art even
 With Him below: here thou art lord alone,
 Boundless and absolute: hell is thine own.

If usual wit and strength will do no good,
Virtues of stones, nor herbs: use stronger charms,
Anger, and love, best hooks of human blood.
If all fail, we'll put on our proudest arms,
And pouring on heav'n's face the sea's huge flood,
Quench his curl'd fires; we'll wake with our alarms
 Ruin, where'er she sleeps at Nature's feet,
 And crush the world till his wide corners meet.

Replied the proud king, O my crown's defence!
Stay of whose strong hopes, you of whose brave wortl
The frighted stars took faint experience,
When 'gainst the thunder's mouth we marchèd forth
Still you are prodigal of your love's expence
In our great projects, both 'gainst heav'n and earth:
 I thank you all, but one must single out,—
 Cruelty, she alone shall cure my doubt.

Fourth of the cursèd knot of hags is she,
Or rather all the other three in one;
Hell's shop of slaughter she does oversee,
And still assists the execution:

But chiefly there does she delight to be
Where hell's capacious cauldron is set on:
And while the black souls boil in their own gore,
To hold them down, and look that none seethe o'er.

Thrice howl'd the caves of night, and thrice the sound,
Thund'ring upon the banks of those black lakes,
Rung through the hollow vaults of hell profound:
At last her list'ning ears the noise o'ertakes,
She lifts her sooty lamps, and looking round,
A gen'ral hiss, from the whole tire of snakes
Rebounding, through hell's inmost caverns came,
In answer to her formidable name.

'Mongst all the palaces in hell's command,
No one so merciless as this of hers.
The adamantine doors for ever stand
Impenetrable, both to pray'rs and tears;
The wall's inexorable steel no hand
Of Time or teeth of hungry Ruin fears.
Their ugly ornaments are the bloody stains
Of ragged limbs, torn skulls, and dash'd out brains.

There has the purple Vengeance a proud seat,
Whose ever-brandish'd sword is sheath'd in blood:
About her Hate, Wrath, War, and Slaughter sweat,
Bathing their hot limbs in life's precious flood.
There rude, impetuous Rage does storm and fret:
And there, as master of this murd'ring brood,
Swinging a huge scythe, stands impartial Death,
With endless business almost out of breath.

For hangings and for curtains, all along
The walls—abominable ornaments!—
Are tools of wrath, anvils of torments hung;
Fell executioners of foul intents,
Nails, hammers, hatchets sharp, and halters strong,
Swords, spears, with all the fatal instruments
  Of sin, and death, twice dipp'd in the dire stains
  Of brothers' mutual blood, and fathers' brains.

The tables furnish'd with a cursèd feast,
Which Harpies with lean Famine feed upon,
Unfill'd for ever. Here, among the rest,
Inhuman Erisichthon, too, makes one;
Tantalus, Atreus, Progne, here are guests:
Wolvish Lycaon here a place hath won.
  The cup they drink in is Medusa's skull,
  Which, mix'd with gall and blood, they quaff brim full.

The foul queen's most abhorrèd maids of honour,
Medea, Jezebel, many a meagre witch,
With Circe, Scylla, stand to wait upon her;
But her best housewives are the Parcæ, which
Still work for her, and have their wages from her;
They prick a bleeding heart at every stitch;
  Her cruel clothes of costly threads they weave,
  Which short-cut lives of murder'd infants leave.

The house is hears'd about with a black wood,
Which nods with many a heavy-headed tree;
Each flower's a pregnant poison, tried and good:
Each herb a plague: the winds' sighs timèd be

By a black fount, which weeps into a flood.
Through the thick shades obscurely might you see
  Minotaurs, Cyclopses, with a dark drove
  Of Dragons, Hydras, Sphinxes, fill the grove.

Here Diomed's horses, Phereus' dogs appear,
With the fierce lions of Therodamas;
Busiris has his bloody altar here;
Here Sylla his severest prison has;
The Lestrigonians here their table rear;
Here strong Procrustes plants his bed of brass;
  Here cruel Scyron boasts his bloody rocks,
  And hateful Schinas his so fearèd oaks.

Whatever schemes of blood, fantastic frames
Of death Mezentius, or Geryon drew;
Phalaris, Ochus, Ezelinus, names
Mighty in mischief, with dread Nero too;
Here are they all; here all the swords or flames
Assyrian tyrants, or Egyptian knew.
  Such was the house, so furnish'd was the hall,
  Whence the fourth Fury answer'd Pluto's call.

Scarce to this monster could the shady king
The horrid sum of his intentions tell;
But she, swift as the momentary wing
Of lightning, or the words he spoke, left hell.
She rose, and with her to our world did bring
Pale proof of her fell presence, th' air too well,
  With a changed countenance, witnessèd the fight,
  And poor fowls intercepted in their flight.

Heav'n saw her rise, and saw hell in the sight.
The fields' fair eyes saw her, and saw no more,
But shut their flow'ry lids; for ever night
And winter strow her way: yea, such a sore
Is she to nature, that a general fright,
An universal palsy spreading o'er
  The face of things, from her dire eyes had run,
  Had not her thick snakes hid them from the sun.

Now had the night's companion from her den,
Where all the busy day she close doth lie,
With her soft wing wiped from the brows of men
Day's sweat; and by a gentle tyranny,
And sweet oppression, kindly cheating them
Of all their cares, tamed the rebellious eye
  Of sorrow; with a soft and downy hand
  Sealing all breasts in a Lethæan band.

When the Erinnys her black pinions spread,
And came to Bethle'm, where the cruel king
Had now retired himself, and borrowèd
His breast awhile from care's unquiet sting.
Such as at Thebes' dire feast she show'd her head,
Her sulphur-breathèd torches brandishing,
  Such to the frighted palace now she comes,
  And with soft feet searches the silent rooms.

By proud usurping Herod now was borne
The sceptre, which of old great David sway'd.
Whose right by David's lineage so long worn,
Himself a stranger to, his own had made:

And from the head of Judah's house quite torn
The crown; for which upon their necks he laid
  A sad yoke, under which they sigh'd in vain,
  And, looking on their lost state, sigh'd again.

Up through the spacious palace passèd she,
To where the king's proudly-reposèd head—
If any can be soft to Tyranny
And self-tormenting sin—had a soft bed.
She thinks not fit such he her face should see,
As it is seen by hell; and seen with dread:
  To change her face's style she doth devise,
  And in a pale ghost's shape to spare his eyes.

Herself awhile she lays aside, and makes
Ready to personate a mortal part.
Joseph the king's dead brother's shape she takes,
What he by nature was, she is by art.
She comes to th' king, and with her cold hand slakes
His spirits, the sparks of life, and chills his heart,
  Life's forge; feign'd is her voice, and false, too, be
  Her words—Sleep'st thou, fond man? Sleep'st thou?
        said she.

So sleeps a pilot whose poor bark is press'd
With many a merciless o'er-mast'ring wave;
For whom, as dead, the wrathful winds contest,
Which of them deep'st shall dig her wat'ry grave.
Why dost thou let thy brave soul lie suppress'd
In death-like slumbers, while thy dangers crave
  A waking eye and hand? Look up, and see
  The fates ripe in their great conspiracy.

Know'st thou not how of th' Hebrew's royal stem—
That old dry stock—a despair'd branch is sprung,
A most strange babe! who here, conceal'd by them,
In a neglected stable lies, among
Beasts and base straw: already is the stream
Quite turn'd: th' ingrateful rebels this their young
  Master, with voice free as the trump of Fame,
  Their new king, and thy successor proclaim.

What busy motions, what wild engines stand
On tiptoe in their giddy brains? th' have fire
Already in their bosoms; and their hand
Already reaches at a sword: they hire
Poisons to speed thee; yet through all the land
What one comes to reveal what they conspire?
  Go now, make much of these; wage still their wars,
  And bring home on thy breast more thankless scars.

Why did I spend my life, and spill my blood,
That thy firm hand for ever might sustain
A well-pois'd sceptre? Does it now seem good
Thy brother's blood be spilt, life spent in vain?
'Gainst thy own sons and brothers thou hast stood
In arms, when lesser cause was to complain:
  And now cross fates a watch about thee keep—
  Can'st thou be careless now, now can'st thou sleep?

Where art thou, man? What cowardly mistake
Of thy great self hath stol'n king Herod from thee?
O, call thyself home to thyself; wake, wake,
And fence the hanging sword heav'n throws upon thee:

Redeem a worthy wrath; rouse thee, and shake
Thyself into a shape that may become thee:
  Be Herod, and thou shalt not miss from me
  Immortal stings to thy great thoughts and thee.

So said, her richest snake, which to her wrist
For a beseeming bracelet she had tied—
A special worm it was as ever kiss'd
The foamy lips of Cerberus—she applied
To the king's heart; the snake no sooner hiss'd,
But virtue heard it, and away she hied;
  Dire flames diffuse themselves through every vein:
  This done, home to her hell she hied amain.

He wakes, and with him, ne'er to sleep, new fears:
His sweat-bedewèd bed had now betray'd him
To a vast field of thorns; ten thousand spears,
All pointed in his heart, seem'd to invade him:
So mighty were th' amazing characters
With which his feeling dream had thus dismay'd him,
  He his own fancy-framèd foes defies:
  In rage, My arms! Give me my arms! he cries.

As when a pile of food-preparing fire
The breath of artificial lungs embraves,
The cauldron-prison'd waters straight conspire,
And beat the hot brass with rebellious waves;
He murmurs and rebukes their bold desire;
Th' impatient liquor frets, and foams, and raves;
  Till his o'erflowing pride suppress the flame,
  Whence his high spirits and hot courage came.

So boils the firèd Herod's blood-swoll'n breast,
Not to be slaked but by a sea of blood:
His faithless crown he feels loose on his crest,
Which on false tyrant's head ne'er firmly stood:
The worm of jealous envy and unrest,
To which his gnaw'd heart is the growing food,
  Makes him impatient of the ling'ring light,
  Hate the sweet peace of all-composing night.

A thousand prophecies that talk strange things
Had sown of old these doubts in his deep breast;
And now of late came tributary kings,
Bringing him nothing but new fears from th' East;
More deep suspicions, and more deadly stings,
With which his fev'rous cares their cold increased:
  And now his dream, hell's firebrand, still more bright,
  Show'd him his fears, and kill'd him with the sight.

No sooner, therefore, shall the morning see—
Night hangs yet heavy on the lids of day—
But all his councillors must summon'd be,
To meet their troublèd lord: without delay
Heralds and messengers immediately
Are sent about, who, posting every way
  To th' heads and officers of every band,
  Declare who sends, and what is his command.

Why art thou troubled, Herod? What vain fear
Thy blood-revolving breast to rage doth move?
Heav'n's King, who doffs Himself weak flesh to wear,
Comes not to rule in wrath, but serve in love:

Nor would He this thy fear'd crown from thee tear,
But give Thee a better with Himself above.
  Poor jealousy! Why should He wish to prey
  Upon thy crown, who gives His own away?

Make to thy reason, man, and mock thy doubts;
Look how below thy fears their causes are.
Thou art a soldier, Herod! Send thy scouts,
See how He's furnish'd for so fear'd a war.
What armour does He wear? a few thin clouts.
His trumpets? tender cries. His men to dare
  So much? rude shepherds. What his steeds? alas,
  Poor beasts! a slow ox, and a simple ass.

IL FINE DEL LIBRO PRIMO.

ON A PRAYER-BOOK SENT TO MRS. M. R.

LO, here a little volume, but great book!
  A nest of new-born sweets,
  Whose native pages disdaining
To be thus folded, and complaining
Of these ignoble sheets,
Affect more comely bands,
Fair one, from thy kind hands,
And confidently look
To find the rest
Of a rich binding in your breast.*

* So in the Paris edition of 1652. In all the others—
Fear it not, sweet,
It is no hypocrite,
Much larger in itself, than in its look!

It is in one choice handful, heaven ; and all
  Heaven's royal hosts encamp'd, thus small
  To prove that true schools use to tell,
A thousand angels in one point can dwell.

It is love's great artillery,
Which here contracts itself, and comes to lie
Close couch'd in their white bosom ; and from thence,
As from a snowy fortress of defence,
Against their ghostly foe to take their part,
And fortify the hold of your chaste heart.

It is an armoury of light;
Let constant use but keep it bright,
  You'll find it yields
To holy hands and humble hearts,
  More swords and shields
Than sin hath snares, or hell hath darts.

  Only be sure
  The hands be pure
That hold these weapons, and the eyes
Those of turtles, chaste, and true,
  Wakeful, and wise.
Here's a friend shall fight for you;
Hold but this book before your heart,
Let prayer alone to play his part.

But, O! the heart
That studies this high art
Must be a sure housekeeper,
And yet no sleeper.

Dear soul, be strong,
Mercy will come ere long,
And bring her bosom full of blessings,
Flowers of never-fading graces;
To make immortal dressings
For worthy souls, whose wise embraces
Store up themselves for Him who is alone
The spouse of virgins, and the Virgin's Son.

But if the noble bridegroom when He comes
  Shall find the wand'ring heart from home,
    Leaving her chaste abode
      To gad abroad:
Amongst the gay mates of the god of flies
  To take her pleasure, and to play
    And keep the Devil's holy day;
To dance in the sunshine of some smiling,
      But beguiling

Spheres of sweet and sugar'd lies,
    Some slippery pair
    Of false, perhaps, as fair
Flattering, but foreswearing eyes.

Doubtless some other heart
    Will get the start
Meanwhile, and, stepping in before,
Will take possession of that sacred store
    Of hidden sweets, and holy joys,
    Words which are not heard with ears—

These tumultuous shops of noise—
        Effectual whispers, whose still voice
The soul itself more feels than hears.

Amorous languishments, luminous trances,
        Sights which are not seen with eyes,
Spiritual and soul-piercing glances:
        Whose pure and subtle lightning flies
Home to the heart, and sets the house on fire;
And melts it down in sweet desire:
        Yet does not stay
To ask the windows leave to pass that way.

Delicious deaths, soft exhalations
Of soul; dear and divine annihilations;
        A thousand unknown rites
        Of joys, and rarified delights.

A hundred thousand goods, glories, and graces,
        And many a mystic thing,
        Which the divine embraces
Of the dear spouse of spirits with them will bring;
        For which it is no shame
That dull mortality must not know a name.

Of all this store
Of blessings, and ten thousand more,
        If when He come
He find the heart from home,
        Doubtless He will unload
Himself some otherwhere,

And pour abroad
His precious sweets,
On the fair soul whom first he meets.

O fair! O fortunate! O rich! O dear!
O happy, and thrice happy she,
Dear silver-breasted dove
Whoe'er she be,
Whose early love,
With wingèd vows,
Makes haste to meet her morning spouse,
And close with his immortal kisses!
Happy, indeed, who never misses
To improve that precious hour:
And every day
Seize her sweet prey,
All fresh and fragrant as he rises,
Dropping, with a balmy shower,
A delicious dew of spices.

O, let the blessful heart hold fast
Her heavenly armful, she shall taste
At once ten thousand paradises;
She shall have power
To rifle and deflower
The rich and roseal spring of those rare sweets,
Which with a swelling bosom there she meets,
Boundless and infinite, bottomless treasures
Of pure inebriating pleasures;
Happy proof she shall discover,
What joy, what bliss,

How many heavens at once it is,
To have a God become her lover!

ON MR. G. HERBERT'S BOOK,

Entitled, "The Temple of Sacred Poems," sent to a Gentlewoman.

KNOW you, fair, on what you look?
Divinest love lies in this book,
Expecting fire from your eyes,
To kindle this His sacrifice.
When your hands untie these strings,
Think you've an angel by the wings;
One that gladly will be nigh
To wait upon each morning sigh,
To flutter in the balmy air
Of your well-perfumèd prayer.
These white plumes of His He'll lend you,
Which every day to heaven will send you;
To take acquaintance of the sphere,
And all the smooth-faced kindred there.
And though Herbert's name do owe
These devotions, fairest, know
That while I lay them on the shrine
Of your white hand, they are mine.

A HYMN TO THE NAME AND HONOUR OF THE ADMIRABLE SAINT TERESA,

Foundress of the Reformation of the discalced Carmelites, both men and women; a woman for angelical height of speculation, for masculine courage of performance, more than a woman; who, yet a child, outran maturity, and durst plot a martyrdom.

LOVE, thou art absolute, sole Lord
Of life and death. To prove the word,
We'll now appeal to none of all
Those thy old soldiers, great and tall,
Ripe men of martyrdom, that could reach down
With strong arms their triumphant crown:
Such as could with lusty breath
Speak loud, unto the face of death,
Their great Lord's glorious name; to none
Of those whose spacious bosoms spread a throne
For love at large to fill; spare blood and sweat:
We'll see Him take a private seat,
And make His mansion in the mild
And milky soul of a soft child.

Scarce has she learnt to lisp a name
Of martyr, yet she thinks it shame
Life should so long play with that breath
Which spent can buy so brave a death.

She never undertook to know
What death with love should have to do.
Nor has she e'er yet understood
Why, to show love, she should shed blood;
Yet, though she cannot tell you why,
She can love, and she can die.
Scarce has she blood enough to make
A guilty sword blush for her sake;
Yet has a heart dares hope to prove
How much less strong is death than love.

Be love but there; let poor six years
Be posed with the maturest fears
Man trembles at, we straight shall find
Love knows no nonage, nor the mind.
'Tis love, not years or limbs, that can
Make the martyr, or the man.
Love touch'd her heart, and lo! it beats
High, and burns with such brave heats;
Such thirst to die, as dares drink up
A thousand cold deaths in one cup.
Good reason, for she breathes all fire;
Her weak breast heaves with strong desire
Of what she may, with fruitless wishes,
Seek for amongst her mother's kisses.

Since 'tis not to be had at home,
She'll travel to a martyrdom.
No home for her confesses she,
But where she may a martyr be.
She'll to the Moors, and trade with them,
For this unvalued diadem;

She offers them her dearest breath,
With Christ's name in't, in change for death:
She'll bargain with them, and will give
Them God, and teach them how to live
In Him; or, if they this deny,
For Him she'll teach them how to die.
So shall she leave amongst them sown,
Her Lord's blood, or at least her own.

Farewell then, all the world, adieu!
Teresa is no more for you.
Farewell all pleasures, sports, and joys,
Never till now esteemèd toys!
Farewell whatever dear may be,
Mother's arms, or father's knee!
Farewell house, and farewell home!
She's for the Moors and martyrdom.

Sweet, not so fast; lo! thy fair spouse,
Whom thou seek'st with so swift vows,
Calls the back, and bids thee come
T' embrace a milder martyrdom.

Blest pow'rs forbid, thy tender life
Should bleed upon a barbarous knife,
Or some base hand have power to rase
Thy breast's chaste cabinet, and uncase
A soul kept there so sweet. O, no,
Wise heaven will never have it so:
Thou art love's victim, and must die
A death more mystical and high!

Into love's arms thou shalt let fall
A still surviving funeral.

His is the dart must make the death,
Whose stroke will taste thy hallow'd breath;
A dart thrice dipp'd in that rich flame
Which writes thy spouse's radiant name
Upon the roof of heaven, where aye
It shines, and, with a sovereign ray,
Beats bright upon the burning faces
Of souls, which in that name's sweet graces
Find everlasting smiles. So rare,
So spiritual, pure and fair,
Must be the immortal instrument
Upon whose choice point shall be spent
A life so loved: and that there be
Fit executioners for thee,
The fairest first-born sons of fire,
Blest seraphim, shall leave their quire,
And turn love's soldiers, upon thee
To exercise their archery.

O, how oft shalt thou complain
Of a sweet and subtle pain!
Of intolerable joys!
Of a death, in which who dies
Loves his death, and dies again,
And would for ever so be slain;
And lives and dies, and knows not why
To live, but that he still may die!

How kindly will thy gentle heart
Kiss the sweetly-killing dart!
And close in his embraces keep
Those delicious wounds, that weep
Balsam, to heal themselves with thus,
When these thy deaths, so numerous,
Shall all at once die into one,
And melt thy soul's sweet mansion;
Like a soft lump of incense, hasted
By too hot a fire, and wasted
Into perfuming clouds, so fast
Shalt thou exhale to heaven at last
In a resolving sigh, and then,—
O, what? Ask not the tongues of men.

Angels cannot tell; suffice,
Thyself shalt feel thine own full joys,
And hold them fast for ever there.
So soon as thou shalt first appear,
The moon of maiden stars, thy white
Mistress, attended by such bright
Souls as thy shining self, shall come,
And in her first ranks make thee room;
Where, 'mongst her snowy family,
Immortal welcomes wait for thee.
O, what delight, when she shall stand
And teach thy lips heaven, with her hand,
On which thou now mayst to thy wishes
Heap up thy consecrated kisses.
What joy shall seize thy soul, when she,

Bending her blessed eyes on thee,
Those second smiles of heaven, shall dart
Her mild rays through thy melting heart!

Angels, thy old friends, there shall greet thee,
Glad at their own home now to meet thee.
All thy good works which went before,
And waited for thee at the door,
Shall own thee there: and all in one
Weave a constellation
Of crowns, with which the king, thy spouse,
Shall build up thy triumphant brows.
All thy old woes shall now smile on thee,
And thy pains sit bright upon thee:
All thy sorrows here shall shine,
And thy sufferings be divine.
Tears shall take comfort, and turn gems,
And wrongs repent to diadems.
Even thy death shall live; and new
Dress the soul which late they slew.
Thy wounds shall blush to such bright scars
As keep account of the Lamb's wars.

Those rare works, where thou shalt leave writ
Love's noble history, with wit
Taught thee by none but Him, while here
They feed our souls, shall clothe thine there.
Each heavenly word by whose hid flame
Our hard hearts shall strike fire, the same
Shall flourish on thy brows; and be
Both fire to us and flame to thee:
Whose light shall live bright in thy face

By glory, in our hearts by grace.
Thou shalt look round about, and see
Thousands of crown'd souls throng to be
Themselves thy crown, sons of thy vows,
The virgin-births with which thy spouse
Made fruitful thy fair soul; go now,
And with them all about thee bow
To Him; put on, He'll say, put on
My rosy love, that thy rich zone,
Sparkling with the sacred flames
Of thousand souls, whose happy names
Heaven keeps upon thy score: thy bright
Life brought them first to kiss the light
That kindled them to stars; and so
Thou with the Lamb, thy Lord, shalt go.
And, wheresoe'er He sets His white
Steps, walk with Him those ways of light,
Which who in death would live to see,
Must learn in life to die like thee.

AN APOLOGY FOR THE PRECEDENT HYMN,

As having been written when the Author was yet a Protestant.

THUS have I back again to thy bright name,
Fair flood of holy fires! transfused the flame
I took from reading thee. 'Tis to th[illegible]rong,
I know, that in my weak and worthless son[illegible]
Thou here art set to shine, where thy full [illegible]

Scarce dawns. O, pardon, if I dare to say
Thine own dear books are guilty: for from thence
I learnt to know that love is eloquence,
That heavenly maxim gave me heart to try
If, what to other tongues is tuned so high,
Thy praise might not speak English, too; forbid,
By all thy mysteries that here lie hid,
Forbid it, mighty love! let no fond hate
Of names and words so far prejudicate;
Souls are not Spaniards, too, one friendly flood
Of baptism blends them all into one blood.
Christ's faith makes but one body of all souls,
And love's that body's soul; no law controls
Our free traffic for heaven; we may maintain
Peace, sure, with piety, though it come from Spain.
What soul soe'er in any language can
Speak heaven like hers is my soul's countryman.
O, 'tis not Spanish, but 'tis heaven she speaks,
'Tis heaven that lies in ambush there, and breaks
From thence into the wond'ring reader's breast,
Who finds his warm heart hatch into a nest
Of little eagles and young loves, whose high
Flights scorn the lazy dust, and things that die.
There are enow, whose draughts, as deep as hell,
Drink up all Spain in sack. Let my soul swell
With thee, strong wine of love! let others swim
In puddles; we will pledge this Seraphim
Bowls full of richer blood than blush of grape
Was ever guilty of; change we, too, our shape,
My soul! Some drink from men to beasts; O, then,
Drink we till we prove more, not less, than men:

And turn not beasts, but angels. Let the king
Me ever into these His cellars bring,
Where flows such wine as we can have of none
But Him who trod the winepress all alone:
Wine of youth's life, and the sweet deaths of love;
Wine of immortal mixture, which can prove
Its tincture from the rosy nectar; wine
That can exalt weak earth; and so refine
Our dust, that at one draught mortality
May drink itself up, and forget to die.

ON A TREATISE OF CHARITY.

RISE, then, immortal maid! religion rise!
Put on thyself in thine own looks: t' our eyes
Be what thy beauties, not our blots, have
made thee;
Such as, ere our dark sins to dust betray'd thee,
Heav'n set thee down new-dress'd; when thy bright birth
Shot thee like lightning to th' astonish'd earth.
From th' dawn of thy fair eyelids wipe away
Dull mists and melancholy clouds: take day
And thine own beams about thee: bring the best
Of whatsoe'er perfumed thy eastern nest.
Gird all thy glories to thee: then sit down,
Open this book, fair queen, and take thy crow[illegible]
These learned leaves shall vindicate to thee
Thy holiest, humblest, handmaid, Charity;
She'll dress thee like thyself, set thee on hi[illegible]
Where thou shalt reach all hearts, comma[illegible]

Lo! where I see thy off'rings wake, and rise
From the pale dust of that strange sacrifice
Which they themselves were; each one putting on
A majesty that may beseem thy throne.
The holy youth of heav'n, whose golden rings
Girt round thy awful altars, with bright wings
Fanning thy fair locks, which the world believes
As much as sees, shall with these sacred leaves
Trick their tall plumes, and in that garb shall go
If not more glorious, more conspicuous though.
——Be it enacted, then,
By the fair laws of thy firm-pointed pen,
God's services no longer shall put on
A sluttishness for pure religion:
No longer shall our churches' frighted stones
Lie scatter'd like the burnt and martyr'd bones
Of dead devotion; nor faint marbles weep
In their sad ruins; nor religion keep
A melancholy mansion in those cold
Urns; like God's sanctuaries they look'd of old;
Now seem they temples consecrate to none,
Or to a new god, Desolation.
No more th' hypocrite shall th' upright be
Because he's stiff, and will confess no knee:
While others bend their knee, no more shalt thou,
Disdainful dust and ashes, bend thy brow,
Nor on God's altar cast two scorching eyes,
Baked in hot scorn, for a burnt sacrifice;
But, for a lamb, thy tame and tender heart,
New struck by love, still trembling on his dart;
Or, for two turtle-doves, it shall suffice

To bring a pair of meek and humble eyes;
This shall from henceforth be the masculine theme
Pulpits and pens shall sweat in; to redeem
Virtue to action; that life-feeding flame
That keeps religion warm: not swell a name
Of faith, a mountain-word, made up of air,
With those dear spoils that want to dress the fair
And fruitful charity's full breasts, of old,
Turning her out to tremble in the cold.
What can the poor hope from us? when we be
Uncharitable even to Charity.

ON THE GLORIOUS ASSUMPTION OF THE BLESSED VIRGIN.

HARK! she is call'd, the parting hour is come;
Take thy farewell, poor world, Heaven must go home.
A piece of heavenly light, purer and brighter
Than the chaste stars, whose choice lamps come to light her,
While through the crystal orbs, clearer than they,
She climbs, and makes a far more milky way.
She's call'd again; hark! how th' immortal dove
Sighs to his silver mate: rise up, my love,
Rise up, my fair, my spotless one!
The winter's past, the rain is gone:
The spring is come, the flowers appear,
No sweets, since thou are wanting here.

Come away, my love;
Come away, my dove;
Cast off delay:
The court of heav'n is come,
To wait upon thee home;
Come away, come away.

She's call'd again, and will she go?
When heav'n bids come, who can say no?
Heav'n calls her, and she must away;
Heav'n will not, and she cannot stay.
Go then, go, glorious, on the golden wings
Of the bright youth of heaven, that sings
Under so sweet a burden: go,
Since thy great Son will have it so:
And while thou go'st, our song and we
Will, as we may, reach after thee.
Hail! holy queen of humble hearts,
We in thy praise will have our parts;
And though thy dearest looks must now be light
To none but the blest heavens, whose bright
Beholders, lost in sweet delight,
Feed for ever their fair sight
With those divinest eyes, which we
And our dark world no more shall see.
Though our poor joys are parted so,
Yet shall our lips never let go
Thy gracious name, but to the last
Our loving song shall hold it fast.

Thy sacred name shall be
Thyself to us, and we

With holy cares will keep it by us;
We to the last
Will hold it fast,
And no assumption shall deny us.
All sweetest showers
Of fairest flowers
We'll strew upon it:
Though our sweetness cannot make
It sweeter, they may take
Themselves new sweetness from it.

Maria, men and angels sing,
Maria, mother of our King.
Live, rarest princess, and may the bright
Crown of a most incomparable light
Embrace thy radiant brows! O, may the best
Of everlasting joys bathe thy white breast!
Live our chaste love, the holy mirth
Of heaven, and humble pride of earth:
Live crown of women, queen of men:
Live mistress of our song; and when
Our weak desires have done their best,
Sweet angels come, and sing the rest!

A HYMN ON THE CIRCUMCISION OF OUR LORD.

RISE, thou best and brightest mor
Rosy with a double red;
With thine own blush thy chee
And the dear drops this day were sh

All the purple pride of laces,
  The crimson curtains of thy bed;
Gild thee not with so sweet graces,
  Nor set thee in so rich a red.

Of all the fair-cheek'd flowers that fill thee,
  None so fair thy bosom strews,
As this modest maiden lily
  Our sins have shamed into a rose.

Bid the golden god, the sun,
  Burnish'd in his best beams rise,
Put all his red-eyed rubies on,—
  These rubies shall put out his eyes.

Let him make poor the purple East,
  Search what the world's close cabinets keep,
Rob the rich births of each bright nest
  That flaming in their fair beds sleep.

Let him embrace his own bright tresses
  With a new morning made of gems;
And wear, in those his wealthy dresses,
  Another day of diadems.

When he hath done all he may,
  To make himself rich in his rise,
All will be darkness to the day
  That breaks from one of these bright eyes.

And soon this sweet truth shall appear,
  Dear babe, ere many days be done:

The morn shall come to meet thee here,
  And leave the long-adorèd sun.

Here are beauties shall bereave him
  Of all his eastern paramours:
His Persian lovers all shall leave him,
  And swear faith to thy sweeter powers.

Nor while they leave him shall they lose the sun,
But in thy fairest eyes find two for one.*

ON HOPE.

By way of Question and Answer, between A. Cowley and R. Crashaw.

COWLEY.

HOPE, whose weak being ruin'd is,
  Alike, if it succeed and if it miss:
  Whom ill and good doth equally confound,
And both the horns of fate's dilemma wound:
  Vain shadow! that doth vanish quite
  Both at full noon and perfect night:
  The Fates have not a possibility
    Of blessing thee.
If things, then, from their ends we happy call,
'Tis Hope is the most hopeless thing of all.

CRASHAW.

  Dear Hope! earth's dowry, and heaven's debt,
The entity of things that are not yet:

* These two lines are not in the version of the Paris edition of 1652.

Subtlest, but surest being! Thou by whom
Our nothing hath a definition:
  Fair cloud of fire! both shade and light,
  Our life in death, our day in night:
  Fates cannot find out a capacity
    Of hurting thee.
From thee their thin dilemma with blunt horn
Shrinks, like the sick moon at the wholesome morn.

COWLEY.

  Hope, thou bold taster of delight,
Who, stead of doing so, devour'st it quite;
Thou bring'st us an estate, yet leav'st us poor
By clogging it with legacies before.
  The joys which we entire should wed
  Come deflower'd virgins to our bed:
  Good fortunes without gain imported be,
    So mighty custom's paid to thee!
For joy, like wine kept close, doth better taste,
If it take air before its spirits waste.

CRASHAW.

  Thou art love's legacy under lock
Of faith: the steward of our growing stock:
Our crown-lands lie above, yet each meal brings
A seemly portion for the sons of kings.
  Nor will the virgin-joys we wed
  Come less unbroken to our bed,
  Because that from the bridal cheek of bliss
    Thou thus steal'st down a distant kiss;
Hope's chaste kiss wrongs no more joy's maidenhead,
Than spousal rites prejudge the marriage-bed.

COWLEY.

Hope, Fortune's cheating lottery,
Where for one prize an hundred blanks there be:
Fond archer, Hope, who tak'st thine aim so far,
That still or short or wide thine arrows are:
Thine empty cloud the eye itself deceives
With shapes that our own fancy gives:
A cloud which gilt and painted now appears,
But must drop presently in tears.
When thy false beams o'er reason's light prevail,
By *ignes fatui*, not North stars, we sail.

CRASHAW.

Fair Hope! our earlier heaven, by thee
Young Time is taster to Eternity.
The generous wine with age grows strong, not sour;
Nor need we kill thy fruit to smell thy flower.
Thy golden head never hangs down,
Till in the lap of love's full noon
It falls and dies. O, no, it melts away
As doth the dawn into the day:
As lumps of sugar lose themselves, and twine
Their subtle essence with the soul of wine.

COWLEY.

Brother of Fear! more gaily clad,
The merrier fool o' th' two, yet quite as mad:
Sire of repentance! shield of fond desire,
That blows the chymic's and the lover's fire,
Still leading them insensibly on,
With the strange witchcraft of Anon!

By thee the one doth changing nature through
Her endless labyrinths pursue,
And th' other chases woman, while she goes
More ways and turns than hunted Nature knows.

Crashaw.

Fortune, alas! above the world's law wars:
Hope kicks the curled heads of conspiring stars:
Her keel cuts not the waves where our winds stir,
And Fate's whole lottery is one blank to her.
Her shafts and she fly far above,
And forage in the fields of light and love.
Sweet Hope! kind cheat! fair fallacy! by thee
We are not where or what we be,
But what and where we would: thus art thou
Our absent presence, and our future now.

Crashaw.

Faith's sister! nurse of fair desire!
Fear's antidote! a wise, a well-stay'd fire
Temper'd 'twixt cold despair and torrid joy:
Queen regent in young love's minority!
Though the vex'd chymic vainly chases
His fugitive gold through all her faces,
And love's more fierce, more fruitless fires assay
One face more fugitive than they,
True Hope's a glorious huntress, and her chase,—
The God of nature in the field of grace!

THE

DELIGHTS OF THE MUSES;

OR, OTHER POEMS

WRITTEN ON SEVERAL OCCASIONS,

BY RICHARD CRASHAW.

MART. DIC MIHI QUID MELIUS DESIDIOSUS AGAS.

THE DELIGHTS OF THE MUSES.

MUSIC'S DUEL.

NOW westward Sol had spent the richest beams
Of noon's high glory, when, hard by the streams
Of Tiber, on the scene of a green plat,
Under protection of an oak, there sat
A sweet lute's master: in whose gentle airs
He lost the day's heat, and his own hot cares.
Close in the covert of the leaves there stood
A nightingale, come from the neighbouring wood:—
The sweet inhabitant of each glad tree,
Their muse, their Syren, harmless Syren she,—
There stood she list'ning, and did entertain
The music's soft report, and mould the same
In her own murmurs, that whatever mood
His curious fingers lent, her voice made good.
The man perceived his rival, and her art;
Disposed to give the light-foot lady sport,
Awakes his lute, and 'gainst the fight to come
Informs it, in a sweet *prœludium*

Of closer strains; and ere the war begin
He slightly skirmishes on every string,
Charged with a flying touch; and straightway she
Carves out her dainty voice as readily
Into a thousand sweet distinguish'd tones;
And reckons up in soft divisions
Quick volumes of wild notes, to let him know
By that shrill taste she could do something too.
His nimble hand's instinct then taught each string
A cap'ring cheerfulness; and made them sing
To their own dance; now negligently rash
He throws his arm, and with a long-drawn dash
Blends all together, then distinctly trips
From this to that, then, quick returning, skips
And snatches this again, and pauses there.
She measures every measure, everywhere
Meets art with art; sometimes, as if in doubt—
Not perfect yet, and fearing to be out—
Trails her plain ditty in one long-spun note
Through the sleek passage of her open throat:
A clear unwrinkled song; then doth she point it
With tender accents, and severely joint it
By short diminutives, that, being rear'd
In controverting warbles evenly shared,
With her sweet self she wrangles; he, amazed
That from so small a channel should be raised
The torrent of a voice, whose melody
Could melt into such sweet variety,
Strains higher yet, that tickled with rare art
The tattling strings—each breathing in his part—
Most kindly do fall out; the grumbling base

In surly groans disdains the treble's grace;
The high-perch'd treble chirps at this, and chides
Until his finger—moderator—hides
And closes the sweet quarrel, rousing all,
Hoarse, shrill, at once: as when the trumpets call
Hot Mars to th' harvest of death's field, and woo
Men's hearts into their hands; this lesson, too,
She gives him back, her supple breast thrills out
Sharp airs, and staggers in a warbling doubt
Of dallying sweetness, hovers o'er her skill,
And folds in waved notes, with a trembling bill,
The pliant series of her slippery song;
Then starts she suddenly into a throng
Of short thick sobs, whose thund'ring vollies float
And roll themselves over her lubric throat
In panting murmurs, 'still'd out of her breast,
That ever-bubbling spring, the sugar'd nest
Of her delicious soul, that there does lie
Bathing in streams of liquid melody,—
Music's best seed-plot; when in ripen'd airs
A golden-headed harvest fairly rears
His honey-dropping tops, plough'd by her breath,
Which there reciprocally laboureth.
In that sweet soil it seems a holy quire
Founded to th' name of great Apollo's lyre;
Whose silver roof rings with the sprightly notes
Of sweet-lipp'd angel-imps, that swill their throats
In cream of morning Helicon; and then
Prefer soft anthems to the ears of men,
To woo them from their beds, still murmuring
That men can sleep while they their matins sing;—

Most divine service! whose so early lay
Prevents the eyelids of the blushing day.
There might you hear her kindle her soft voice
In the close murmur of a sparkling noise,
And lay the ground-work of her hopeful song;
Still keeping in the forward stream so long,
Till a sweet whirlwind, striving to get out,
Heaves her soft bosom, wanders round about,
And makes a pretty earthquake in her breast;
Till the fledged notes at length forsake their nest,
Fluttering in wanton shoals, and to the sky,
Wing'd with their own wild echos, pratt'ling fly.
She opes the floodgate, and lets loose a tide
Of streaming sweetness, which in state doth ride
On the waved back of every swelling strain,
Rising and falling in a pompous train;
And while she thus discharges a shrill peal
Of flashing airs, she qualifies their zeal
With the cool epode of a graver note;
Thus high, thus low, as if her silver threat
Would reach the brazen voice of war's hoarse bird;
Her little soul is ravish'd: and so pour'd
Into loose ecstasies, that she is placed
Above herself—music's enthusiast!
  Shame now and anger mixed a double stain
In the musician's face; yet once again,
Mistress, I come. Now reach a strain, my lute,
Above her mock, or be for ever mute;
Or tune a song of victory to me,
Or to thyself sing thine own obseqny!
So said, his hands sprightly as fire he flings,

And with a quivering coyness tastes the strings:
The sweet-lipp'd sisters, musically frighted,
Singing their fears, are fearfully delighted:
Trembling as when Apollo's golden hairs
Are fann'd and frizzled in the wanton airs
Of his own breath, which, married to his lyre,
Doth tune the spheres, and make heaven's self look higher;
From this to that, from that to this, he flies,
Feels music's pulse in all her arteries;
Caught in a net which there Apollo spreads,
His fingers struggle with the vocal threads,
Following those little rills, he sinks into
A sea of Helicon; his hand does go
Those parts of sweetness which with nectar drop,
Softer than that which pants in Hebe's cup:
The humourous strings expound his learnèd touch
By various glosses; now they seem to grutch
And murmur in a buzzing din, then gingle
In shrill-tongued accents, striving to be single;
Every smooth turn, every delicious stroke,
Gives life to some new grace: thus doth he invoke
Sweetness by all her names; thus, bravely thus—
Fraught with a fury so harmonious—
The lute's light Genius now does proudly rise,
Heaved on the surges of swoll'n rhapsodies,
Whose flourish, meteor-like, doth curl the air
With flash of high-born fancies; here and there
Dancing in lofty measures, and anon
Creeps on the soft touch of a tender tone,
Whose trembling murmurs, melting in wild airs,
Run to and fro, complaining his sweet cares;

Because those precious mysteries that dwell
In music's ravish'd soul he dare not tell,
But whisper to the world: thus do they vary
Each string his note, as if they meant to carry
Their master's blest soul, snatch'd out at his ears
By a strong ecstasy, through all the spheres
Of music's heaven; and seat it there on high
In th' *empyrœum* of pure harmony.
At length—after so long, so loud a strife
Of all the strings, still breathing the best life
Of blest variety, attending on
His fingers' fairest revolution,
In many a sweet rise, many as sweet a fall—
A full-mouth'd diapason swallows all.
This done, he lists what she would say to this;
And she, although her breath's late exercise
Had dealt too roughly with her tender throat,
Yet summons all her sweet powers for a note.
Alas, in vain! for while, sweet soul, she tries
To measure all those wild diversities
Of chatt'ring strings, by the small size of one
Poor simple voice, raised in a natural tone,
She fails; and failing, grieves; and grieving, dies;—
She dies, and leaves her life the victor's prize,
Falling upon his lute. O, fit to have—
That lived so sweetly—dead, so sweet a grave!

UPON THE DEATH OF A GENTLEMAN.

FAITHLESS and fond mortality,
Who will ever credit thee?
Fond and faithless thing! that thus
In our best hopes beguilest us,
What a reckoning hast thou made
Of the hopes in him we laid!
For life by volumes lengthenèd,
A line or two to speak him dead.
For the laurel in his verse,
The sullen cypress o'er his hearse.
For a silver-crownèd head,
A dirty pillow in death's bed.
For so dear, so deep a trust,
Sad requital, thus much dust!
Now though the blow that snatch'd him hence
Stopp'd the mouth of eloquence,
Though she be dumb e'er since his death,
Not used to speak but in his breath;
Yet if, at least, she not denies
The sad language of our eyes,
We are contented; for than this
Language none more fluent is.
Nothing speaks our grief so well,
As to speak nothing. Come, then, tell
Thy mind in tears, whoe'er thou be
That ow'st a name to misery;

Eyes are vocal, tears have tongues,
And there be words not made with lungs ;—
Sententious showers! O, let them fall,
Their cadence is rhetorical.
Here's a theme will drink th' expence
Of all thy wat'ry eloquence;
Weep then, only be express'd
Thus much, He's dead; and weep the rest.

UPON THE DEATH OF MR. HERRYS.

A PLANT of noble stem, forward and fair,
As ever whisper'd to the morning air,
Thrived in these happy grounds; the
earth's just pride,
Whose rising glories made such haste to hide
His head in clouds, as if in him alone
Impatient nature had taught motion
To start from time, and cheerfully to fly
Before, and seize upon maturity.
Thus grew this gracious plant, in whose sweet shade
The sun himself oft wish'd to sit, and made
The morning Muses perch like birds, and sing
Among his branches; yea, and vow'd to bring
His own delicious phœnix from the blest
Arabia, there to build her virgin nest,
To hatch herself in 'mongst his leaves: the day
Fresh from the rosy East rejoiced to play:
To them she gave the first and fairest beam

That waited on her birth ; she gave to them
The purest pearls, that wept her evening death ;
The balmy Zephyrus got so sweet a breath,
By often kissing them, and now begun
Glad time to ripen expectation :
The timorous maiden-blossoms on each bough
Peep'd forth from their first blushes : so that now
A thousand ruddy hopes smiled in each bud,
And flatter'd every greedy eye that stood
Fix'd in delight, as if already there
Those rare fruits dangled, whence the golden year
His crown expected ; when—O Fate ! O Time !
That seldom lett'st a blushing youthful prime
Hide his hot beams in shade of silver age !
So rare is hoary virtue—the dire rage
Of a mad storm these bloomy joys all tore,
Ravish'd the maiden blossoms, and down bore
The trunk ; yet in this ground his precious root
Still lives, which, when weak time shall be poured out
Into eternity, and circular joys
Dance in an endless round, again shall rise,
The fair sun of an ever-youthful spring,
To be a shade for angels while they sing !
Meanwhile, whoe'er thou art that passest here,
O, do thou water it with one kind tear !

UPON THE DEATH OF THE MOST DESIRED MR. HERRYS.

DEATH, what dost? O, hold thy blow;
What thou dost, thou dost not know.
Death, thou must not here be cruel,
This is Nature's choicest jewel!
This is he in whose rare frame
Nature labour'd for a name;
And meant to leave his precious feature
The pattern of a perfect creature.
Joy of goodness, love of art,
Virtue wears him next her heart:
Him the Muses love to follow,
Him they call their vice-Apollo!
Apollo, golden though thou be,
Th' art not fairer than is he;
Nor more lovely lift'st thy head,
Blushing from thine Eastern bed;
The glories of thy youth ne'er knew
Brighter hopes than he can show!
Why, then, should it ere be seen,
That his should fade while thine is green?
And wilt thou, O cruel boast,
Put poor Nature to such cost?
O, 'twill undo our common mother,
To be at charge of such another.
What! think we to no other end,

Gracious heavens do use to send
Earth her best perfection,
But to vanish and be gone?
Therefore, only give to-day,
To-morrow to be snatch'd away?
I've seen, indeed, the hopeful bud
Of a ruddy rose, that stood
Blushing to behold the ray
Of the new-saluted day—
His tender top not fully spread—
The sweet dash of a shower now shed,
Invited him no more to hide
Within himself the purple pride
Of his forward flower, when, lo!
While he sweetly 'gan to show
His swelling glories, Auster spied him,
Cruel Auster thither hied him,
And with the rush of one rude blast
Shamed not spitefully to waste
All his leaves, so fresh, so sweet,
And lay them trembling at his feet.
I've seen the morning's lovely ray
Hover o'er the new-born day,
With rosy wings so richly bright,
As if he scorn'd to think of night;
When a ruddy storm, whose scowl
Made heaven's radiant face look foul,
Call'd for an untimely night
To blot the newly-blossom'd light.
But were the rose's blush so rare,
Were the morning's smile so fair

As is he, nor cloud nor wind
But would be courteous, would be kind.
  Spare him, Death, O, spare him then,
Spare the sweetest among men:
Let not Pity with her tears
Keep such distance from thine ears;
But, O, thou wilt not, can'st not spare,
Haste hath never time to hear;
Therefore, if he needs must go,
And the Fates will have it so,
Softly may he be possess'd
Of his monumental rest!
Safe, thou dark home of the dead,
Safe, O hide his lovèd head!
For pity's sake, O hide him quite,
From his mother Nature's sight:
Lest, for the grief his loss may move,
All her births abortive prove.

IN EUNDEM SCAZON.

HUC hospes, oculos flecte, sèd lacrimis cæcos,
Legit optime hæc, quem legere non sinit flectus.
Ars nuper et natura, forma, virtusque
Æmulatione fervidæ, paciscuntur
Probare in uno juvene quid queant omnes,
Fuere tantæ terra nuper fuit liti
Ergo hic ab ipso judicem maneat cœlo.*

* From the edition of 1648.

ANOTHER.

IF ever Pity were acquainted
With stern death; if e'er he fainted
Or forgot the cruel vigour
Of an adamantine rigour,
Here, O, here, we should have known it,
Here or nowhere he'd have shown it.
For he whose precious memory
Bathes in tears of every eye:
He to whom our sorrow brings
All the streams of all her springs,
Was so rich in grace and nature,
In all the gifts that bless a creature;
The fresh hopes of his lovely youth
Flourish'd in so fair a growth;
So sweet the temple was that shrined
The sacred sweetness of his mind;
That could the Fates know to relent;
Could they know what mercy meant;
Or had ever learnt to bear
The soft tincture of a tear;
Tears would now have flow'd so deep
As might have taught grief how to weep;
Now all their steely operation
Would quite have lost the cruel fashion:
Sickness would have gladly been
Sick himself to have saved him:
And his fever wish'd to prove

Burning only in his love;
Him when wrath itself had seen,
Wrath itself had lost his spleen;
Grim destruction here amazed,
Instead of striking would have gazed;
Even the iron-pointed pen,
That notes the tragic dooms of men,
Wet with tears still'd from the eyes
Of the flinty destinies,
Would have learnt a softer style,
And have been ashamed to spoil
His life's sweet story, by the haste
Of a cruel stop ill placed
In the dark volume of our fate,
Whence each leaf of life hath date;
Where, in sad particulars,
The total sum of man appears;
And the short clause of mortal breath
Bound in the period of death.
In all the book if anywhere
Such a term as this, "Spare here,"
Could have been found, 'twould have been read,
Writ in white letters o'er his head:
Or close unto his name annex'd
The fair gloss of a fairer text.
In brief, if any one were free,
He was that one, and only he.
  But he, alas! even he is dead,
And our hopes' fair harvest spread
In the dust! pity now spend
All the tears that grief can lend:

Sad mortality may hide
In his ashes all her pride,
With this inscription o'er his head:—
All hope of never dying here lies dead.

HIS EPITAPH.

PASSENGER, whoe'er thou art,
Stay awhile, and let thy heart
Take acquaintance of this stone,
Before thou passest further on.
This stone will tell thee that beneath
Is entomb'd the crime of death;
The ripe endowments of whose mind
Left his years so much behind,
That, numb'ring of his virtue's praise,
Death lost the reckoning of his days;
And, believing what they told,
Imagined him exceeding old.
In him perfection did set forth
The strength of her united worth;
Him his wisdom's pregnant growth
Made so reverend, even in youth,
That in the centre of his breast—
Sweet as is the Phœnix' nest—
Every reconcilèd grace
Had their general meeting-place;
In him goodness joy'd to see
Learning learn humility.

The splendour of his birth and blood
Was but the gloss of his own good;
The flourish of his sober youth
Was the pride of naked truth;
In composure of his face
Lived a fair but manly grace;
His mouth was rhetoric's best mould,
His tongue the touchstone of her gold;
What word soe'er his breast kept warm
Was no word now, but a charm:
For all persuasive graces thence
Suck'd their sweetest influence.
His virtue, that within had root,
Could not choose but shine without;
And th' heart-bred lustre of his worth,
At each corner peeping forth,
Pointed him out in all his ways,
Circled round in his own rays:
That to his sweetness all men's eyes
Were vow'd love's flaming sacrifice.
  Him while fresh and fragrant time
Cherish'd in his golden prime;
Ere Hebe's hand had overlaid
His smooth cheeks with a downy shade;
The rush of death's unruly wave
Swept him off into his grave.
  Enough, now, if thou canst, pass on;
For now, alas! not in this stone,
Passenger, whoe'er thou art,
Is he entomb'd, but in thy heart.

AN EPITAPH UPON HUSBAND AND WIFE,

Who died and were buried together.

TO these whom death again did wed,
This grave's the second marriage-bed.
For though the hand of Fate could force
'Twixt soul and body a divorce,
It could not sever man and wife,
Because they both lived but one life.
Peace, good reader, do not weep;
Peace, the lovers are asleep.
They, sweet turtles, folded lie
In the last knot that love could tie.
Let them sleep, let them sleep on,
Till the stormy night be gone,
And the eternal morrow dawn;
Then the curtains will be drawn,
And they wake into a light
Whose day shall never die in night.

AN EPITAPH UPON DOCTOR BROOK.

A BROOK, whose stream so great, so good,
Was loved, was honour'd as a flood;
Whose banks the Muses dwelt upon
More than their own Helicon;
Here, at length, hath gladly found
A quiet passage underground;

Meanwhile, his lovèd banks, now dry,
The Muses with their tears supply.

UPON MR. STANINOUGH'S DEATH.*

DEAR relics of a dislodged soul, whose lack
Makes many a mourning paper put on black,
O, stay awhile, ere thou draw in thy head,
And wind thyself up close in thy cold bed;
Stay but a little while, until I call
A summons worthy of thy funeral!
Come then, youth, beauty, blood! all ye soft pow'rs,
Whose silken flatteries swell a few fond hours
Into a false eternity! Come, man—
Hyperbolized nothing!—know thy span!
Take thine own measure here; down, down, and bow
Before thyself in thy idea! thou
Huge emptiness! contract thy bulk, and shrink
All thy wild circle to a point! O, sink
Lower, and lower yet; till thy small size
Call heaven to look on thee with narrow eyes!
Lesser, and lesser yet; till thou begin
To show a face fit to confess thy kin,
Thy neighbourhood to nothing!
Proud looks, and lofty eyelids, here put on
Yourselves in this unfeign'd reflection!

* Repeated, with alterations, at the end of the edition of 1670, under the title, "Death's Lecture—the Funeral of a Young Gentleman."

Here, gallant ladies, this impartial glass,
Though you be painted, shows you your own face.
These death-seal'd lips do dare to give the lie
To the proud hopes of poor mortality.
These curtain'd windows, this self-prison'd eye
Out-stares the lids of large-look'd tyranny.
This posture is the brave one! this that lies
Thus low stands up, methinks, thus, and defies
The world. All-daring dust and ashes! only you,
Of all interpreters, read nature true!

UPON THE DUKE OF YORK'S* BIRTH.

A Panegyric.

BRITAIN, the mighty ocean's lovely bride,
Now stretch thyself, fair isle, and grow; spread wide
Thy bosom, and make room; thou art oppress'd
With thine own glories: and art strangely bless'd
Beyond thyself: for lo! the gods, the gods,
Come fast upon thee, and those glorious odds
Swell thy full glories to a pitch so high,
As sits above thy best capacity!

Are they not odds? and glorious? that to thee
Those mighty Genii throng, which well might be
Each one an age's labour; that thy days
Are gilded with the union of those rays,
Whose each divided beam would be a sun,
To glad the sphere of any nation.

* Afterwards king James II.

O, if for these thou mean'st to find a seat,
Th' hast need, O Britain, to be truly great!
And so thou art, their presence makes thee so;
They are thy greatness; gods, where'er they go,
Bring their heav'n with them, their great footsteps place
An everlasting smile upon the face
Of the glad earth they tread on; while with thee
Those beams that ampliate mortality,
And teach it to expatiate, and swell
To majesty and fulness, deign to dwell;
Thou by thyself may'st sit, blest isle, and see
How thy great mother Nature doats on thee!
Thee, therefore, from the rest apart she hurl'd,
And seem'd to make an isle, but made a world!
Great Charles! thou sweet dawn of a glorious day,
Centre of those thy grandsires, shall I say,
Henry, and James, or Mars and Phœbus rather?
If this were wisdom's god, that war's stern father,
'Tis but the same, is said, Henry and James
Are Mars and Phœbus under divers names.
O thou full mixture of those mighty souls
Whose vast intelligences tuned the poles
Of peace and war; thou for whose manly brow
Both laurels twine into one wreath, and woo
To be thy garland; see, sweet prince, O see
Thou and the lovely hopes that smile in thee
Are ta'en out, and transcribed by thy great mother!
See, see thy real shadow, see thy brother,
Thy little self in less, read in these eyne
The beams that dance in those full stars of thine.
From the same snowy alabaster rock

These hands and thine were hewn, these cherries mock
The coral of thy lips. Thou art of all
This well-wrought copy the fair principal.
  Justly, great Nature, may'st thou brag and tell
How even th' hast drawn this faithful parallel,
And match'd thy master-piece: O, then, go on,
Make such another sweet comparison:—
See'st thou that Mary there? O, teach her, mother,
To show her to herself in such another.
Fellow this wonder, too, nor let her shine
Alone; light such another star, and twine
Their rosy beams, so that the morn for one
Venus may have a constellation.
  So have I seen, to dress their mistress, May,
Two silken sister-flowers consult, and lay
Their bashful cheeks together; newly they
Peep'd from their buds, show'd like the garden's eyes
Scarce waked: like was the crimson of their joys,
Like were the pearls they wept; so like, that one
Seem'd but the other's kind reflection.
  But stay, what glimpse was that? why blush'd the day?
Why trembling ran the started air away?
Who's this that comes circled in rays that scorn
Acquaintance with the sun? what second morn
At mid-day opes a presence, which heaven's eye
Stands off and points at? is't some deity,
Stepp'd from her throne of stars, deigns to be seen?
Is it some deity? or is't our queen?
'Tis she, 'tis she, her awful beauties chase
The day's abashèd glories, and in face
Of noon wear their own sunshine! O, thou bright

Mistress of wonders! Cynthia's is the night;
But thou at noon dost shine, and art all day—
Nor does the sun deny 't—our Cynthia.
Illustrious sweetness! in thy faithful womb,
That nest of heroes, all our hopes find room;
Thou art the mother Phœnix, and thy breast
Chaste as that virgin honour of the East,
But much more fruitful is; nor does, as she,
Deny to mighty love a deity.
Then let the Eastern world brag and be proud
Of one coy Phœnix, while we have a brood,
A brood of Phœnixes, and still the mother;*
And may we long; long may'st thou live, t' increase
The house and family of Phœnixes:
Nor may the light that gives their eyelids light
E'en prove the dismal morning of thy night;
Ne'er may a birth of thine be bought so dear
To make his costly cradle of thy bier.
O, may'st thou thus make all the year thine own,
And see such names of joy sit white upon
The brow of every month; and when that's done,
May'st in a son of his find every son
Repeated, and that son still in another,
And so in each child often prove a mother!
Long may'st thou, laden with such clusters, lean
Upon thy royal elm, fair vine! and when
The heavens will stay no longer, may thy glory
And name dwell sweet in some eternal story!
Pardon, bright excellence! an untuned string,
That in thy ears thus keeps a murmuring;

* Here a line seems deficient.

O, speak a lowly muse's pardon; speak
Her pardon or her sentence; only break
Thy silence! speak; and she shall take from thence
Numbers, and sweetness, and an influence
Confessing thee! or, if too long I stay,
O, speak thou, and my pipe hath nought to say.
For see, Apollo all this while stands mute,
Expecting by thy voice to tune his lute.
But gods are gracious, and their altars make
Precious their offerings that their altars take;
Give, then, this rural wreath fire from thine eyes:
This rural wreath dares be thy sacrifice.

UPON FORD'S TWO TRAGEDIES,

Love's Sacrifice, and the Broken Heart.

THOU cheat'st us, Ford, mak'st one seem
two by art:
What is love's sacrifice but the broken heart?

ON A FOUL MORNING,

Being then to take a Journey.

WHERE art thou, Sol, while thus the blind-
fold day
Staggers out of the East, losing her way,
Stumbling on night? Rouse thee, illustrious youth,
And let no dull mists choke the light's fair growth.

Point here thy beams, O, glance on yonder flocks,
And make their fleeces golden as thy locks.
Unfold thy fair front, and there shall appear
Full glory flaming in her own free sphere.
Gladness shall clothe the earth, we will instile
The face of things an universal smile:
Say to the sullen morn, thou com'st to court her,
And wilt demand proud Zephyrus to sport her,
With wanton gales; his balmy breath shall lick
The tender drops which tremble on her cheek;
Which rarified, and in a gentle rain
On those delicious banks distill'd again,
Shall rise in a sweet harvest, which discloses
In every blush a bed of new-born roses.
He'll fan her bright locks, teaching them to flow
And frisk in curled meanders: he will throw
A fragrant breath, suck'd from the spicy nest
O' th' precious Phœnix, warm upon her breast:
He with a dainty and soft hand will trim
And brush her azure mantle, which shall swim
In silken volumes; wheresoe'er she'll tread,
Bright clouds, like golden fleeces, shall be spread.
  Rise then, fair blue-eyed maid, rise and discover
Thy silver brow, and meet thy golden lover.
See how he runs, with what a hasty flight
Into thy bosom, bathed with liquid light.
Fly, fly, profane fogs, far hence fly away,
Taint not the pure streams of the springing day
With your dull influence; it is for you
To sit and scowl upon night's heavy brow;
Not on the fresh cheeks of the virgin morn,

Where nought but smiles and ruddy joys are worn:
Fly, then, and do not think with her to stay;
Let it suffice, she'll wear no mask to-day.

UPON THE FAIR ETHIOPIAN,

Sent to a Gentlewoman.

LO, here, the fair Chariclia! in whom strove
So false a fortune and so true a love.
Now, after all her toils by sea and land,
O, may she but arrive at your white hand,
Her hopes are crown'd; only she fears that then
She shall appear true Ethiopian!

ON MARRIAGE.

I WOULD be married, but I'd have no wife;
I would be married to a single life.

TO THE MORNING.

Satisfaction for Sleep.

WHAT succour can I hope the Muse will send,
Whose drowsiness hath wrong'd the Muse's friend?
What hope, Aurora, to propitiate thee,
Unless the Muse sing my apology?
O! in that morning of my shame, when I
Lay folded up in sleep's captivity;

How at the sight didst thou draw back thine eyes
Into thy modest veil! how didst thou rise
Twice dyed in thine own blushes, and didst run
To draw the curtains and awake the sun!
Who, rousing his illustrious tresses, came,
And seeing the loath'd object, hid for shame
His head in thy fair bosom, and still hides
Me from his patronage; I pray, he chides;
And, pointing to dull Morpheus, bids me take
My own Apollo, try if I can make
His Lethe be my Helicon: and see
If Morpheus have a Muse to wait on me.
Hence 'tis my humble fancy finds no wings,
No nimble raptures, starts to heaven and brings
Enthusiastic flames, such as can give
Marrow to my plump genius, make it live
Dress'd in the glorious madness of a Muse,
Whose feet can walk the milky-way, and choose
Her starry throne; whose holy heats can warm
The grave, and hold up an exalted arm
To lift me from my lazy urn, and climb
Upon the stoopèd shoulders of old Time,
And trace eternity. But all is dead,
All these delicious hopes are buriѐd
In the deep wrinkles of his angry brow,
Where mercy cannot find them; but, O thou
Bright lady of the morn, pity doth lie
So warm in thy soft breast, it cannot die;
Have mercy, then, and when he next doth rise,
O, meet the angry god, invade his eyes,
And stroke his radiant cheeks; one timely kiss

Will kill his anger, and revive my bliss.
So to the treasure of thy pearly dew
Thrice will I pay three tears, to show how true
My grief is; so my wakeful lay shall knock
At th' oriental gates, and duly mock
The early lark's shrill orisons to be
An anthem at the day's nativity.
And the same rosy-finger'd hand of thine,
That shuts night's dying eyes, shall open mine.
  But thou, faint god of sleep, forget that I
Was ever known to be thy votary.
No more my pillow shall thine altar be,
Nor will I offer any more to thee
Myself a melting sacrifice; I'm born
Again a fresh child of the buxom morn.
Heir of the sun's first beams, why threat'st thou so?
Why dost thou shake thy leaden sceptre? Go,
Bestow thy poppy upon wakeful woe,
Sickness and sorrow, whose pale lids ne'er know
Thy downy finger dwell upon their eyes;
Shut in their tears, shut out their miseries.

LOVE'S HOROSCOPE.

LOVE, brave virtue's younger brother,
Erst hath made my heart a mother.
She consults the conscious spheres,
To calculate her young son's years;
She asks if sad or saving pow'rs
Gave omen to his infant hours;

She asks each star that then stood by
If poor Love shall live or die.

Ah, my heart, is that the way?
Are these the beams that rule thy day?
Thou know'st a face in whose each look
Beauty lays ope Love's fortune-book,
On whose fair revolutions wait
The obsequious motions of Love's fate.
Ah, my heart! her eyes and she
Have taught thee new astrology.
Howe'er Love's native hours were set,
Whatever starry synod met,
'Tis in the mercy of her eye,
If poor Love shall live or die.

If those sharp rays, putting on
Points of death, bid Love begone;
Though the heavens in council sat
To crown an uncontrollèd fate;
Though their best aspects twined upon
The kindest constellation,
Cast amorous glances on his birth,
And whisper'd the confederate earth
To pave his paths with all the good
That warms the bed of youth and blood:—
Love has no plea against her eye;
Beauty frowns, and Love must die.

But if her milder influence move,
And gild the hopes of humble Love;—

Though heaven's inauspicious eye
Lay black on Love's nativity;
Though every diamond in Jove's crown
Fix'd his forehead to a frown;—
Her eye a strong appeal can give,
Beauty smiles, and Love shall live.

O, if Love shall live, O, where
But in her eye, or in her ear,
In her breast, or in her breath,
Shall I hide poor Love from death?
For in the life aught else can give,
Love shall die, although he live.

Or, if Love shall die, O, where,
But in her eye, or in her ear,
In her breath, or in her breast,
Shall I build his funeral nest?
While Love shall thus entombèd lie,
Love shall live, although he die!

OUT OF VIRGIL, IN THE PRAISE OF THE SPRING.

ALL trees, all leafy groves confess the spring
Their gentlest friend; then, then the lands begin
To swell with forward pride, and seed desire
To generation; heaven's almighty sire

Melts on the bosom of his love, and pours
Himself into her lap in fruitful showers;
And by a soft insinuation, mix'd
With earth's large mass, doth cherish and assist
Her weak conceptions; no lone shade, but rings
With chattering birds' delicious murmurings.
Then Venus' mild instinct, at set times, yields
The herds to kindly meetings, then the fields,
Quick with warm Zephyr's lively breath, lay forth
Their pregnant bosoms in a fragrant birth;
Each body's plump and juicy, all things full
Of supple moisture: no coy twig but will
Trust his belovèd bosom to the sun,
Grown lusty now; no vine so weak and young
That fears the foul-mouth'd Auster, or those storms
That the south-west wind hurries in his arms,
But hastes her forward blossoms, and lays out,
Freely lays out her leaves; nor do I doubt,
But when the world first out of Chaos sprang,
So smiled the days, and so the tenour ran
Of their felicity: a spring was there,
An everlasting spring; the jolly year
Led round in his great circle; no wind's breath,
As then, did smell of winter, or of death.
When light's sweet light first shone on beasts, and when
From their hard mother earth sprang hardy men;
When beasts took up their lodging in the wood,
Stars in their higher chambers; never could
The tender growth of things endure the sense
Of such a change, but that the heav'n's indulgence
Kindly supplies sick nature, and doth mould
A sweetly-temper'd mean, nor hot nor cold.

WITH A PICTURE SENT TO A FRIEND.

I PAINT so ill, my piece had need to be
Painted again by some good poesy;
I write so ill, my slender line is scarce
So much as th' picture of a well-limn'd verse:
Yet may the love I send be true, though I
Send not true picture nor true poesy:
Both which away, I should not need to fear
My love or feign'd or painted should appear.

IN PRAISE OF LESSIUS'S RULE OF HEALTH.*

GO now, and with some daring drug,
Bait the disease, and, while they tug,
Thou to maintain their precious strife
Spend the dear treasure of thy life:
Go, take physic, doat upon
Some big-named composition,—
The oraculous doctors' mystic bills,
Certain hard words made into pills;
And what at last shalt get by these?
Only a costlier disease.

* Repeated, with some additional lines, at the end of the edition of 1670; and printed, from "Hark hither," among the commendatory verses in praise of the translation of "The Temperate Man, &c. the right Way of preserving Life and Health," &c. of Lessius and others, London, 1678, 12mo.

Go, poor man, think what shall be
Remedy against thy remedy.
That which makes us have no need
Of physic, that's physic indeed.
  Hark hither, reader, would'st thou see
Nature her own physician be?
Would'st see a man all his own wealth,
His own physic, his own health?
A man whose sober soul can tell
How to wear her garments well?
Her garments, that upon her sit,
As garments should do, close and fit?
A well-clothed soul, that's not oppress'd,
Nor choked with what she should be dress'd?
A soul sheathed in a crystal shrine,
Through which all her bright features shine?
As when a piece of wanton lawn,
A thin aërial veil is drawn,
O'er beauty's face, seeming to hide,
More sweetly shows the blushing bride.
A soul whose intellectual beams
No mists do mask, no lazy streams?
A happy soul, that all the way
To heaven hath a summer's day?
Would'st see a man whose well-warm'd blood
Bathes him in a genuine flood?
A man whose tunèd humours be
A seat of rarest harmony?
Would'st see blithe looks, fresh cheeks beguile
Age? Would'st see December smile?
Would'st see a nest of roses grow

In a bed of reverend snow?
Warm thoughts, free spirits, flattering
Winter's self into a spring?
In sum, would'st see a man that can
Live to be old, and still a man?
Whose latest, and most leaden hours,
Fall with soft wings, stuck with soft flow'rs;
And, when life's sweet fable ends,
Soul and body part like friends:—
No quarrels, murmurs, no delay;
A kiss, a sigh, and so away?
This rare one, reader, would'st thou see,
Hark hither; and—thyself be he!

THE BEGINNING OF HELIODORUS.

THE smiling morn had newly waked the day,
And tipp'd the mountains in a tender ray:
When, on a hill, whose high imperious brow
Looks down, and sees the humble Nile below
Lick his proud feet, and haste into the seas,
Through the great mouth that's named from Hercules,
A band of men, rough as the arms they wore,
Look'd round, first to the sea, then to the shore:—
The shore that show'd them what the sea denied,
Hope of a prey. There to the main land tied
A ship they saw, no men she had; yet press'd
Appear'd with other lading, for her breast
Deep in the groaning waters wallowèd

Up to the third ring; o'er the shore was spread
Death's purple triumph; on the blushing ground
Life's late forsaken houses all lay drown'd
In their own blood's dear deluge; some new dead,
Some panting in their yet warm ruins bled,
While their affrighted souls, now wing'd for flight,
Lent them the last flash of her glimmering light:
Those yet fresh streams which crawlèd everywhere,
Show'd that stern war had newly bathed him there:
Nor did the face of this disaster show
Marks of a fight alone, but feasting too;
A miserable and a monstrous feast,
Where hungry war had made himself a guest;
And, coming late, had eat up guest and all,
Who proved the feast to their own funeral, &c.

CUPID'S CRYER. OUT OF THE GREEK.

LOVE is lost, nor can his mother
Her little fugitive discover:
She seeks, she sighs, but nowhere spies him;
Love is lost; and thus she cries him.
O yes! if any happy eye
This roving wanton shall descry:
Let the finder surely know
Mine is the wag; 'tis I that own
The wingèd wand'rer; and that none
May think his labour vainly gone,
The glad descryer shall not miss
To taste the nectar of a kiss

From Venus' lips; but as for him
That brings him to me, he shall swim
In riper joys; more shall be his,
Venus assures him, than a kiss.
But lest your eye discerning slide,
These marks may be your judgment's guide:
His skin, as with a fiery blushing,
High-coloured is; his eyes still flushing
With nimble flames; and though his mind
Be ne'er so cursed, his tongue is kind:
For never were his words in aught
Found the pure issue of his thought.
The working bees' soft-melting gold,
That which their waxen mines enfold,
Flows not so sweet as do the tones
Of his tuned accents; but if once
His anger kindle, presently
It boils out into cruelty
And fraud: he makes poor mortals' hurts
The objects of his cruel sports;
With dainty curls his froward face
Is crown'd about; but, O, what place,
What farthest nook of lowest hell,
Feels not the strength, the reaching spell
Of his small hand? yet not so small
As 'tis powerful therewithal;
Though bare his skin, his mind he covers,
And, like a saucy bird, he hovers
With wanton wing, now here, now there,
'Bout men and women; nor will spare
Till at length he, perching, rest

In the closet of their breast.
His weapon is a little bow,
Yet such a one as, Jove knows how,
Ne'er suffer'd yet his little arrow
Of heav'n's highest arches to fall narrow.
The gold that on his quiver smiles
Deceives men's fears with flattering wiles:
But, O, too well my wounds can tell,
With bitter shafts 'tis sauc'd too well;
He is all cruel, cruel all;
His torch imperious, though but small,
Makes the sun, of flames the sire,
Worse than sun-burnt in his fire:
Wheresoe'er you chance to find him,
Seize him, bring him, but first bind him;
Pity not him, but fear thyself,
Though thou see the crafty elf
Tell down his silver drops unto thee,
They're counterfeit, and will undo thee;
With baited smiles if he display
His fawning cheeks, look not that way:
If he offer sugared kisses,
Start, and say the serpent hisses;
Draw him, drag him, though he pray,
Woo, intreat, and, crying, say
Prithee, sweet, now let me go,
Here's my quiver, shafts and bow;
I'll give thee all, take all:—take heed,
Lest his kindness make thee bleed.
Whate'er it be love offers, still presume
That, though it shines, 'tis fire, and will consume.

HIGH mounted on an ant, Nanus the tall
Was thrown, alas! and got a deadly fall.
Under th' unruly beast's proud feet he lies
All torn; with much ado yet e'er he dies,
He strains these words: Base envy, do laugh on,
Thus did I fall, and thus fell Phaeton.

UPON VENUS PUTTING ON MARS'S ARMS.

WHAT! Mars's sword! fair Cytherea, say,
Why art thou arm'd so desperately to-day?
Mars thou hast beaten naked, and, O, then,
What need'st thou put on arms against poor men?

UPON THE SAME.

PALLAS saw Venus arm'd, and straight she cried,
"Come, if thou dar'st, thus, thus let us be tried."
"Why, fool!" says Venus, "thus provok'st thou me,
That being naked, thou know'st could conquer thee?"

UPON BISHOP ANDREWS'S PICTURE BEFORE HIS SERMONS.

THIS reverend shadow cast that setting sun,
Whose glorious course through our horizon run,
Left the dim face of this dull hemisphere,
All one great eye, all drown'd in one great tear!
Whose fair illustrious soul led his free thought
Through learning's universe, and, vainly, sought
Room for her spacious self, until at length
She found the way home; and, with holy strength,
Snatch'd herself hence to heaven: fill'd a bright place,
'Mongst those immortal fires, and on the face
Of her great Maker fix'd her flaming eye,
There still to read true pure divinity.
And now that grave aspect hath deign'd to shrink
Into this less appearance, if you think
'Tis but a dead face art doth here bequeath,
Look on the following leaves, and see them breathe.

OUT OF MARTIAL.

FOUR teeth thou had'st, that ranked in goodly state,
Kept thy mouth's gate.

The first blast of thy cough left two alone;
The second none.

This last cough, Ælia, cough'd out all thy fear—
Th' hast left the third cough now no business here.

A SONG. OUT OF THE ITALIAN.

TO thy lover,
Dear, discover
That sweet blush of thine, that shameth,
When the roses
It discloses,
All the flowers that nature nameth!

In free air,
Flow thy hair;
That no more summer's best dresses
Be beholden,
For their golden
Locks, to Phœbus' flaming tresses.

O, deliver
Love his quiver;
From thy eyes he shoots his arrow,
Where Apollo
Cannot follow,
Feather'd with his mother's sparrows!

O, envy not,
That we die not,
Those dear lips, whose door encloses

All the Graces
In their places,
Brother pearls, and sister roses!

From these treasures
Of ripe pleasures,
One bright smile to clear the weather:
Earth and heaven,
Thus made even,
Both will be good friends together.

The air does woo thee,
Winds cling to thee;
Might a word once fly from out thee,
Storms and thunder
Would sit under,
And keep silence round about thee!

But if Nature's
Common creatures
So dear glories dare not borrow;
Yet thy beauty
Owes a duty
To my loving, ling'ring sorrow!

When, to end me,
Death shall send me
All his terrors, to affright me;
Thine eyes' graces
Gild their faces,
And those terrors shall delight me!

When my dying
Life is flying,
Those sweet airs, that often slew me,
Shall revive me,
Or reprieve me,
And to many deaths renew me!

OUT OF THE ITALIAN.

LOVE now no fire hath left him,
We two betwixt us have divided it;
Your eyes the light hath reft him;
The heart commanding in my heart doth sit:
O, that poor love be not for ever spoil'd,
Let my heat to your light be reconciled!

So shall these flames, whose worth
Now all obscurèd lies,
Dress'd in those beams start forth,
And dance before your eyes.

Or else partake my flames,
I care not whether,
And so in mutual names,
O love, burn both together!

OUT OF THE ITALIAN.

WOULD any one the true cause find
How love came naked, a boy, and blind?
'Tis this: list'ning one day too long
To th' Syrens in my mistress' song,
The ecstasy of a delight
So much o'ermast'ring all his might,
To that one sense made all else thrall;
And so he lost his clothes, eyes, heart, and all!

ON THE FRONTISPIECE OF ISAACSON'S CHRONOLOGY EXPLAINED.

IF with distinctive eye and mind you look
Upon the front, you see more than one book.
Creation is God's book, wherein He writ
Each creature as a letter filling it.
History is creation's book; which shows
To what effects the series of it goes.
Chronology's the book of history, and bears
The just account of days, of months, and years.
But resurrection, in a later press
And new edition, is the sum of these:
The language of these books had all been one
Had not th' aspiring tow'r of Babylon
Confused the tongues, and in a distance hurl'd
As far the speech, as men, o' th' new-fill'd world.

Set then your eyes in method, and behold
Time's emblem, Saturn; who, when store of gold
Coin'd the first age, devour'd that birth he fear'd;
Till history, time's eldest child, appear'd,
And, phœnix-like, in spite of Saturn's rage,
Forced from her ashes heirs in every age.
From th' rising sun, obtaining by just suit,
A spring's ingender, and an autumn's fruit.
Who in those volumes, at her motion penn'd,
Unto creation's Alpha doth extend.
Again ascend, and view chronology,
By optic skill pulling far history
Nearer; whose hand the piercing eagle's eye
Strengthens to bring remotest objects nigh.
Under whose feet you see the setting sun,
From the dark gnomon, o'er her volumes run,
Drown'd in eternal night, never to rise
Till resurrection show it to the eyes
Of earth-worn men; and her shrill trumpet's sound
Affright the bones of mortals from the ground:
The columns both are crown'd with either sphere,
To show chronology and history bear
No other culmen than the double art
Astronomy, geography impart.

OR THUS.

LET hoary Time's vast bowels be the grave
To what his bowels birth, and being gave;
Let Nature die, and, phœnix-like, from
death,
Revivèd Nature take a second breath;
If, on Time's right hand sit fair history;
If, from the seed of empty ruin she
Can raise so fair an harvest, let her be
Ne'er so far distant, yet chronology,
Sharp-sighted as the eagle's eye, that can
Outstare the broad-beam'd day's meridian,
Will have a perspicil to find her out;
And, through the night of error, and dark doubt,
Discern the dawn of truth's eternal ray,
As when the rosy morn buds into day!
Now that Time's empire might be amply fill'd,
Babel's bold artists strive, below, to build
Ruin a temple; on whose fruitful fall
History rears her pyramids, more tall
Than were th' Egyptian! by the life, these give,
Th' Egyptian pyramids themselves must live:
On these she lifts the world; and, on their base,
Shows the two terms and limits of Time's race:
That the creation is; the judgment this;
That the world's morning; this her midnight is!

AN EPITAPH UPON MR. ASHTON, A CONFORMABLE CITIZEN.

THE modest front of this small floor,
Believe me, reader, can say more
Than many a braver marble can,—
"Here lies a truly honest man!"
One whose conscience was a thing
That troubled neither church nor king;
One of those few that in this town
Honour all preachers; hear their own.
Sermons he heard, yet not so many
As left no time to practise any;
He heard them reverendly, and then
His practise preach'd them o'er again;
His parlour-sermons rather were
Those to the eye, than to the ear;
His prayers took their price and strength
Not from the loudness nor the length;
He was a protestant at home,
Not only in despite of Rome;
He loved his father, yet his zeal
Tore not off his mother's veil;
To th' church he did allow her dress,
True beauty to true holiness;
Peace, which he loved in life, did lend
Her hand to bring him to his end;
When age and death call'd for the score,
No surfeits were to reckon for;

Death tore not, therefore, but, sans strife,
Gently untwined his thread of life.
What remains, then, but that thou
Write these lines, reader, on thy brow,
And, by his fair example's light
Burn in thy imitation bright?
So, while these lines can but bequeath
A life, perhaps, unto his death,
His better epitaph shall be—
His life still kept alive in thee.

OUT OF CATULLUS.

COME, and let us live, my dear,
Let us love and never fear
What the sourest fathers say;
Brightest Sol, that dies to day,
Lives again as blithe to-morrow;
But if we, dark sons of sorrow,
Set, O then, how long a night
Shuts the eyes of our short light!
Then let amorous kisses dwell
On our lips, begin and tell
A thousand and a hundred score,
A hundred and a thousand more,
Till another thousand smother
That, and that wipe off another.
Thus at last, when we have number'd
Many a thousand, many a hundred,

We'll confound the reckoning quite,
And lose ourselves in wild delight:
While our joys so multiply,
As shall mock the envious eye.

WISHES TO HIS SUPPOSED MISTRESS.

WHOE'ER she be,
That not impossible she,
That shall command my heart and me:

Where'er she lie,
Lock'd up from mortal eye,
In shady leaves of destiny:

Till that ripe birth
Of studied fate, stand forth,
And teach her fair steps to our earth:

Till that divine
Idea take a shrine
Of crystal flesh, through which to shine:

Meet you her, my Wishes,
Bespeak her to my blisses,
And be ye call'd my absent kisses.

I wish her beauty,
That owes not all its duty
To gaudy tire, or glist'ring shoe-tie.

Something more than
Taffata or tissue can,
Or rampant feather, or rich fan.

More than the spoil
Of shop, or silkworm's toil,
Or a bought blush, or a set smile.

A face, that's best
By its own beauty dress'd,
And can alone command the rest.

A face, made up
Out of no other shop,
Than what Nature's white hand sets ope.

A cheek, where youth
And blood, with pen of truth,
Write what the reader sweetly rueth.

A cheek, where grows
More than a morning rose,
Which to no box his being owes.

Lips, where all day
A lover's kiss may play,
Yet carry nothing thence away.

Looks, that oppress
Their richest tires, but dress
And clothe their simplest nakedness.

Eyes, that displace
The neighbour diamond, and out-face
That sunshine by their own sweet grace.

Tresses, that wear
Jewels, but to declare
How much themselves more precious are.

Whose native ray
Can tame the wanton day
Of gems that in their bright shades play.

Each ruby there,
Or pearl that dare appear,
Be its own blush, be its own tear.

A well-tamed heart,
For whose more noble smart
Love may be long choosing a dart.

Eyes, that bestow
Full quivers on love's bow,
Yet pay less arrows than they owe.

Smiles, that can warm
The blood, yet teach a charm,
That chastity shall take no harm.

Blushes, that bin
The burnish of no sin,
Nor flames of aught too hot within.

Joys, that confess
Virtue their mistress,
And have no other head to dress.

Fears, fond and slight,
As the coy bride's, when night
First does the longing lover right.

Tears, quickly fled,
And vain, as those are shed
For a dying maidenhead.

Days, that need borrow
No part of their good morrow,
From a fore-spent night of sorrow.

Days, that in spite
Of darkness, by the light
Of a clear mind, are day all night.

Nights; sweet as they
Made short by lovers' play,
Yet long by th' absence of the day.

Life, that dares send
A challenge to his end,
And when it comes, say, Welcome, friend!

Sydneian showers
Of sweet discourse, whose powers
Can crown old winter's head with flowers.

Soft silken hours,
Open suns, shady bowers,
'Bove all—nothing within that lowers.

Whate'er delight
Can make day's forehead bright,
Or give down to the wings of night.

In her whole frame,
Have Nature all the name,
Art and ornament the shame.

Her flattery,
Picture and poesy,
Her counsel her own virtue be.

I wish her store
Of worth may leave her poor
Of wishes; and I wish——no more.

Now, if Time knows
That her, whose radiant brows
Weave them a garland of my vows;

Her, whose just bays
My future hopes can raise,
A trophy to her present praise;

Her, that dares be
What these lines wish to see:
I seek no further, it is she.

'Tis she, and here,
Lo, I unclothe and clear
My Wish's cloudy character!

May she enjoy it,
Whose merit dare apply it,
But modesty dares still deny it!

Such worth as this is
Shall fix my flying wishes,
And determine them to kisses.

Let her full glory,
My fancies, fly before ye,
Be ye my fictions but—her story.

UPON TWO GREEN APRICOCKS SENT TO COWLEY BY SIR CRASHAW.

TAKE these, Time's tardy truants, sent by me
To be chastised, sweet friend, and chid by thee.
Pale sons of our Pomona! whose wan cheeks
Have spent the patience of expecting weeks,
Yet are scarce ripe enough at best to show
The red, but of the blush to thee they owe.
By thy comparison they shall put on
More summer in their shame's reflection,

Than e'er the fruitful Phœbus' flaming kisses
Kindled on their cold lips. O, had my wishes,
And the dear merits of your Muse, their due,
The year had found some fruit early as you;
Ripe as those rich composures, time computes
Blossoms, but our blest taste confesses fruits.
How does thy April-autumn mock those cold
Progressions 'twixt whose terms poor Time grows old!
With thee alone he wears no beard; thy brain
Gives him the morning world's fresh gold again.
'Twas only Paradise, 'tis only thou,
Whose fruit and blossoms both bless the same bough.
Proud in the pattern of thy precious youth,
Nature, methinks, might easily mend her growth.
Could she in all her births but copy thee,
Into the public year's proficiency,
No fruit should have the face to smile on thee,
Young master of the world's maturity!
But such whose sun-born beauties what they borrow
Of beams to-day, pay back again to-morrow,
Nor need be double-gilt. How, then, must these
Poor fruits look pale at thy Hesperides!
Fain would I chide their slowness, but in their
Defects I draw mine own dull character.
Take them, and me in them, acknowledging
How much my summer waits upon thy spring!*

* From the edition of 1648.

CARMEN DEO NOSTRO,

TE DECET HYMNUS.

SACRED POEMS,

COLLECTED,
CORRECTED,
AUGMENTED,
Most humbly PRESENTED,

TO MY LADY THE COUNTESS OF DENBIGH.

BY HER MOST DEVOTED SERVANT

RICH. CRASHAW.

In hearty acknowledgement of his immortal obligation to her goodness and charity.

CRASHAWE,

THE ANAGRAM "HE WAS CAR."

WAS Car then Crashaw, or was Crashaw Car,
Since both within one name combinèd are?
Yes, Car's Crashaw, he Car; 'tis love alone
Which melts two hearts, of both composing one;
So Crashaw's still the same: so much desired
By strongest wits; so honour'd, so admired;
Car was but he that enter'd as a friend
With whom he shared his thoughts, and did commend,
While yet he lived, this work; they loved each other:
Sweet Crashaw was his friend: he Crashaw's brother;
So Car hath title then; 'twas his intent
That what his riches penn'd, poor Car should print;
Nor fears he check, praising that happy one
Who was beloved by all; disprais'd by none.
To wit, being pleased with all things, he pleased all.
Nor would he give nor take offence; befall
What might, he would possess himself, and live
As dead, devoid of interest, t' all might give

Diseased his well-composèd mind, forestall'd
With heavenly riches, which had wholly call'd
His thoughts from earth, to live above in th' air
A very bird of paradise. No care
Had he of earthly trash. What might suffice
To fit his soul to heavenly exercise,
Sufficèd him; and may we guess his heart
By what his lips bring forth, his only part
Is God and godly thoughts. Leaves doubt to none
But that to whom one God is all, all's one.
What he might eat or wear he took no thought,
His needful food he rather found than sought.
He seeks no downs, no sheets, his bed's still made;
If he can find a chair or stool, he's laid;
When day peeps in, he quits his restless rest;
And still, poor soul, before he's up, he's dress'd.
Thus dying did he live, yet lived to die
In th' Virgin's lap, to whom he did apply
His virgin thoughts and words, and thence was styled
By foes, the chaplain of the virgin mild,
While yet he lived without: his modesty
Imparted this to some, and they to me.
Live happy, then, dear soul! enjoy thy rest
Eternally by pains thou purchasedst,
While Car must live in care, who was thy friend,
Nor cares he how he live, so in the end
He may enjoy his dearest Lord and thee;
And sit and sing more skilful songs eternally.

THOMAS CAR.

AN EPIGRAM

Upon the Pictures in the following Poems which the Author first made with his own hand admirably well, as may be seen in his Manuscript dedicated to the Right Honourable Lady the Lady Denbigh.

TWIXT pen and pencil rose a holy strife
Which might draw virtue better to the life;
But wits gave votes to that: but painters swore
They never saw pieces so sweet before
As these: fruits of pure nature; where no art
Did lead the untaught pencil, nor had part
In th' work.
The hand grown bold, with wit will needs contest.
Doth it prevail? ah, wo! say each is best.
This to the ear speaks wonders; that will try
To speak the same, yet louder, to the eye.
Both their aims are holy, both conspire
To wound, to burn the heart with heavenly fire.
This then's the doom, to do both parties right:
This, to the ear speaks best; that, to the sight!*

THOMAS CAR.

* Printed only in the edition of 1652.

TO THE NOBLEST AND BEST OF LADIES THE COUNTESS OF DENBIGH:

Persuading her to resolution in Religion, and to render herself without further delay into the communion of the Catholic Church.

WHAT heaven-entreated heart is this
Stands trembling at the gate of bliss?
Holds fast the door, yet dares not venture
Fairly to open it and enter?
Whose definition is a doubt
'Twixt life and death, 'twixt in and out?
Say, ling'ring fair! why comes the birth
Of your brave soul so slowly forth?
Plead your pretences, O you strong
In weakness, why you choose so long
In labour of yourself to lie,
Nor daring quite to live nor die.
Ah, linger not, loved soul! a slow
And late consent was a long no;
Who grants at last, long time had tried
And did his best to have denied.

What magic bolts, what mystic bars
Maintain the will in these strange wars!
What fatal, what fantastic bands
Keep the free heart from its own hands!
So, when the year takes cold, we see
Poor waters their own prisoners be;
Fetter'd and lock'd up fast they lie
In a sad self-captivity;
Th' astonish'd nymphs their floods' strange fate deplore,
To see themselves their own severer shore.
Thou that alone canst thaw this cold,
And fetch the heart from its strong hold,
Almighty Love! end this long war,
And of a meteor make a star.
O, fix this fair indefinite,
And 'mongst thy shafts of sovereign light
Choose out that sure decisive dart,
Which has the key of this close heart,
Knows all the corners of't, and can control
The self-shut cabinet of an unsearch'd soul!
O, let it be at last Love's hour;
Raise this tall trophy of thy pow'r;
Come once the conquering way, not to confute,
But kill this rebel-word—Irresolute;
That so, in spite of all this peevish strength
Of weakness, she may write—Resolved at length!
Unfold at length, unfold fair flow'r,
And use the season of Love's show'r;
Meet his well-meaning wounds, wise heart!
And haste to drink the wholesome dart;
That healing shaft, which heav'n till now

Has in Love's quiver hid for you.
O dart of love! arrow of light!
O, happy you, if it hit right!
It must not fall in vain, it must
Not mark the dry regardless dust.
Fair one, it is your fate; and brings
Eternal worlds upon its wings.
Meet it with wide-spread arms; and see
Its seat your soul's just centre be.
Disband dull fears; give Faith the day;
To save your life, kill your delay;
It is Love's siege, and sure to be
Your triumph, though his victory.
'Tis cowardice that keeps this field,
And want of courage not to yield.
Yield then, O yield, that Love may win
The fort at last, and let Life in.
Yield quickly, lest perhaps you prove
Death's prey, before the prize of Love.
This fort of your fair self, if't be not won,
He is repuls'd indeed, but you're undone.

TO THE NAME ABOVE EVERY NAME, THE NAME OF JESUS. A HYMN.

I SING the name which none can say
But touch'd with an interior ray;
The name of our new peace; our good:
Our bliss, and supernatural blood:

The name of all our lives and loves.
Hearken, and help, ye holy doves!
The high-born brood of day; you bright
Candidates of blissful light,
The heirs elect of love; whose names belong
Unto the everlasting life of song;
All ye wise souls, who in the wealthy breast
Of this unbounded name build your warm nest.
Awake, my glory, soul, if such thou be,
And that fair word at all refer to thee,
Awake and sing,
And be all wing;
Bring hither thy whole self; and let me see
What of thy parent heav'n yet speaks in thee.
O, thou art poor
Of noble pow'rs, I see,
And full of nothing else but empty me;
Narrow, and low, and infinitely less
Than this great morning's mighty business.
One little world or two,
Alas! will never do;
We must have store.
Go, soul, out of thyself, and seek for more;
Go and request
Great Nature for the key of her huge chest
Of heav'n's, the self-involving set of spheres,
Which dull mortality more feels than hears;
Then rouse the nest
Of nimble art, and traverse round
The airy shop of soul-appeasing sound:
And beat a summons in the same

All-sovereign name,
To warn each several kind
And shape of sweetness, be they such
As sigh with supple wind,
Or answer artful touch,
That they convene and come away
To wait at the love-crownèd doors of that
Illustrious day.
Shall we dare this, my soul? We'll do 't, and bring
No other note for 't, but the Name we sing.
Wake, lute and harp,
And every sweet-lipp'd thing
That talks with tuneful string;
Start into life, and leap with me
Into a hasty fit-tuned harmony.
Nor must you think it much
T' obey my bolder touch;
I have authority in Love's name to take you
And to the work of love this morning wake you;
Wake, in the name
Of Him who never sleeps, all things that are,
Or what's the same,
Are musical;
Answer my call
And come along;
Help me to meditate mine immortal song.
Come, ye soft ministers of sweet sad mirth,
Bring all your household-stuff of heav'n on earth:
O you, my soul's most certain wings,
Complaining pipes, and prattling strings,
Bring all the store

Of sweets you have, and murmur that you have no more.
Come, ne'er to part,
Nature and art!
Come, and come strong,
To the conspiracy of our spacious song.
Bring all the pow'rs of praise
Your provinces of well-united worlds can raise;
Bring all your lutes and harps of heav'n and earth;
Whate'er co-operates to the common mirth;
Vessels of vocal joys,
Or you, more noble architects of intellectual noise,
Cymbals of heav'n, or human spheres,
Solicitors of souls or ears;
And when you are come, with all
That you can bring, or we can call,
O, may you fix
For ever here, and mix
Yourselves into the long
And everlasting series of a deathless song!
Mix all your many worlds above,
And loose them into one of love.
Cheer thee, my heart!
For thou, too, hast thy part
And place in the great throng
Of this unbounded, all-embracing song.
Pow'rs of my soul, be proud!
And speak loud
To all the dear-bought nations this redeeming name;
And in the wealth of one rich word proclaim
New smiles to nature.
May it be no wrong,

Blest heav'ns, to you, and your superior song,
That we dark sons of dust and sorrow
Awhile dare borrow
The name of your delights, and our desires,
And fit it to so far inferior lyres!
Our murmurs have their music, too,
Ye mighty orbs, as well as you,
Nor yields the noblest nest
Of warbling seraphim to the ears of love,
A choicer lesson than the joyful breast
Of a poor panting turtle-dove.
And we, low worms, have leave to do
The same bright business, ye third Heav'ns, with you.
Gentle spirits, do not complain,
We will have care
To keep it fair,
And send it back to you again.
Come, lovely name! appear from forth the bright
Regions of peaceful light;
Look from Thine own illustrious home,
Fair king of names, and come:
Leave all thy native glories in their gorgeous nest,
And give thyself awhile the gracious guest
Of humble souls, that seek to find
The hidden sweets
Which man's heart meets
When Thou art master of the mind.
Come, lovely name! life of our hope!
Lo, we hold our hearts wide ope!
Unlock thy cabinet of day,
Dearest sweet, and come away.

Lo, how the thirsty lands
Gasp for thy golden showers with long-stretch'd hands!
Lo, how the labouring earth,
That hopes to be
All heaven by thee,
Leaps at thy birth!
Th' attending world, to wait thy rise,
First turn'd to eyes,
And then, not knowing what to do,
Turn'd them to tears, and spent them, too.
Come, royal name! and pay th' expence
Of all this precious patience;
O, come away,
And kill the death of this delay!
O, see so many worlds of barren years
Melted and measured out in seas of tears!
O, see the weary lids of wakeful hope,
Love's eastern windows, all wide ope,
With curtains drawn,
To catch the day-break of thy dawn!
O, dawn, at last, long-look'd for day!
Take thine own wings and come away.
Lo, where aloft it comes! It comes, among
The conduct of adoring spirits, that throng,
Like diligent bees, and swarm about it.
O, they are wise,
And know what sweets are suck'd from out it!
It is the hive
By which they thrive,
Where all their hoard of honey lies.
Lo, where it comes, upon the snowy dove's

Soft back, and brings a bosom big with loves!
Welcome to our dark world, thou
Womb of day!
Unfold thy fair conceptions, and display
The birth of our bright joys.
O, thou compacted
Body of blessings: spirit of souls extracted!
O, dissipate thy spicy pow'rs,
Cloud of condensèd sweets, and break upon us
In balmy show'rs!
O, fill our senses, and take from us
All force of so profane a fallacy
To think aught sweet but that which smells of thee!
Fair, flow'ry name, in none but thee,
And thy nectareal fragrancy,
Hourly there meets
An universal synod of all sweets;
By whom it is definèd thus
That no perfume
For ever shall presume
To pass for odoriferous,
But such alone whose sacred pedigree
Can prove itself some kin, sweet name, to thee.
Sweet name, in thy each syllable
A thousand blest Arabias dwell;
A thousand hills of frankincense,
Mountains of myrrh, and beds of spices,
And ten thousand paradises,
The soul that tastes thee takes from thence.
How many unknown worlds there are
Of comforts, which thou hast in keeping!

How many thousand mercies there
In Pity's soft lap lie a-sleeping!
Happy he who has the art
To awake them,
And to take them
Home, and lodge them in his heart.
O, that it were as it was wont to be!
When thy old friends of fire, all full of thee,
Fought against frowns with smiles; gave glorious chase
To persecutions; and against the face
Of death and fiercest dangers durst, with brave
And sober pace, march on to meet a grave.
On their bold breasts about the world they bore thee,
And to the teeth of hell stood up to teach thee;
In centre of their inmost souls they wore thee,
Where racks and torments strived in vain to reach thee.
Little, alas! thought they
Who tore the fair breasts of thy friends,
Their fury but made way
For thee, and served them in thy glorious ends.
What did their weapons, but with wider pores
Enlarge thy flaming-breasted lovers,
More freely to transpire
That impatient fire,
The heart that hides thee hardly covers!
What did their weapons, but set wide the doors
For thee; fair purple doors, of Love's devising,
The ruby windows which enrich'd the east
Of thy so oft-repeated rising!
Each wound of theirs was thy new morning,
And re-enthroned thee in thy rosy nest,

With blush of thine own blood thy day adorning:
It was the wit of love o'erflow'd the bounds
Of wrath, and made the way through all these wounds.
Welcome, dear, all-adorèd name!
For sure there is no knee
That knows not thee.
Or, if there be such sons of shame,
Alas! what will they do
When stubborn rocks shall bow,
And hills hang down their heav'n-saluting heads
To seek for humble beds
Of dust, where, in the bashful shades of night,
Next to their own low nothing they may lie,
And couch before the dazz'ling light of thy dread Majesty!
They that by Love's mild dictate now
Will not adore thee,
Shall then, with just confusion, bow
And break before thee.

IN THE GLORIOUS EPIPHANY OF OUR LORD GOD.

A Hymn sung as by the Three Kings.

First King.

BRIGHT babe, whose awful beauties make
The morn incur a sweet mistake;
2nd. For whom th' officious heav'ns devise

To disinherit the sun's rise,
3rd. Delicately to displace
The day, and plant it fairer in Thy face;
1st. O, Thou born King of loves,
2nd. Of lights,
3rd. Of joys!
Cho. Look up, sweet babe, look up, and see
For love of Thee,
Thus far from home,
The East is come
To seek herself in Thy sweet eyes!
1st. We, who strangely went astray,
Lost in a bright
Meridian night,
2nd. A darkness made of too much day,
3rd. Beckon'd from far
By Thy fair star,
Lo, at last have found our way!
Cho. To Thee, thou day of night; thou East of West!
Lo, we at last have found the way
To Thee, the world's great universal East;
The general and indifferent day!
1st. All-circling point, all-cent'ring sphere,
The world's one, round, eternal year;
2nd. Whose full and all-unwrinkled face
Nor sinks nor swells with time or place;
3rd. But everywhere, and everywhile,
Is one consistent solid smile;
1st. Not vex'd and tost
2nd. 'Twixt spring and frost,
3rd. Nor by alternate shreds of light

Sordidly shifting hands with shades and night.
Cho. O, little all, in Thy embrace
The world lies warm, and likes his place;
Nor does his full globe fail to be
Kiss'd on both his cheeks by Thee:
Time is too narrow for Thy year,
Nor makes the whole world Thy half sphere.
1st. To Thee, to Thee,
From him we flee;
2nd. From him, whom, by a more illustrious lie,
The blindness of the world did call the eye;
3rd. To him, who by these mortal clouds hast made
Thyself our sun, though Thine own shade.
1st. Farewell, the world's false light;
Farewell, the white
Egypt, a long farewell to thee,
Bright idol; black idolatry;
The dire face of inferior darkness kiss'd
And courted in the pompous mask of a more
specious mist.
2nd. Farewell, farewell,
The proud and misplaced gates of hell,
Perch'd in the morning's way,
And double-gilded as the doors of day;
The deep hypocrisy of death and night
More desperately dark, because more bright.
3rd. Welcome, the world's sure way;
Heav'n's wholesome ray!
Cho. Welcome, to us; and we,
Sweet, to ourselves in Thee,
1st. The deathless heir of all thy Father's day;

2nd. Decently born,
Embosom'd in a much more rosy morn—
The blushes of thy all-unblemish'd mother.
3rd. No more that other
Aurora shall set ope
Her ruby casements, or hereafter hope
From mortal eyes
To meet religious welcomes at her rise.
Cho. We, precious ones, in you have won
A gentler morn, a juster sun.
1st. His superficial beams sun-burnt our skin;
2nd. But left within
3rd. The night and winter still of death and sin.
Cho. Thy softer, yet more certain darts
Spare our eyes, but pierce our hearts.
1st. Therefore, with his proud Persian spoils
2nd. We court Thy more concerning smiles.
3rd. Therefore, with his disgrace
We gild the humble cheek of this chaste place;
Cho. And at Thy feet pour forth his face.
1st. The doting nations now no more
Shall any day but Thine adore;
2nd. Nor, much less, shall they leave these eyes
For cheap Egyptian deities.
3rd. In whatsoe'er more sacred shape
Of ram, he-goat, or reverend ape,
Those beauteous ravishers oppress'd so sore
The too-hard-tempted nations.
1st. Never more
By wanton heifer shall be worn
2nd. A garland, or a gilded horn.

The altar-stall'd ox, fat Osiris now,
With his fair sister-cow,
3rd. Shall kick the clouds no more; but lean and tame
Cho. See his horn'd face, and die for shame,
And Mithra now shall be no name.
1st. No longer shall the immodest lust
Of adulterous godless dust
2nd. Fly in the face of heav'n; as if it were
The poor world's fault that he is fair.
3rd. Nor with perverse loves and religious rapes
Revenge Thy bounties in their beauteous shapes,
And punish best things worst; because they stood
Guilty of being much for them too good.
1st. Proud sons of death, that durst compel
Heav'n itself to find them hell;
2nd. And by strange wit of madness wrest
From this world's East the other's West.
3rd. All-idolizing worms, that thus could crowd
And urge their sun into Thy cloud;
Forcing his sometimes eclipsed face to be
A long deliquium to the light of Thee.
Cho. Alas! with how much heavier shade
The shamefaced lamp hung down his head,
For that one eclipse he made,
Than all those he suffered!
1st. For this he look'd so big, and every morn
With a red face confess'd this scorn;
Or hiding his vex'd cheeks in a hirèd mist,
Kept them from being so unkindly kiss'd:
2nd. It was for this the day did rise
So oft with blubber'd eyes.

For this the evening wept; and we ne'er knew,
But call'd it dew.
This daily wrong
Silenced the morning sons, and damp'd their song.
Nor was 't our deafness, but our sins, that thus
Long made th' harmonious orbs all mute to us.
Time has a day in store,
When this so proudly poor
And self-oppressèd spark, that has so long
By the love-sick world been made
Not so much their sun as shade,
Weary of this glorious wrong,
From them and from himself shall flee
For shelter to the shadow of Thy tree!
Proud to have gain'd this precious loss,
And changed his false crown for Thy cross.
That dark day's clear doom shall define
Whose is the master fire, which sun would shine;
That sable judgment-seat shall by new laws
Decide and settle the great cause
Of controverted light;
And Nature's wrongs rejoice to do Thee right.
That forfeiture of noon to-night shall pay
All the idolat'rous theft done by this night of day;
And the great penitent press his own pale lips
With an elaborate love-eclipse,
To which the low world's laws
Shall lend no cause,
Save those domestic which He borrows
From our sins and His own sorrows.
Three sad hours' sackcloth, then, shall show to us

His penance, as our fault, conspicuous.
2nd. And he more needfully and nobly prove
The nations' terror now, than erst their love,
3rd. Their hated loves changed into wholesome fears.
Cho. The shutting of his eye shall open theirs.
1st. As by a fair-eyed fallacy of day
Misled before they lost their way,
So shall they, by the seasonable fright
Of an unseasonable night,
Losing it once again, stumble on true light;
2nd. And as before his too-bright eye
Was their more blind idolatry,
So his officious blindness now shall be
Their black, but faithful perspective of Thee;
3rd. His new prodigious night,
Their new and admirable light;
The supernatural dawn of thy pure day,
While wond'ring they,
The happy converts now of Him
Whom they compell'd before to be their sin,
Shall henceforth see
To kiss him only as their rod,
Whom they so long courted as God;
Cho. And their best use of him they worshipp'd be
To learn of him at least to worship Thee.
1st. It was their weakness woo'd his beauty;
But it shall be
Their wisdom now, as well as duty,
T' enjoy his blot; and, as a large black letter,
Use it to spell Thy beauties better;
And make the night itself their torch to Thee.

2nd. By the oblique ambush of this close night,
Couch'd in that conscious shade,
The right-eyed Areopagite
Shall with a vigorous guess invade
And catch thy quick reflex; and sharply see
On this dark ground
To descant Thee.
3rd. O price of the rich spirit! with that fierce chase
Of this strong soul shall he
Leap at Thy lofty face,
And seize the swift flash, in rebound
From this obsequious cloud,
Once call'd a sun;
Till dearly thus undone,
Cho. Till thus triumphantly tamed, O ye two
Twin suns! and taught now to negotiate you.
1st. Thus shall that reverend child of light,
2nd. By being scholar first of that new night,
Come forth great master of the mystic day;
3rd. And teach obscure mankind a more close way,
By the frugal negative light
Of a most wise and well-abusèd night,
To read more legible Thine original ray,
Cho. And make our darkness serve thy day;
Maintaining 'twixt Thy world and ours
A commerce of contrary pow'rs;
A mutual trade
'Twixt sun and shade,
By confederate black and white,
Borrowing day and lending night.
1st. Thus we, who when with all the noble pow'rs

That, at Thy cost, are call'd, not vainly, ours;
We vow to make brave way
Upwards, and press on for the pure intelligential prey;
2nd. At least, to play
The amorous spies,
And peep and proffer at Thy sparkling throne;
3rd. Instead of bringing in the blissful prize,
And fast'ning on thine eyes,
Forfeit our own,
And nothing gain,
But more ambitious loss, at least of brain;
Cho. Now by abasèd lids shall learn to be
Eagles, and shut our eyes that we may see.

The Close.

Therefore to Thee and Thine auspicious ray,
Dread sweet! lo, thus
At least by us,
The delegated eye of day
Does first his sceptre, then himself in solemn tribute pay.
Thus he undresses
His sacred unshorn tresses;
At Thy adorèd feet, thus, he lays down
1st. His gorgeous tire
Of flame and fire,
2nd. His glittering robe,
3rd. His sparkling crown,
1st. His gold,
2nd. His myrrh,

3rd. His frankincense,
Cho. To which he now has no pretence.
For being show'd by this day's light, how far
He is from sun enough to make Thy star,
His best ambition now is but to be
Something a brighter shadow, sweet, of Thee;
Or on heaven's azure forehead high to stand
Thy golden index; with a duteous hand
Pointing us home to our own sun,
The world's and his Hyperion!

TO THE QUEEN'S MAJESTY ON TWELFTH-DAY.

MADAM,
'Mongst those long rows of crowns that gild your race
These royal sages sue for decent place.
The day-break of the nations; their first ray;
When the dark world dawn'd into Christian day,
And smiled i' th' babe's bright face, the purpling bud
And rosy dawn of the right royal blood;
Fair first-fruits of the Lamb; sure kings in this;
They took a kingdom while they gave a kiss:
But the world's homage, scarce in these well blown,
We read in you, rare queen, ripe and full grown.
For from this day's rich seed of diadems
Does rise a radiant crop of royal stems,

A golden harvest of crown'd heads, that meet
And crowd for kisses from the Lamb's white feet.
In this illustrious throng, your lofty flood
Swells high, fair confluence of all high-born blood!
With your bright head whose groves of sceptres bend
Their wealthy tops; and for these feet contend.
So swore the Lamb's dread sire, and so we see't,
Crowns, and the heads they kiss, must court these feet.
Fix here, fair majesty! May your heart ne'er miss
To reap new crowns and kingdoms from that kiss!
Nor may we miss the joy to meet in you
The aged honours of this day still new.
May the great time in you still greater be,
While all the year is your Epiphany;
While your each day's devotion duly brings
Three kingdoms to supply this day's three kings!

THE OFFICE OF THE HOLY CROSS.

FOR THE HOUR OF MATINS.

The Versicle.

LORD, by Thy sweet and saving sign,

The Responsor.

Defend us from our foes and Thine.

Ver. Thou shalt open my lips, O Lord;
Res. And my mouth shall declare Thy praise.
Ver. O God, make speed to save me.

Res. O Lord, make haste to help me.
Ver. Glory be to the Father,
And to the Son,
And to the Holy Ghost,
Res. As it was in the beginning, is now, and ever shall be, world without end. *Amen.*

The Hymn.

The wakeful matins haste to sing
The unknown sorrows of our King;
The Father's word and wisdom made
Man for man, by man's betray'd;
The world's price set to sale, and by the bold
Merchants of death and sin is bought and sold;
Of His best friends, yea of Himself, forsaken,
By his worst foes, because he would, besieg'd and taken.

The Antiphon.

All hail, fair tree,
Whose fruit we be!
What song shall raise
Thy seemly praise,
Who brought'st to light
Life out of death, day out of night!

The Versicle.

Lo, we adore Thee,
Dread Lamb! and bow thus low before Thee;

The Responsor.

'Cause by the covenant of Thy Cross
Thou hast saved at once the whole world's loss.

The Prayer.

O, my Lord Jesu Christ, Son of the living God! interpose, I pray Thee, Thine own precious death, Thy Cross and Passion, betwixt my soul and Thy judgment, now and in the hour of my death. And vouchsafe to grant me Thy grace and mercy; to the living and dead remission and rest; to Thy Church, peace and concord; to us sinners, life and glory everlasting. Who livest and reignest with the Father, in the unity of the Holy Ghost, one God, world without end. *Amen.*

FOR THE HOUR OF PRIME.

The Versicle.

LORD, by Thy sweet and saving sign,

The Responsor.

Defend us from our foes and Thine.

Ver. Thou shalt open my lips, O Lord;
Res. And my mouth shall declare Thy praise.
Ver. O God, make speed to save me.
Res. O Lord, make haste to help me.
Ver. Glory be to, &c.
Res. As it was in, &c.

The Hymn.

The early prime blushes to say
She could not rise so soon as they
Call'd Pilate up, to try if he
Could lend them any cruelty.
Their hands with lashes arm'd, their tongues with lies,
And loathsome spittle blot those beauteous eyes,
The blissful springs of joy, from whose all-cheering ray
The fair stars fill their weakful fires, the sun himself
drinks day.

The Antiphon.

Victorious sign
That now dost shine,
Transcrib'd above
Into the land of light and love;
O, let us twine
Our roots with thine,
That we may rise
Upon thy wings and reach the skies!

The Versicle.

Lo, we adore Thee,
Dread Lamb! and fall
Thus low before Thee;

The Responsor.

'Cause by the covenant of Thy Cross
Thou hast saved at once the whole world's loss.

to us sinners, life and glory everlasting. Who livest and reignest with the Father, in the unity of the Holy Ghost, one God, world without end. *Amen.*

THE SIXTH.

The Versicle.

LORD, by Thy sweet and saving sign,

The Responsor.

Defend us from our foes and Thine.

Ver. Thou shalt open my lips, O Lord;
Res. And my mouth shall declare Thy praise.
Ver. O God, make speed to save me.
Res. O Lord, make haste to help me.
Ver. Glory be to, &c.
Res. As it was in, &c.

The Hymn.

Now is the noon of sorrow's night
High in His patience as their spite.
Lo, the faint Lamb, with weary limb,
Bears that huge tree which must bear Him!
That fatal plant, so great of fame
For fruit of sorrow and of shame,
Shall swell with both for Him, and mix
All woes into one crucifix.
Is tortur'd thirst itself too sweet a cup?
Gall and more bitter mocks shall make it up.

Are nails blunt pens of superficial smart?
Contempt and scorn can send sure wounds to search
the inmost heart.

The Antiphon.

O, dear and sweet dispute
'Twixt death's and love's far different fruit!
Different as far
As antidotes and poisons are.
By that first fatal tree
Both life and liberty
Were sold and slain;
By this they both look up and live again!

The Versicle.

Lo, we adore Thee,
Dread Lamb! and bow thus low before Thee;

The Responsor.

'Cause by the covenant of Thy Cross
Thou hast saved the world from certain loss.

The Prayer.

O, my Lord Jesu Christ, Son of the living God! interpose, I pray Thee, Thine own precious death, Thy Cross and Passion, betwixt my soul and Thy judgment, now and in the hour of my death. And vouchsafe to grant me Thy grace and mercy; to the living and dead, remission and rest; to Thy Church, peace and concord; to us sinners, life and glory everlasting. Who livest and reignest with the Father, in the unity of the Holy Ghost, one God, world without end. *Amen.*

THE NINTH.

The Versicle.

LORD, by Thy sweet and saving sign,

The Responsor.

Defend us from our foes and Thine.
Ver. Thou shalt open my lips, O Lord;
Res. And my mouth shall declare Thy praise.
Ver. O God, make speed to save me.
Res. O Lord, make haste to help me.
Ver. Glory be to, &c.
Res. As it was in, &c.

The Hymn.

The ninth with awful horror hark'ned to those groans
Which taught attention even to rocks and stones.
Hear, Father, hear! Thy Lamb, at last, complains
Of some more painful thing than all His pains.
Then bows His all-obedient head, and dies,
His own love's and our sin's great sacrifice.
The sun saw that, and would have seen no more;
The centre shook, her useless veil th' inglorious temple
tore.

The Antiphon.

O, strange mysterious strife
Of open death and hidden life!

When on the Cross my King did bleed
Life seem'd to die, death died indeed.

The Versicle.

Lo, we adore Thee,
Dread Lamb! and fall
Thus low before Thee;

The Responsor.

'Cause by the covenant of Thy Cross
Thou hast saved at once the whole world's loss.

The Prayer.

O, my Lord Jesu Christ, Son of the living God! interpose, I pray Thee, Thine own precious death, Thy Cross and Passion, betwixt my soul and Thy judgment, now and in the hour of my death. And vouchsafe to grant me Thy grace and mercy; to the living and dead, remission and rest; to Thy Church, peace and concord; to us sinners, life and glory everlasting. Who livest and reignest with the Father, in the unity of the Holy Ghost, one God, world without end. *Amen.*

EVENSONG.

The Versicle.

LORD, by Thy sweet and saving sign,

The Responsor.

Defend us from our foes and Thine.

Ver. Thou shalt open my lips, O Lord;
Res. And my mouth shall declare Thy praise.
Ver. O God, make speed to save me.
Res. O Lord, make haste to help me.
Ver. Glory be to, &c.
Res. As it was in, &c.

The Hymn.

But there were rocks would not relent at this.
Lo, for their own hearts they rend His!
Their deadly hate lives still, and hath
A wild reserve of wanton wrath;
Superfluous spear! but there's a heart stands by
Will look no wounds be lost, no death shall die.
Gather now thy grief's ripe fruit, great Mother-maid!
Then sit thee down, and sing thy evensong in the sad
tree's shade.

The Antiphon.

O sad, sweet tree!
Woeful and joyful, we

Both weep and sing in shade of thee:
When the dear nails did lock
And graft into thy gracious stock
The hope, the health,
The worth, the wealth
Of all the ransom'd world, thou hadst the power,
In that propitious hour,
To poise each precious limb,
And prove how light the world was when it weigh'd with Him.
Wide may'st thou spread
Thine arms; and with thy bright and blissful head
O'erlook all Libanus! Thy lofty crown
The King Himself is; thou His humble throne.
Where yielding, and yet conquering, He
Proved a new path of patient victory,
When wond'ring death by death was slain,
And our captivity His captive ta'en.

The Versicle.

Lo, we adore Thee,
Dread Lamb! and bow thus low before Thee;

The Responsor.

'Cause by the covenant of Thy Cross
Thou hast saved the world from certain loss.

The Prayer.

O, my Lord Jesu Christ, Son of the living God! interpose, I pray Thee, Thine own precious death, Thy Cross and Passion, betwixt my soul and Thy judgment, now and in the hour of my death. And vouchsafe to grant me Thy grace and mercy; to the living and dead, remission and rest; to Thy Church, peace and concord; to us sinners, life and glory everlasting. Who livest and reignest with the Father, in the unity of the Holy Ghost, one God, world without end. *Amen.*

COMPLIN.

The Versicle.

LORD, by Thy sweet and saving sign,

The Responsor.

Defend us from our foes and Thine.

Ver. Thou shalt open my lips, O Lord;
Res. And my mouth shall declare Thy praise.
Ver. O God, make speed to save me.
Res. O Lord, make haste to help me.
Ver. Glory be to, &c.
Res. As it was in, &c.

The Hymn.

The complin hour comes last, to call
Us to our own life's funeral.
Ah, heartless task! yet hope takes heed,
And lives in Him that here lies dead.
Run, Mary, run! bring hither all the blest
Arabia, for thy royal phœnix' nest;

Pour on thy noblest sweets, which, when they touch
This sweeter body, shall indeed be such.
But must Thy bed, Lord, be a borrow'd grave,
Who lend'st to all things all the life they have?
O, rather use this heart, thus far a fitter stone,
'Cause, though a hard and cold one, yet it is Thine own.
Amen.

The Antiphon.

O, save us, then,
Merciful King of men!
Since thou would'st needs be thus
A Saviour, and at such a rate, for us;
Save us, O save us, Lord!
We now will own no shorter wish, nor name a narrower word.
Thy blood bids us be bold;
Thy wounds give us fair hold;
Thy sorrows chide our shame;
Thy Cross, Thy nature, and Thy name
Advance our claim
And cry with one accord,
Save them, O save them, Lord!

The Versicle.

Lo, we adore Thee,
Dread Lamb! and bow thus low before Thee;

The Responsor.

'Cause by the covenant of Thy Cross
Thou hast saved the world from certain loss.

The Prayer.

O, my Lord Jesu Christ, Son of the living God! interpose, I pray Thee, Thine own precious death, Thy Cross and Passion, betwixt my soul and Thy judgment, now and in the hour of my death. And vouchsafe to grant me Thy grace and mercy; to the living and dead, remission and rest; to Thy Church, peace and concord; to us sinners, life and glory everlasting. Who livest and reignest with the Father, in the unity of the Holy Ghost, one God, world without end. *Amen.*

THE RECOMMENDATION.

THESE hours, and that which hovers o'er
my end,
Into Thy hands and heart, Lord, I commend!

Take both to Thine account, that I and mine
In that hour, and in these, may be all Thine.

That as I dedicate my devoutest breath,
To make a kind of life for my Lord's death,

So from His living, and life-giving death,
My dying life may draw a new and never-fleeting breath!

VEXILLA REGIS.

The Hymn of the Holy Cross.

LOOK up, languishing soul! Lo, where the
fair
Badge of thy faith calls back thy care,
And bids thee ne'er forget
Thy life is one long debt
Of love to Him who, on this painful tree,
Paid back the flesh He took for thee.

Lo, how the streams of life from that full nest
Of loves, thy Lord's too liberal breast,
Flow in an amorous flood
Of water wedding blood!
With these He wash'd thy stain, transferr'd thy smart,
And took it home to His own heart.

But thou, great love, greedy of such sad gain,
Usurp'd the portion of Thy pain,
And from the nails and spear
Turn'd the steel point of fear,
Their use is changed, not lost; and now they move
Not stings of wrath, but wounds of love.

Tall tree of life! Thy truth makes good
What was till now ne'er understood,
Though the prophetic King

Struck loud his faithful string;
It was thy wood he meant should make the throne
For a more than Solomon.

Large throne of Love! royally spread
With purple of too rich a red:
Thy crime is too much duty;
Thy burthen too much beauty!
Glorious or grievous more? thus to make good
Thy costly excellence with thy King's own blood.

Even balance of both worlds! our world of sin,
And that of grace heav'n weigh'd in Him,
Us with our price thou weighed'st;
Our price for us thou payed'st;
Soon as the right-hand scale rejoiced to prove
How much death weigh'd more light than Love.

Hail, our alone Hope! let Thy fair head shoot
Aloft; and fill the nations with Thy noble fruit.
The while our hearts and we
Thus graft ourselves on Thee,
Grow Thou, and they; and be Thy fair increase
The sinner's pardon, and the just man's peace.

Live, O, for ever live and reign,
The Lamb whom His own love has slain!
And let Thy lost sheep live t' inherit
That kingdom which this Cross did merit. *Amen.*

CHARITAS NIMIA,

Or the Dear Bargain.

LORD, what is man? why should he cost
Thee
So dear? what had his ruin lost Thee?
Lord, what is man? that Thou hast over-bought
So much a thing of nought?

Love is too kind, I see, and can
Make but a simple merchantman.
'Twas for such sorry merchandise
Bold painters have put out his eyes.

Alas, sweet Lord! what were't to Thee
If there were no such worms as we?
Heav'n ne'ertheless still heav'n would be.
Should mankind dwell
In the deep hell,
What have his woes to do with Thee?

Let him go weep
O'er his own wounds;
Seraphim will not sleep,
Nor spheres let fall their faithful rounds.

Still would the youthful spirits sing,
And still Thy spacious palace ring;

Still would those beauteous ministers of light
Burn all as bright,

And bow their flaming heads before Thee;
Still thrones and dominations would adore Thee;
Still would those ever-wakeful sons of fire
Keep warm Thy praise
Both nights and days,
And teach Thy loved name to their noble lyre.

Let froward dust then do its kind,
And give itself for sport to the proud wind.
Why should a piece of peevish clay plead shares
In the eternity of Thy old cares?
Why shouldst Thou bow Thy awful breast to see
What mine own madnesses have done with me?

Should not the king still keep his throne
Because some desperate fool's undone?
Or will the world's illustrious eyes
Weep for every worm that dies?

Will the gallant sun
E'er the less glorious run?
Will he hang down his golden head,
Or e'er the sooner seek his western bed,
Because some foolish fly
Grows wanton, and will die?

If I were lost in misery,
What was it to Thy heav'n, and Thee?

What was it to Thy precious blood
If my foul heart call'd for a flood?

What if my faithless soul and I
Would needs fall in
With guilt and sin,
What did the Lamb that He should die?
What did the Lamb that He should need,
When the wolf sins, Himself to bleed?

If my base lust
Bargain'd with death and well-beseeming dust,
Why should the white
Lamb's bosom write
The purple name
Of my sin's shame?

Why should His unstain'd breast make good
My blushes with His own heart blood?

O, my Saviour, make me see
How dearly Thou hast paid for me,

That, lost again, my life may prove
As then in death, so now in love!

SANCTA MARIA DOLORUM,

Or the Mother of Sorrows; a Pathetical descant upon the devout plainsong of "Stabat Mater dolorosa."

IN shade of death's sad tree
Stood doleful she;
Ah, she! now by none other
Name to be known, alas! but Sorrow's Mother.
Before her eyes
Her's, and the whole world's joys,
Hanging all torn, she sees, and in His woes
And pains her pangs and throes.
Each wound of His from every part,
All, more at home in Her own heart.

What kind of marble, then,
Is that cold man
Who can look on and see,
Nor keep such noble sorrow's company?
Sure even from you,
My flints, some drops are due,
To see so many unkind swords contest
So fast for one soft breast;
While with a faithful, mutual flood
Her eyes bleed tears, His wounds weep blood!

O, costly intercourse
Of death's, and worse
Divided loves: while Son and Mother
Discourse alternate wounds to one another!
Quick deaths that grow
And gather as they come and go;
His nails write swords in Her; which soon Her heart
Pays back, with more than their own smart;
Her swords, still growing with His pain,
Turn spears, and straight come home again.

She sees Her Son, Her God,
Bow with a load
Of borrow'd sins, and swim
In woes that were not made for Him.
Ah! hard command
Of Love! Here must She stand
Charged to look on, and with a steadfast eye
See Her life die;
Leaving Her only so much breath
As serves to keep alive Her death.

O, Mother turtle-dove!
Soft source of love!
That these dry lids might borrow
Something from Thy full seas of sorrow!
O, in that breast
Of Thine, the noblest nest
Both of Love's fires and floods, might I recline
This hard, cold heart of mine,
The chill lump would relent, and prove
Soft subject for the siege of Love!

O, teach those wounds to bleed
In me; me, so to read
This book of loves, thus writ
In lines of death, my life may copy it
With loyal cares.
O, let me here claim shares!
Yield something in thy sad prerogative,
Great Queen of griefs, and give
Me to my tears; who, though all stone,
Think much that Thou should'st mourn alone.

Yea, let my life and me
Fix here with Thee,
And at the humble foot
Of this fair tree take our eternal root.
That so we may
At least be in Love's way;
And in these chaste wars while the wing'd wounds flee
So fast 'twixt Him and Thee,
My breast may catch the kiss of some kind dart,
Though as at second hand from either heart.

O you, your own best darts,
Dear doleful hearts!
Hail, and strike home and make me see
That wounded bosoms their own weapons be!
Come, wounds! come, darts!
Nail'd hands! and piercèd hearts!
Come, your whole selves, Sorrow's great Son and
Mother,
Nor grudge a younger brother

Of griefs his portion, who, had all their due,
One single wound should not have left for you.

Shall I set there
So deep a share,
Dear wounds, and only now
In sorrows draw no dividend with you!
O, be more wise,
If not more soft, mine eyes!
Flow, tardy founts! and into decent show'rs
Dissolve my days and hours:
And if thou yet, faint soul, defer
To bleed with Him, fail not to weep with Her.

Rich Queen, lend some relief,
At least in alms of grief,
To a heart who, by a sad right of sin,
Could prove the whole sum, too sure, due to him.
By all those stings
Of love, sweet bitter things,
Which these torn hands transcribed on Thy true heart;
O, teach mine, too, the art
To study him so, till we mix
Wounds, and become one crucifix.

O, let me suck the wine
So long of this chaste vine,
Till, drunk of the dear wounds, I be
A lost thing to the world, as it to me!
O, faithful friend
Of me and of my end!

Fold up my life in love, and lay't beneath
My dear Lord's vital death.
Lo, heart, thy hope's whole plea! Her precious breath
Pour'd out in prayers for thee; thy Lord's in death.

THE HYMN OF SAINT THOMAS IN ADORATION OF THE BLESSED SACRAMENT.

WITH all the pow'rs my poor heart hath,
Of humble love and loyal faith,
Thus low, my hidden life! I bow to Thee,
Whom too much love hath bow'd more low for me.
Down, down, proud sense! discourses die,
Keep close, my soul's enquiring eye!
Nor touch nor taste must look for more,
But each sit still in his own door.

Your ports are all superfluous here,
Save that which lets in faith—the ear.
Faith is my skill, faith can believe
As fast as love new laws can give.
Faith is my force, faith strength affords
To keep pace with those pow'rful words:
And words more sure, more sweet than they
Love could not think, truth could not say.

O, let Thy wretch find that relief
Thou didst afford the faithful thief;

Plead for me, Love! allege and show
That faith has farther here to go,
And less to lean on; because then,
Though hid as God, wounds write Thee man;
Thomas might touch none but might see,
At least, the suff'ring side of Thee;
And that, too, was Thyself which Thee did cover,
But here even that's hid, too, which hides the other.

Sweet, consider then, that I,
Though allow'd not hand nor eye
To teach at Thy loved face, nor can
Taste Thee God, or touch Thee man,
Both yet believe and witness Thee,
My Lord, too, and my God, as loud as He.

Help, Lord, my hope increase,
And fill my portion in Thy peace.
Give love for life, nor let my days
Grow, but in new powers to name Thy praise.

O, dear memorial of that death
Which lives still, and allows us breath!
Rich, royal flood! bountiful bread!
Whose use denies us to the dead;
Whose vital gust alone can give
The same leave both to eat and live;
Live ever, bread of loves, and be
My life, my soul, my surer self to me!

O, soft self-wounding pelican,
Whose breast weeps balm for wounded man!

Ah, this way bend thy benign flood,
To a bleeding heart that gasps for blood;
That blood whose least drop sovereign be
To wash my worlds of sins from me!
Come, love! come, Lord! and that long day
For which I languish, come away;
When this dry soul those eyes shall see,
And drink the unseal'd source of Thee;
When glory's sun faith's shade shall chase,
Then for Thy veil give me Thy face. *Amen.*

THE HYMN FOR THE BLESSED SACRAMENT.

LAUDA SION SALVATOREM.

RISE, royal Sion! rise and sing
Thy soul's kind shepherd, thy heart's King.
Stretch all thy powers, call, if you can,
Harps of heav'n to hands of man—
This sovereign subject sits above
The best ambition of thy love.

Lo, the bread of life! this day's
Triumphant text provokes Thy praise—
The living and life-giving bread
To the great twelve distributed,
When Life Himself at point to die,
Of Love, was his own legacy.

Come, Love! and let us work a song
Loud and pleasant, sweet and long;
Let lips and hearts lift high the noise
Of so just and solemn joys,
Which on His white brows this bright day
Shall hence for ever bear away.

Lo, the new law of a new Lord,
With a new Lamb blesses the board!
The aged Pascha pleads not years,
But spies love's dawn, and disappears.
Types yield to truths, shades shrink away,
And their night dies into our day.

But, lest that die too, we are bid
Ever to do what he once did;
And, by a mindful, mystic breath,
That we may live, revive His death;
With a well-blest bread and wine
Transumed and taught to turn divine.

The heav'n-instructed house of faith
Here a holy dictate hath,
That they but lend their form and face,
Themselves with reverence leave their place,
Nature and name, to be made good
By nobler bread, more needful blood.

Where Nature's laws no leave will give,
Bold faith takes heart, and dares believe
In different species, name not things,

Himself to me my Saviour brings,
As meat in that, as drink in this;
But still in both one Christ He is.

The receiving mouth here makes
Nor wound nor breach in what He takes.
Let one, or one thousand be
Here dividers, single he
Bears home no less, all they no more,
Nor leave they both less than before.

Though in itself this sovereign feast
Be all the same to every guest,
Yet on the same, life-meaning, bread
The child of death eats himself dead.
Nor is't Love's fault, but sin's dire skill
That thus from life can death distil.

When the blest signs thou broke shalt see,
Hold but thy faith entire as He,
Who, howsoe'er clad, cannot come
Less than whole Christ in every crumb.
In broken forms a stable faith
Untouch'd her precious total hath.

Lo, the life-food of angels then
Bow'd to the lowly mouths of men!
The childrens' bread, the bridegroom's wine,
Not to be cast to dogs or swine.

Lo, the full, final sacrifice
On which all figures fix'd their eyes,

The ransom'd Isaac and his ram,
The manna, and the Paschal Lamb!

Jesu, Master, just and true!
Our food, and faithful Shepherd too!
O, by Thyself vouchsafe to keep,
As with Thyself Thou feed'st Thy sheep.

O, let that love which thus makes Thee
Mix with our low mortality,
Lift our lean souls, and set us up
Convictors of Thine own full cup,
Co-heirs of saints, that so all may
Drink the same wine, and the same way;
Nor change the pasture, but the place,
To feed of Thee in Thine own face! *Amen.*

THE HYMN "DIES IRÆ DIES ILLA."

In Meditation of the Day of Judgment.

HEAR'ST thou, my soul, what serious things
Both the Psalm and Sibyl sings,
Of a sure Judge, from whose sharp ray
The world in flames shall fly away?

O, that Fire! before whose face
Heav'n and earth shall find no place:
O, these Eyes! whose angry light
Must be the day of that dread night.

O, that Trump! whose blast shall run
An even round with th' circling sun,
And urge the murmuring graves to bring
Pale mankind forth to meet his King.

Horror of nature, hell and death!
When a deep groan from beneath
Shall cry, "we come, we come," and all
The caves of night answer one call.

O, that Book! whose leaves so bright
Will set the world in severe light.
O, that Judge! whose hand, whose eye
None can endure, yet none can fly.

Ah, then, poor soul! what wilt thou say?
And to what patron choose to pray,
When stars themselves shall stagger, and
The most firm foot no more than stand?

But Thou giv'st leave, dread Lord, that we
Take shelter from Thyself in Thee;
And with the wings of Thine own dove
Fly to Thy sceptre of soft love!

Dear, remember in that day
Who was the cause Thou cam'st this way;
Thy sheep was stray'd, and Thou wouldst be
Even lost Thyself in seeking me!

Shall all that labour, all that cost
Of love, and even that loss, be lost?

And this loved soul judged worth no less
Than all that way and weariness?

Just Mercy, then, Thy reck'ning be
With my price, and not with me;
'Twas paid at first with too much pain,
To be paid twice, or once in vain.

Mercy, my Judge! mercy, I cry,
With blushing cheek and bleeding eye;
The conscious colours of my sin
Are red without, and pale within.

O, let Thine own soft bowels pay
Thyself, and so discharge that day!
If Sin can sigh, Love can forgive,
O, say the word, my soul shall live!

Those mercies which Thy Mary found,
Or who Thy cross confess'd and crown'd,
Hope tells my heart the same loves be
Still alive, and still for me.

Though both my pray'rs and tears combine,
Both worthless are, for they are mine;
But Thou Thy bounteous self still be,
And show Thou art by saving me.

O, when Thy last frown shall proclaim
The flocks of goats to folds of flame,
And all Thy lost sheep found shall be,
Let "Come ye blessed" then call me!

When the dread "Ite" shall divide
Those limbs of death from Thy left side,
Let those life-speaking lips command
That I inherit Thy right hand!

O, hear a suppliant heart, all crush'd
And crumbled into contrite dust!
My hope, my fear! my Judge, my Friend!
Take charge of me, and of my end!

THE HYMN "O GLORIOSA DOMINA."

HAIL, most high, most humble one!
Above the world, below thy Son,
Whose blush the moon beauteously mars
And stains the timorous light of stars.
He that made all things had not done
Till He had made Himself thy Son.
The whole world's host would be thy guest
And board Himself at thy rich breast.
O, boundless hospitality!
The feast of all things feeds on thee.
The first Eve, mother of our fall,
Ere she bore any one, slew all.
Of her unkind gift might we have
The inheritance of a hasty grave;
Quick buried in the wanton tomb
Of one forbidden bit,

Had not a better fruit forbidden it;
Had not thy healthful womb
The world's new Eastern window been
And given us heav'n again in giving Him:
Thine was the rosy dawn that sprung the day
Which renders all the stars she stole away.
Let then th' aged world be wise, and all
Prove nobly, here, unnatural:
'Tis gratitude to forget that other,
And call the maiden Eve their mother.
Ye redeem'd nations far and near,
Applaud your happy selves in her,
All you to whom this love belongs,
And keep 't alive with lasting songs.
Let hearts and lips speak loud, and say,
Hail, door of life, and source of day!
The door was shut, the fountain seal'd,
Yet light was seen, and life revealed;
The fountain seal'd, yet life found way.
Glory to Thee, great Virgin's Son,
In bosom of Thy Father's bliss!
The same to Thee, sweet Spirit, be done,
As ever shall be, was, and is! *Amen.*

THE FLAMING HEART,

Upon the Book and Picture of the Seraphical Saint Teresa, as she is usually expressed with a Seraphim beside her.

WELL-MEANING readers! you that come as friends
And catch the precious name this piece pretends,
Make not too much haste t' admire
That fair-cheek'd fallacy of fire.
That is a seraphim, they say,
And this the great Teresia.
Readers, be ruled by me, and make
Here a well-placed and wise mistake;
You must transpose the picture quite,
And spell it wrong to read it right;
Read Him for Her, and Her for Him,
And call the saint the seraphim.
Painter, what didst thou understand
To put her dart into his hand?
See, even the years and size of him
Shows this the mother seraphim.
This is the mistress flame, and duteous he
Her happy fireworks, here, comes down to see:
O, most poor-spirited of men!
Had thy cold pencil kiss'd her pen,
Thou couldst not so unkindly err

To show us this faint shade for her.
Why, man, this speaks pure mortal frame;
And mocks with female frost love's manly flame,
One would'st suspect thou mean'st to print
Some weak, inferior woman Saint.
But, had thy pale-faced purple took
Fire from the burning cheeks of that bright book,
Thou would'st on her have heap'd up all
That could be found seraphical;
Whate'er this youth of fire wears fair,
Rosy fingers, radiant hair,
Glowing cheek, and glist'ring wings,
All those fair and flagrant things;
But, before all, that fiery dart
Had fill'd the hand of this great heart.
Do, then, as equal right requires,
Since his the blushes be, and her's the fires;
Resume and rectify thy rude design,
Undress thy seraphim into mine;
Redeem this injury of thy art,
Give him the veil, give her the dart.
Give him the veil, that he may cover
The red cheeks of a rivall'd lover,
Ashamed that our world now can show
Nests of new seraphims here below.
Give her the dart, for it is she,
Fair youth, shoots both thy shaft and thee;
Say, all ye wise and well-pierced hearts
That live and die amidst her darts,
What is't your tasteful spirits do prove
In that rare life of her and love?

Say and bear witness. Sends she not
A seraphim at every shot?
What magazines of immortal arms there shine!
Heav'n's great artillery in each love-spun line.
Give, then, the dart to her who gives the flame,
Give him the veil who gives the shame.
  But if it be the frequent fate
Of worst faults to be fortunate,
If all's prescription, and proud wrong
Hearkens not to an humble song,
For all the gallantry of him,
Give me the suff'ring seraphim.
His be the bravery of those bright things,
The glowing cheeks, the glistering wings,
The rosy hand, the radiant dart;
Leave her alone the flaming heart.
  Leave her that, and thou shalt leave her
Not one loose shaft, but Love's whole quiver.
For in Love's field was never found
A nobler weapon than a wound.
Love's passives are his activ'st part,
The wounded is the wounding heart.
O, heart! the equal poise of Love's both parts,
Big alike with wounds and darts,
Live in these conquering leaves, live all the same,
And walk through all tongues one triumphant flame;
Live here, great heart, and love, and die, and kill,
And bleed, and wŏund, and yield, and conquer still.
Let this immortal Life, where'er it comes,
Walk in a crowd of loves and martyrdoms.
Let mystic deaths wait on't, and wise souls be

The love-slain witnesses of this life of thee.
O, sweet incendiary! show here thy art
Upon this carcass of a hard, cold heart;
Let all thy scatter'd shafts of light, that play
Among the leaves of thy large books of day,
Combined against this breast, at once break in
And take away from me myself and sin;
This gracious robbery shall thy bounty be,
And my best fortunes such fair spoils of me.
O, thou undaunted daughter of desires!
By all thy dower of lights and fires,
By all the eagle in thee, all the dove,
By all thy lives and deaths of love,
By thy large draughts of intellectual day,
And by thy thirsts of love more large than they;
By all thy brim-fill'd bowls of fierce desire,
By thy last morning's draught of liquid fire,
By the full kingdom of that final kiss
That seiz'd thy parting soul, and seal'd thee his;
By all the heav'ns thou hast in him,
Fair sister of the seraphim!
By all of him we have in thee,
Leave nothing of myself in me:
Let me so read thy life that I
Unto all life of mine may die.

A SONG.

LORD, when the sense of Thy sweet grace
Sends up my soul to seek Thy face,
Thy blessed eyes breed such desire,
I die in love's delicious fire.
O Love! I am thy sacrifice,
Be still triumphant, blessed eyes;
Still shine on me, fair suns! that I
Still may behold though still I die.

SECOND PART.

Though still I die, I live again,
Still longing so to be still slain;
So gainful is such loss of breath,
I die even in desire of death.
Still live in me this loving strife
Of living death and dying life:
For while Thou sweetly slayest me,
Dead to myself, I live in Thee.

TO MISTRESS M. R.* COUNSEL CONCERNING HER CHOICE.

DEAR, heav'n-designèd soul!
Amongst the rest
Of suitors that besiege your maiden breast,
Why may not I
My fortune try,
And venture to speak one good word,
Not for myself, alas! but for my dearer Lord?
You've seen already, in this lower sphere
Of froth and bubbles, what to look for here.
Say, gentle soul, what can you find
But painted shapes,
Peacocks and apes,
Illustrious flies,
Gilded dunghills, glorious lies,
Goodly surmises
And deep disguises,
Oaths of water, words of wind?
Truth bids me say, 'tis time you ceased to trust
Your soul to any son of dust.
'Tis time you listen to a braver love,
Which from above
Calls you up higher,
And bids you come
And choose your room

* See antea, p. 61.

Among his own fair sons of fire,
Where you among
The golden throng,
That watches at his palace doors,
May pass along
And follow those fair stars of yours;
Stars much too fair and pure to wait upon
The false smiles of a sublunary sun.
Sweet, let me prophesy that at last 'twill prove
Your wary love
Lays up his purer and more precious vows,
And means them for a far more worthy spouse
Than this world of lies can give ye,
Ev'n for him with whom nor cost,
Nor love, nor labour can be lost;
Him who never will deceive ye.
Let not my Lord, the mighty lover
Of souls, disdain that I discover
The hidden art
Of His high stratagem to win your heart.
It was His heav'nly art
Kindly to cross you
In your mistaken love,
That, at the next remove,
Thence He might toss you,
And strike your troublèd heart
Home to Himself, to hide it in His breast,
The bright ambrosial nest,
Of love, of life, and everlasting rest.
Happy mistake!
That thus shall wake

Your wise soul, never to be won
Now with a love below the sun.
Your first choice fails; O, when you choose again,
May it not be among the sons of men!

ALEXIAS.

The Complaint of the forsaken wife of Saint Alexis.

THE FIRST ELEGY.

I LATE the Roman youth's loved praise and pride,
Whom long none could obtain, though thousands tried,
Lo, here am left, alas! for my lost mate
T' embrace my tears, and kiss an unkind fate.
Sure in my early woes stars were at strife,
And tried to make a widow ere a wife.
Nor can I tell, and this new tears doth breed,
In what strange path my Lord's fair footsteps bleed.
O, knew I where he wander'd, I should see
Some solace in my sorrow's certainty;
I'd send my woes in words should weep for me.
Who knows how pow'rful well-writ pray'rs would be!
Sending's too slow a word, myself would fly;
Who knows my own heart's woes so well as I?
But how shall I steal hence? Alexis, thou,
Ah, thou thyself, alas! has taught me how
Love, too, that leads thee would lend me the wings

To bear me harmless through the hardest things:
And where love lends the wing, and leads the way,
What dangers can there be dare say me nay?
If I be shipwreck'd, love shall teach to swim;
If drown'd, sweet is the death endured for him;
The noted sea shall change his name with me,
I 'mongst the blest stars a new name shall be;
And sure where lovers make their wat'ry graves
The weeping mariner will augment the waves.
For who so hard, but, passing by that way,
Will take acquaintance of my woes, and say,
Here't was the Roman maid found a hard fate,
While through the world she sought her wand'ring mate;
Here perish'd she, poor heart! heav'ns, be my vows
As true to me as she was to her spouse!
O, live so rare a love! live! and in thee
The too frail life of female constancy.
Farewell, and shine, fair soul, shine there above,
Firm in thy crown as here fast in thy love.
There thy lost fugitive thou hast found at last;
Be happy, and for ever hold him fast!

THE SECOND ELEGY.

THOUGH all the joys I had fled hence with thee,
Unkind! yet are my tears still true to me;
I'm wedded o'er again since thou art gone,
Nor could'st thou, cruel, leave me quite alone.

Alexis's widow now is Sorrow's wife,
With him shall I weep out my weary life.
Welcome, my sad, sweet mate! now have I got
At last a constant love that leaves me not:
Firm he, as thou art false, nor need my cries
Thus vex the earth, and tear the [lofty] skies.
For him, alas! ne'er shall I need to be
Troublesome to the world, thus, as for thee,
For thee I talk to trees; with silent groves
Expostulate my woes and much-wrong'd loves.
Hills and relentless rocks, or if there be
Things that in hardness more allude to thee;
To these I talk in tears, and tell my pain,
And answer, too, for them in tears again.
How oft have I wept out the weary sun!
My wat'ry hour-glass hath old time outrun.
O, I am learnèd grown, poor love and I
Have studied over all astrology.
I'm perfect in heav'n's state, with every star
My skilful grief is grown familiar.
Rise, fairest of those fires, whate'er thou be
Whose rosy beam shall point my sun to me;
Such as the sacred light that erst did bring
The eastern princes to their infant King.
O rise, pure lamp! and lend thy golden ray
That weary love at last may find his way.

THE THIRD ELEGY.

RICH, churlish land! that hid'st so long in thee,
My treasures, rich, alas! by robbing me.
Needs must my miseries owe that man a spite
Whoe'er he be was the first wand'ring knight.
O, had he ne'er been at that cruel cost
Nature's virginity had ne'er been lost.
Seas had not been rebuked by saucy oars,
But lain lock'd up safe in their sacred shores;
Men had not spurn'd at mountains, nor made wars
With rocks; nor bold hands struck the world's strong bars;
Nor lost in too large bounds, our little Rome
Full sweetly with itself had dwelt at home.
My poor Alexis then in peaceful life
Had under some low roof loved his plain wife;
But now, ah me! from where he has no foes
He flies, and into wilful exile goes.
Cruel, return; or tell the reason why
Thy dearest parents have deserved to die;
And I, what is my crime I cannot tell,
Unless it be a crime t' have loved too well.
If heats of holier love and high desire
Make big thy fair breast with immortal fire,
What needs my virgin lord fly thus from me,
Who only wish his virgin wife to be?
Witness, chaste heav'ns! no happier vows I know
Than to a virgin grave untouch'd to go.

Love's truest knot by Venus is not tied,
Nor do embraces only make a bride.
The queen of angels, and men chaste as you,
Was maiden wife, and maiden mother too.
Cecilia, glory of her name and blood,
With happy gain her maiden vows made good.
The lusty bridegroom made approach: young man,
Take heed, said she, take heed, Valerian!
My bosom's guard, a spirit great and strong,
Stands armed to shield me from all wanton wrong.
My charity is sacred, and my sleep
Wakeful, her dear vows undefiled to keep.
Pallas bears arms, forsooth, and should there be
No fortress built for true virginity?
No gaping gorgon this, none, like the rest
Of your learned lies: here you'll find no such jest.
I'm yours; O, were my God, my Christ so too,
I'd know no name of love on earth but you.
He yields, and straight baptized, obtains the grace
To gaze on the fair soldier's glorious face.
Both mix'd at last their blood in one rich bed
Of rosy martyrdom twice marrièd.
O, burn our Hymen bright in such high flame;
Thy torch, terrestrial love, have here no name.
How sweet the mutual yoke of man and wife,
When holy fires maintain love's heav'nly life!
But I, so help me, Heav'n, my hopes to see,
When thousands sought my love, loved none but thee.
Still as their vain tears my firm vows did try,
Alexis, he alone is mine, said I;
Half true, alas! half false proves that poor line,
Alexis is alone, but is not mine.

DESCRIPTION OF A RELIGIOUS HOUSE AND CONDITION OF LIFE.

Out of Barclay.

NO roofs of gold o'er riotous tables shining,
Whole days and suns devoured with endless dining;
No sails of Tyrian silk proud pavements sweeping;
Nor ivory couches costlier slumbers keeping;
False lights of flaring gem; tumultuous joys;
Halls full of flattering men and frisking boys;
Whate'er false shows of short and slippery good
Mix the mad sons of men in mutual blood.
But walks and unshorn woods, and souls just so
Unforced and genuine, but not shady though;
Our lodgings hard and homely as our fare,
That chaste and cheap as the few clothes we wear.
Those course and negligent, as the natural locks
Of these loose groves, rough as th' unpolish'd rocks.
A hasty portion of prescribèd sleep;
Obedient slumbers that can wake and weep,
And sing, and sigh, and work, and sleep again;
Still rolling a round sphere of still-returning pain;
Hands full of hearty labours do much that more they may,
And work for work, not wages; let to-morrow's
New drops wash off the sweat of this day's sorrows;

A long and daily-dying life, which breathes
A respiration of reviving deaths.
But neither are there those ignoble stings
That nip the bosom of the world's best things,
And lash earth-labouring souls;
No cruel guard of diligent cares, that keep
Crown'd woes awake, as things too wise for sleep:
But reverend discipline, and religious fear,
And soft obedience, find sweet biding here;
Silence and sacred rest, peace and pure joys,
Kind loves keep house, lie close, and make no noise,
And room enough for monarchs, while none swells
Beyond the kingdoms of contentful cells.
The self-rememb'ring soul sweetly recovers
Her kindred with the stars; not basely hovers
Below; but meditates her immortal way
Home to th' original source of light and intellectual day.

POEMATA LATINA.

POEMATA LATINA.

BULLA.

QUID tibi vana suos offert mea bulla timores?
Quid facit ad vestrum pondus inane meum?
Expectat nostros humeros toga fortior; ista
En mea bulla, lares en tua dextera mihi.

Quid tu? quæ nova machina,
Quæ tam fortuito globo
In vitam properas brevem?
Qualis virgineos adhuc
Cypris concutiens sinus,
Cypris jam nova, jam recens,
Et spumis media in suis,
Promsit purpureum latus;
Concha de patria micas,
Pulchroque exsilis impetu;
Statim et millibus ebria
Ducens terga coloribus
Evolvis tumidos sinus
Sphæra plena volubili.

Cujus per varium latus,
Cujus per teretem globum
Iris lubrica cursitans
Centum per species vagas,
Et picti facies chori
Circum regnat, et undique,
Et se Diva volatilis
Jucundo levis impetu
Et vertigine perfida
Lasciva sequitur fuga
Et pulchre dubitat; fluit
Tam fallax toties novis,
Tot se per reduces vias,
Erroresque reciprocos
Spargit vena coloribus;
Et pompa natat ebria.
Tali militia micans
Agmen se rude dividit;
Campis quippe volantibus,
Et campi levis æquore
Ordo insanus obambulans
Passim se fugit, et fugat.
Passim perdit, et invenit.
Pulchrum spargitur hic Chaos.
Hic viva, hic vaga flumina
Ripa non propria meant,
Sed miscent socias vias,
Communique sub alveo
Stipant delicias suas.
Quarum proximitas vaga
Tam discrimine lubrico,

Tam subtilibus arguit
Juncturam tenuem notis,
Pompa ut florida nullibi
Sinceras habeat vias;
Nec vultu nitent suo.
Sed dulcis cumulus novos
Miscens purpureus sinus
Flagrant divitiis suis,
Privatum renuens jubar.
Floris diluvio vagi,
Floris sidere publico
Late ver subit aureum,
Atque effunditur in suæ
Vires undique copiæ.
Nempe omnis quia cernitur,
Nullus cernitur hic color,
Et vicinia contumax
Allidit species vagas.
Illic contiguis aquis
Marcent pallidulæ faces.
Unde hic vena tenellulæ,
Flammis ebria proximis
Discit purpureas vias,
Et rubro salit alveo.
Ostri sanguineum jubar
Lambunt lactea flumina;
Suasu cærulei maris
Mansuescit seges aurea;
Et lucis faciles genæ
Vanas ad nebulas stupent;
Subque avis rubicundulis

Flagrant sobria lilia.
Vicinis adeo rosis
Vicinæ invigilant nives,
Ut sint et nives rosæ,
Ut sint et rosæ nives;
Accenduntque rosæ nives,
Extinguuntque nives rosas.
Illic cum viridi rubet,
Hic et cum rutile viret
Lascivi facies chori.
Et quicquid rota lubrica
Caudæ stelligeræ notat,
Pulchrum pergit et in ambitum.
Hic cœli implicitus labor,
Orbes orbibus obvii;
Hic grex velleris aurei
Grex pellucidus ætheris;
Qui noctis nigra pascua
Puris morsibus atterit;
Hic quicquid nitidum et vagum
Cœli vibrat arenula
Dulci pingitur in joco.
Hic mundus tener impedit
Sese amplexibus in suis.
Succinctique sinu globi
Errat per proprium decus.
Hic nictant subitæ faces,
Et ludunt tremulum diem.
Mox se surripiunt sui et
Quærunt tecta supercili;
Atque abdunt petulans jubar,

Subsiduntque proterviter.
Atque hæc omnia quam brevis
Sunt mendacia machinæ!
Currunt scilicet omnia
Sphæra, non vitrea quidem,
Ut quondam Siculus globus,
Sed vitro nitida magis,
Sed vitro fragili magis,
Et vitro vitrea magis.

Sum venti ingenium breve
Flos sum, scilicet, aëris;
Sidus scilicet æquoris;
Naturæ jocus auréus,
Naturæ vaga fabula,
Naturæ breve somnium.
Nugarum decus et dolor;
Dulcis, doctaque vanitas.
Auræ filia perfidæ;
Et risus facilis parens.
Tantum gutta superbior,
Fortunatius et lutum.

Sum fluxæ pretium spei;
Una ex Hesperidum insulis.
Formæ pyxis, amantium
Clare cæcus ocellulus;
Vanæ et cor leve gloriæ.

Sum cæcæ speculum Deæ,
Sum Fortunæ ego tessera,

Quam dat militibus suis;
Sum Fortunæ ego symbolum,
Quo sancit fragilem fidem
Cum mortalibus ebriis
Obsignatque tabellulas.

Sum blandum, petulans, vagum,
Pulchrum, purpureum, et decens,
Comptum, floridulum, et recens,
Distinctum nivibus, rosis,
Undis, ignibus, aëre,
Pictum, gemmeum, et aureum,
O sum, scilicet, O nihil.

Si piget, et longam traxisse in tædia pompam
  Vivax, et nimium Bulla videtur anus;
Tolle tuos oculos, pensum leve desinet, illam
  Parca metet facili non operosa manu.
Vixit adhuc. Cur vixit? adhuc tu nempe legebas;
  Tempe fuit tempus tum potuisse mori.

THESAURUS MALORUM FŒMINA.

QUIS deus, o quis erat qui te, mala fœmina, finxit?
  Proh! crimen superum, noxa pudenda deûm!
Quæ divum manus est adeo non dextera mundo?
  In nostras clades ingeniosa manus!

Parcite; peccavi: nec enim pia numina possunt
  Tam crudele semel vel voluisse nefas.
Vestrum opus est pietas; opus est concordia vestrum:
  Vos equidem tales haud reor artifices.
Heus inferna cohors! fœtus cògnoscite vestros.
  Num pudet hanc vestrum vincere posse scelus?
Plaudite Tartarei proceres, Erebique potentes,
  (Næ mirum est tantum vos potuisse malum,)
Jam vestras laudate manus. Si forte tacetis,
  Artificum laudes grande loquetur opus.
Quam bene vos omnes speculo contemplor in isto?
  Pietas in angustum cogitur omne malum.
Quin dormi Pluto. Rabidas compesce sorores,
  Jam non poscit opem nostra ruina tuam.
Hæc satis in nostros fabricata est machina muros,
  Mortales furias Tartara nostra dabunt.

IN APOLLINEA DEPEREUNTEM DAPHNEN.

STULTE Cupido,
  Quid tua flamma parat?
  Annos sole sub ipso
Accensæ pereunt faces?
Sed fax nostra potentior istis,
Flammas inflammare potest, ipse uritur ignis,
Ecce flammarum potens
Majore sub flamma gemit.
Eheu! quid hoc est? En Apollo

Lyra tacente (ni sonet dolores)
Coma jacente squallet æternus decor
Ores, en! dominæ quo placeat magis,
Languido tardum jubar igne promit.
Pallente vultu territat æthera.
Mundi oculus lacrymis senescit,
Et solvit pelago debita, quodque hauserat ignibus,
His lacrymis rependit.
Noctis adventu properans se latebris recondit,
Et opacas tenebrarum colit umbras,
Namque suos odit damnans radios, nocensque lumen.
An lateat tenebris dubitat, an educat diem,
Hinc suadet hoc luctus furens, inde repugnat amor.

ÆNEAS PATRIS SUI BAJULUS.

MŒNIA Trojæ—Hostis et ignis
Hostis inter et ignes—Æneas spolium piu
Atque humeris venerabile pondus
Excipit, et sævæ nunc ô nunc parcite flammæ,
Parcite haud (clamat) mihi;
Sacræ favete sarcinæ,
Quod si negatis, nec licebit
Vitam juvare, sed juvabo funus;
Rogusque fiam patris ac bustum mei.
His dictis acies pervolat hostium
Gestit, et partis veluti trophæis
Ducit triumphos. Nam furor hostium

Jam stupet et pietate tanta
Victor vincitur; imo et moritur
Troja libenter funeribusque gaudet,
Ac faces admittit orans, ne lateat tenebras
Per opacas opus ingens pietatis.
Debita sic patri solvis tua, sic pari rependis
Officio. Dederat vitam tibi, tu reddis huic,
Felix! parentis qui pater diceris esse tui.

IN PIGMALIONA.

PŒNITET artis
Pigmaliona suæ,
Quod felix opus esset
Infelix erat artifex.
Sentit vulnera, nec videt ictum.
Quis credit? gelido veniunt de marmore flammæ.
Marmor ingratum nimis
Incendit autorem suum.
Concepit hic vanos furores;
Opus suum miratur atque adorat.
Prius creavit, ecce nunc colit manus,
Tentantes digitos molliter applicat;
Decipit molles caro dura tactus.
An virgo vera est, an sit eburnea;
Reddat an oscula quæ dabantur
Nescit. Sed dubitat, sed metuit, munere supplicat,
Blanditiasque miscet.
Te, miser, pœnas dare vult, hos Venus, hos triumphos

Capit a te, quod amorem fugis omnem.
Cur fugis heu vivos? mortua te necat puella.
Non erit innocua hæc, quamvis tua fingas manu,
Ipsa heu nocens erit nimis, cujus image nocet.

ARION.

SQUAMMEA vivæ
Lubrica terga ratis
Jam conscendet Arion.
Merces tam nova solvitur
Navis quam nova scanditur. Illa
Aërea est merces, hæc est et aquatica navis.
Perdidere illum viri
Mercede magna, servat hic
Mercede nulla piscis: et sic
Salute plus ruina constat illi;
Minoris et servatur hinc quam perditur.
Hic dum findit aquas, findit hic aëra:
Cursibus, piscis; digitis, Arion:
Et sternit undas, sternit et aëra:
Carminis hoc placido Tridente
Abjurat sua jam murmura, ventusque modestior
Auribus ora mutat:
Ora dediscit, minimos et metuit susurros.
(Sonus alter restat, ut fit sonus illis)
Aura strepens circum muta sit lateri adjacente penna,
Ambit et ora viri, nec vela ventis hic egent;
Attendit hanc ventus ratem: non trahit, at trahitur.

PHŒNICIS GENETHLIACON ET EPICEDION.

PHŒNIX alumna mortis,
Quam mira tua puerpera!
Tu scandis haud nidos, sed ignes.
Non parere sed perire ceu parata:
Mors obstetrix; atque ipsa tu teipsum paris.
Tu tuique mater ipsa es,
Tu tuique filia.
Tu sic odora messis
Surgis tuorum funerum;
Tibique per tuam ruinam
Reparata, te succedis ipsa. Mors ô
Fæcunda! Sancta ô lucra pretiosæ necis!
Vive (monstrum dulce) vive
Tu tibique suffice.

EPITAPHIUM.

QUISQUIS nectareo serenus ævo,
Et spe lucidus aureæ juventæ
Nescis purpureos abire soles,
Nescis vincula, ferreamque noctem
Imi carceris, horridumque Ditem,
Et spectas tremulum procul senectam,
Hinc discas lacrymas, et hinc reponas.
Hic, ô scilicet hic brevi sub antro

Spes et gaudia mille, mille longam
(Heu longam miseris) induere noctem.
Flammantem nitidæ facem juventæ,
Submersit Stygiæ paludis unda.
Ergo si lacrymas neges doloris
Huc certo lacrymas feres timoris.

DAMNO AFFICI SÆPE FIT LUCRUM.

DAMNA adsunt multis taciti compendia lucri
Felicique docent plus properare mora,
Luxuriem annorum posita sic pelle redemit
Atque sagax serpens in nova sæcla subit.
Cernis ut ipsa sibi replicato suppetat ævo,
Seque iteret, multa morte perennis avis.
Succrescat generosa sibi, facilesque per ignes
Perque suos cineres, per sua fata ferax.
Quæ solers jactura sui? quis funeris usus?
Flammarumque fides, ingeniumque rogi?
Siccine fraude subis? pretiosaque funera ludis?
Siccine tu mortem, ne moriaris, adis?
Felix cui medicæ tanta experientia mortis,
Cui tam Parcarum est officiosa manus.

HUMANÆ VITÆ DESCRIPTIO.

O VITA, tantum lubricus quidam furor
Spoliumque vitæ! scilicet longi brevis
Erroris hospes! Error ô mortalium!
O certus error! qui sub incerto vagum
Suspendit ævum, mille per dolos viæ
Fugacis, et proterva per volumina
Fluidi laboris, ebrios lactat gradus;
Et irretitos ducit in nihilum dies.
O fata! quantum perfidæ vitæ fugit
Umbris quod imputemus atque auris, ibi
Et umbra et aura serias partes agunt
Miscentque scenam, volvimur ludibrio
Procacis æstus, ut per incertum more
Fragilis protervo cymba cum nutat freto.
Et ipsa vitæ, fila, queis nentes Deæ
Ævi severa texta producunt manu,
Hæc ipsa nobis implicant vestigia
Retrahunt trahuntque donec everso gradu
Ruina lassos alta deducat pedes.
Felix, fugaces quisquis excipiens dies
Gressus serenos fixit, insidiis sui
Nec servit ævi, vita inoffensis huic
Feretur auris, atque clauda rarius
Titubabit hora: vortices anni vagi
Hic extricabit, sanus assertor sui.

TRANQUILLITAS ANIMI, SIMILITUDINE DUCTA AB AVE CAPTIVA ET CANORA TAMEN.

UTcum delicias leves, loquacem
Convivam nemoris, vagamque musam
Observans dubia viator arte
Prendit desuper: horridusve ruris
Eversor, male perfido paratu
(Heu durus !) rapit, atque Io triumphans
Vadit; protinus et sagace nisu
Evolvens digitos, opus tenellum
Ducens pollice lenis erudito,
Virgarum implicat ordinem severum,
Angustam meditans domum volucri.
Illa autem, hospitium licet vestustum
Mentem solicitet minis minisque,
Et suetum nemus, hinc opaca mitis
Umbræ frigora, et hinc aprica puri
Solis fulgura, patrisque sylvæ
Nunquam muta quies; ubi illa dudum
Totum per nemus, arborem per omnem,
Hospes libera liberis querelis
Cognatum bene provocabit agmen:
Quanquam ipsum nemus, arboresque alumnam
Implorant profugam, atque amata multum

Quærant murmura, lubricumque carmen
Blandi gutturis et melos serenum.
Illa autem, tamen, illa jam relictæ
(Simplex !) haud meminit domus, nec ultra.
Sylvas cogitat ; at brevi sub antro,
Ah penna nimium brevis recisa,
Ah ritu vidua, sibique sola,
Privata heu fidicen ! canit, vagoque
Exercens querulam domum susurro
Fallit vincula, carceremque mulcet ;
Nec pugnans placidæ procax quieti
Luctatur gravis, orbe sed reducto
Discursu vaga saltitans tenello,
Metitur spatia invidæ cavernæ.
Sic in se pia mens reposta, secum
Alte tuta sedet, nec ardet extra,
Aut ullo solet æstuare fato :
Quamvis cuncta tumultuentur, atræ
Sortis turbine non movetur illa.
Fortunæ furias onusque triste
Non tergo minus accipit quieto,
Quam vectrix Veneris columba blando
Admittat juga delicata collo.
Torvæ si quid inhorruit procellæ,
Si quid sæviat et minetur, illa
Spernit, nescit, et obviis furorem
Fallit blanditiis, amatque et ambit
Ipsum, quo male vulneratur, ictum.
Curas murmure non fatetur ullo ;
Non lambit lacrymas dolor, nec atræ
Mentis nubila frons iniqua prodit.

Quod si lacryma pervicax rebelli
Erumpit tamen evolatque gutta,
Invitis lacrymis, negante luctu,
Ludunt perspicui per ora risus.

RICHARDI CRASHAWI

POEMATA ET EPIGRAMMATA,

QUÆ SCRIPSIT LATINA

ET GRÆCA,

DUM AULÆ PEMB. ALUMNUS FUIT, ET

COLLEGII PETRENSIS SOCIUS.

EDITIO SECUNDA, AUCTIOR ET EMENDATIOR.

Εἵνεκεν ἐνμαθίης πινυτόφρονος, ἣν ὁ Μέλιχρος
Ἤσκησεν, Μουσῶνἅμμιγα καὶ Χαρίτων.

Ἀνθολ.

CANTABRIGIÆ,
Ex Officina *Joan. Hayes*, Celeberrimæ Academiæ
Typographi. 1670.

REVERENDO ADMODUM VIRO

BENJAMINO LANY

SS. THEOLOGIÆ PROFESSORI, AULÆ PEMBROCHIANÆ

CUSTODI DIGNISSIMO, EX SUORUM

MINIMIS MINIMUS,

R. CRASHAW

CUSTODIAM CŒLESTEM

P.

SUUS est et florum fructus; quibus fruimur, si non utilius, delicatius certe. Neque etiam rarum est quod ad spem veris, de se per flores suos quasi pollicentis, adultioris anni, ipsiusque adeo Autumni exigamus fidem. Ignoscas igitur (vir colendissime) properanti sub ora Apollinis sui, primæque adolescentiæ lascivia exultante Musæ. Teneræ ætatis flores adfert, non fructus seræ: quos quidem exigere ad seram illam et sobriam maturitatem, quam in fructibus expectamus merito, durum fuerit; forsan et ipsa hac præcoci importunitate sua placituros magis: Tibi præsertim quem paternus animus (quod fieri solet) intentum tenet omni suæ spei diluculo, quo tibi de tuorum indole promittas aliquid. Ex more etiam eorum, qui in præmium laboris sui pretiumque patientiæ festini, ex iis quæ severunt ipsi et excoluerunt, quicquid est flosculi prominulum, prima quasi verecundia auras et apertum Jovem experientis arripiunt avidi, saporemque illi non tam ex ipsius indole et ingenio quam ex animi sui affectu, foventis in eo curas suas et spes, affingunt. Patere igitur (reverende custos) hanc tibi ex istiusmodi floribus corollam necti; convivalem vero: nec aliter passuram sidus illud oris tui auspicatissimum, nisi (qua est etiam amœnitate) remissiore radio cum se reclinat, et in tantum de se demit. Neque sane hoc scriptionis genere (modo partes suas satis præstiterit) quid esse potuit otio Theologico accommodatius, quo nimirum res ipsa Theologica Poetica amœnitate delinita majestatem suam venustate commendat. Hoc demum quicquid est, amore tamen poteris, et voles, scio: non ut magnum quid, non ut egregium, non ut te dignum denique, sed ut tuum: tuum summo jure, utpote quo è tua gleba, per tuum radium, in manum denique tuam evocatum fuerit. Quod restat hujus libelli fatis, exorandus es igitur (vir spectatissime) ut quem sinu tum facili privatum excepisti, eum jam ore magis publico alloquentem te non asperneris. Stes illi in limine, non auspicium modo suum, sed et argumentum. Enimvero Epigramma sacrum tuus ille vultus vel est, vel quid sit docet; ubi nimirum amabili diluitur severum, et sanctum suavi demulcetur. Pronum me vides in negatam mihi provinciam; laudum tuarum, intelligo: quas mihi cum modestia tua abstulerit, reliquum mihi est necessario ut sim brevis: imo vero longus nimium; utpote cui argumentum istud abscissum fuerit, in quo unice poteram, et sine tædio, prolixus esse. Vale, virorum ornatissime, neque dedigneris quod colere audeam Genii tui serenitatem supplex tam tenuis, et (quoniam numen quoque hoc de se non negat) amare etiam. Interim vero da veniam Musæ in tantum sibi non temperanti; quin in hanc saltem laudis tuæ partem, quæ tibi ex rebus sacris apud nos ornatis meritissima est, istiusmodi carmine involare ausa sit, qualicunque,

Salve, alme custos Pierii gregis;
Per quem erudito exhalat in otio;
  Seu frigus udi captet antri,
    Sive Jovem nitidosque soles.

Non ipsi custos pulchrior invias
Egit sub umbras Æmonios greges;
  Non ipse Apollo notus illis
    Lege suæ meliore cannæ.

Tu, si sereno des oculo frui,
Sunt rura nobis, sunt juga, sunt aquæ,
  Sunt plectra dulcium sororum;
    (Non alio mihi nota Phœbo)

Te dante, castos composuit sinus;
Te dante, mores sumpsit; et in suo
  Videnda vultu, pulveremque
    Religio cineremque nescit.

Stat cincta digna fronde decens caput:
Suosque per te fassa palam Deos,

Comisque, Diva, vestibusque
Ingenium dedit ordinemque.

Jamque ecce nobis amplior es modo
Majorque cerni. Quale jubar tremit
Sub os! verecundusque quanta
Mole sui Genius laborat!

Jam qui serenas it tibi per genas,
Majore cœlo sidus habet suum;
Majorque circum cuspidatæ
Ora comis tua flos diei.

Stat causa. Nempe hanc ipse Deus, Deus,
Hanc ara, per te pulchra, diem tibi
Tuam refundit, obvioque
It radio tibi se colenti.

Ecce, ecce! sacro in limine, dum pio
Multumque prono poplite amas humum,
Altaria annuunt ab alto;
Et refluis tibi plaudit alis.

Pulchro incalescens officio, puer
Quicunque crispo sidere crinium,
Vultuque non fatente terram,
Currit ibi roseus satelles.

Et jure. Nam cum fana tot inviis
Mœrent ruinis, ipsaque (ceu preces,
Manusque, non decora supplex,
Tendat) opem rogat, heu negatam!

Tibi ipsa voti est ora sui rea.
Et solvet. O quam semper apud Deum
Litabis illum, cujus aræ
Ipse preces prius audiisti!

VENERABILI VIRO MAGISTRO TOURNAY, TUTORI SUO SUMME OBSERVANDO.

MESSIS inauravit Cereri jam quarta capillos,
Vitis habet Bacchum quarta corona suæ,
Nostra ex quo, primis plumæ vix alba pruinis,
Ausa tuo Musa est nidificare sinu.
Hic nemus, hic soles, et cœlum mitius illi:
Hic sua quod Musis umbra vel aura dedit.
Sedit ibi secura malus quid moverit Auster,
Quæ gravis hybernum vixerit ala Jovem.
Nescio quo interea multum tibi murmure nota est:
Nempe sed hoc poteras murmur amare tamen.
Tandem ecce (heu simili de prole puerpera) tandem
Hoc tenero tenera est pignore facta parens.
Jamque meam hanc sobolem (rogo) quis sinus alter haberet?
Quis mihi tam noti nempe teporis erat?
Sed quoque et ipsa meus (de te) meus, improba, tutor
(Quam primum potuit dicere) dixit, erit.
Has ego legitimæ, nec lævo sidere natæ
Non puto degeneres indolis esse notas;
Nempe quod illa suo patri tam semper apertos,

Tam semper faciles nôrit adire sinus.
Ergo tuam tibi sume: tuos est illa sub alas:
Hoc quoque de nostro, quod tueāris, habe.
Sic quæ Suada tuo fontem sibi fecit in ore,
Sancto et securo melle perennis est.
Sic tua, sic nullas Siren non mulceat aures,
Aula cui plausus et sua serta dedit.
Sic tuus ille (precor) Tagus aut est obice nullo,
Aut omni (quod adhuc) obice major est.

ORNATISSIMO VIRO PRÆCEPTORI SUO COLENDISSIMO, MAGISTRO BROOK.

O MIHI qui nunquam nomen non dulce fuisti
Tunc quoque cum domini fronte timendus eras!
Ille ego pars vestri quondam intactissima regno,
De nullo virgæ nota labore tuæ,
Do tibi quod de te per secula longa queretur
Quod de me nimium non metuendas eras:
Quod tibi turpis ego torpentis inertia sceptri
Tam ferulæ tulerim mitia jura tuæ.
Scilicet in foliis quicquid peccabitur istis,
Quod tua virga statim vapulet, illud erit.
Ergo tibi hæc pœnas pro me mea pagina pendat.
Hic agitur virgæ res tibi multa tuæ.
In me igitur quicquid nimis illa pepercerit olim,
Id licet in fœtu vindicet omne meo.
Hic tuus inveniet satis in quo sæviat unguis,

Quodque veru docto trans obeliscus eat.
Scilicet hæc mea sunt; hæc quæ mala scilicet: ô si
(Quæ tua nempe forent) hic meliora forent!
Qualiacunque, suum norunt hæc flumina fontem
(Nilus ab ignoto fonte superbus est)
Nec certe nihil est qua quis sit origine. Fontes
Esse solent fluvii nomen honorque sui.
Hic quoque tam parvus (de me mea secula dicant)
Non parvi soboles hic quoque fontis erat.
Hoc modo et ipse velis de me dixisse, meorum
Ille fuit minimus. Sed fuit ille meus.*

IN PICTURAM REVERENDISSIMI EPISCOPI, D. ANDREWS.

HÆC charta monstrat, fama quem monstrat magis,
Sed et ipsa necdum fama quem monstrat satis,
Ille, ille totam solus implevit tubam,
Tot ora solus domuit et famam quoque
Fecit modestam: mentis igneæ pater
Agilique radio lucis æternæ vigil,
Per alta rerum pondera indomito vagus
Cucurrit animo, quippe naturam ferox
Exhausit ipsam mille fœtus artibus,

* Here follows, in the edition of 1634, the poem "Lectori" which occurs at p. 259, *postea;* but the intervening poems, with the single exception marked, are all added, in the order in which they occur, in the edition of 1670.

Et mille linguis ipse se in gentes procul
Variavit omnes, fuitque toti simul
Cognatus orbi, sic sacrum et solidum jubar
Saturumque cœlo pectus ad patrios libens
Porrexit ignes: hac eum, Lector, vides
Hæc, ecce, charta O utinam et audires quoque.

VOTIVA DOMUS PETRENSIS PRO DOMO DEI.

UT magis in mundi votis, aviumque querelis
Jam veniens solet esse dies, ubi cuspide prima
Palpitat, et roseo lux prævia ludit ab ortu;
Cum nec abest Phœbus, nec Eois lætus habenis
Totus adest, volucrumque procul vaga murmura mulcet:

Nos ita; quos nuper radiis afflavit honestis
Religiosa dies; nostrique per atria cœli
(Sacra domus nostrum est cœlum) jam luce tenella
Libat adhuc trepidæ fax nondum firma diei:
Nos ita jam exercet nimii impatientia voti,
Speque sui propiore premit.
Quis pectora tanti
Tendit amor cœpti! desiderio quam longo
Lentæ spes inhiant! domus o dulcissima rerum!
Plena Deo domus! Ah, quis erit, quis (dicimus) ille
(O bonus, ô ingens meritis, ô proximus ipsi,
Quem vocat in sua dona, Deo!) quo vindice totas
Excutiant tenebras hæc sancta crepuscula?

Quando erit, ut teneræ flos heu tener ille diei,
Qui velut ex oriente suo jam altaria circum
Lambit, et ambiguo nobis procul annuit astro,
Plenis se pandat foliis, et lampade tota
Lætus (ut è medio cum sol micat aureus axe)
Attonitam penetrare domum jam possit adulto.
Sidere, nec dubio pia mœnia mulcent ore?

Quando erit, ut convexa suo quoque pulchra sereno
Florescant, roseoque tremant laquearia risu?
Quæ minium informis tanquam sibi conscia frontis
Perpetuis jam se lustrant lachrymantia guttis.

Quando erit, ut claris meliori luce fenestris
Plurima per vitreos vivat pia pagina vultus?

Quando erit, ut sacrum nobis celebrantibus hymnum
Organicos facili, et nunquam fallente susurro
Nobile murmur agat nervos; pulmonis iniqui
Fistula nec monitus faciat male-fida sinistros?

Denique, quicquid id est, quod res hic sacra requirit,
Fausta illa, et felix (sitque ô tua) dextra, suam cui
Debeat hæc Aurora diem. Tibi supplicat ipsa,
Ipsa tibi facit ora preces. Tu jam illius audi,
Audiet illa tuas. Dubium est (modo porrige dextram,)
Deo magis, an capias: audi tantum esse beatus,
Et damnum hoc lucrare tibi.
Scis ipse volucres
Quæ rota volvit opes; has ergo, hic fige perennis

Fundamenta domus Petrensi in rupe; suamque
Fortunæ sic deme rotam. Scis ipse procaces
Divitias quam prona vagos vehat ala per Euros;
Divitiis illas, age, deme volucribus alas,
Facque suus nostras illis sit motus ad oras:
Remigii ut tandem pennas melioris adaptæ,
Se rapiant dominumque suum super æthera secum.

Felix ô qui sic potuit bene providus uti
Fortunæ pennis et opum levitate suarum,
Divitiisque suis aquilæ sic addidit alas.

IN CÆTERORUM OPERUM DIFFICILI PARTURITIONE GEMITUS.

O FELIX nimis illa, et nostræ nobile nomen
Invidiæ volucris! facili quæ funere surgens
Mater odora sui, nitidæ nova fila juventæ,
Et festinatos peragit sibi fata per ignes.
Illa, haud natalis tot tardis mensibus horas
Tam miseris tenuata moris, saltu velut uno
In nova secla rapit sese, et caput omne decoras
Explicat in frondes, roseoque repullulat ortu.
Cinnameos simul illa rogos conscenderit, omnem
Læta bibit Phœbum, et jam jam victricibus alis
Plaudit humum, cineresque suos.
Heu! dispare fato
Nos ferimur; seniorque suo sub Apolline phœnix
Petrensis mater, dubias librata per auras

Pendet adhuc, quæritque sinum in qua ponat inertes
Exuvias, spoliisque suæ reparata senectæ
Ore pari surgat, similique per omnia vultu.
At nunc heu nixu secli melioris in ipso
Deliquium patitur!—
At nunc heu lentæ longo in molimine vitæ
Interea moritur! Dubio stant mœnia vultu
Parte sui pulchra, et fratres in fœdera muros
Invitant frustra, nec respondentia saxis
Saxa suis. Mœrent opera intermissa, manusque
Implorant.
Succurre piæ, succurre parenti
O quisquis pius es. Illi succurre parenti,
Quam sibi tot sanctæ matres habuere parentem.
Quisquis es, ô tibi, crede, tibi tot hiantia ruptis
Mœnibus ora loqui! Matrem tibi, crede verendam
Muros tam longe laceros senioque situque
Ceu canos monstrare suos. Succurre roganti.
Per tibi plena olim, per jam sibi sicca precatur.
Ubera, ne desis senio. Sic longa juventus
Te foveat, querulæ nunquam cessura senectæ.

EPITAPHIUM IN GULIELMUM HERRISIUM.

SISTE te paulum, viator, ubi longum sisti
Necesse erit, huc nempe properare te scias
quocunque properas.
Moræ pretium erit
Et lachrymæ,

Si jacere hic scias
Gulielmum
Splendidæ Herrisiorum familiæ
Splendorem maximum:
Quem cum talem vixisse intellexeris,
Et vixisse tantum;
Discas licet
In quantas spes possit
Assurgere mortalitas,
De quantis cadere.

Quem { Infantem, Essexia—— / Juvenem, Cantabrigia } vidit

Senem, ah infelix utraque
Quod non vidit.
Qui
Collegii Christi Alumnus
Aulæ Pembrokianæ socius.
Utrique, ingens amoris certamen fuit,
Donec
Dulciss. lites elusit Deus,
Eumque cœlestis collegii,
Cujus semper alumnus fuit
socium fecit;
Qui et ipse collegium fuit,
In quo
Musæ omnes et gratiæ,
Nullibi magis sorores,
Sub præside religione.
In tenacissimum sodalitium coaluere.

Quem	Oratoria	Oratorem	Agnovere.
	Poetica	Poetam	
	Utraque	Philosophum	
	Christianum	Omnes	

Qui	Fide	Mundum	Superavit.
	Spe	Cœlum	
	Charitate	Proximum	
	Humilitate	Seipsum	

Cujus
Sub verna fronte senilis animus,
Sub morum facilitate, severitas virtutis;
Sub plurima indole, pauci anni;
Sub majore modestia, maxima indoles
adeo se occuluerunt
ut vitam ejus
Pulchram dixeris et pudicam dissimulationem:
Imo vero et mortem,
Ecce enim in ipso funere
Dissimulare se passus est,
Sub tantillo marmore tantum hospitem,
Eo nimirum majore monumento
quo minore tumulo.
Eo ipso die occubuit quo Ecclesia
Anglicana ad vesperas legit,
Raptus est ne malitia mutaret intellectum ejus;
Scilicet Id: Octobris, Anno S. 1631.

IN EUNDEM.

ITE meæ lacrymæ (nec enim moror), ite. Sed oro
Tantum ne miseræ claudite vocis iter.
O liceat querulos verbis animare dolores!
Et saltem ah periit, dicere, noster amor.
Ecce negant tamen; ecce negant, lacrymæque rebelles
Pergunt indomita præcipitantque via.
Visne (ô chare!) igitur te nostra silentia dicant?
Vis fleat assiduo murmure mutus amor?
Flebit. Et urna suos semper bibet humida rores,
Et fidas semper semper habebit aquas.
Interea, quicunque estis, ne credite mirum
Si veræ lacrymæ non didicere loqui.*

NATALIS PRINCIPIS MARIÆ.

CRESCE, O dulcibus imputanda divis,
O cresce, et propera, puella princeps,
In matris propera venire partes.
Et eum par breve fulminum minorum,
Illinc Carolus, et Jacobus inde,
In patris faciles subire famam,
Ducent fata furoribus decoris;

* Not in the edition of 1670.

Cum terror sacer, Anglicique magnum
Murmur nominis increpabit omnem
Lato Bosporon, Ottomanicasque
Non picto quatiet tremore Lunas;
Te tunc altera nec timenda paci,
Poscent prælia. Tu potens pudici
Vibratrix oculi, pios in hostes
Late dulcia fata dissipabis.
O cum flos tener ille, qui recenti
Pressus sidere jam sub ora ludit,
Olim fortior omne cuspidatos
Evolvet latus aureum per ignes;
Quique imbellis adhuc, adultus olim;
Puris expatiabitur genarum
Campis imperiosus Cupido;
O quam certa superbiore penna
Ibunt spicula, melleæque mortes,
Exultantibus hinc et inde turmis,
Quoque jusseris, impigre volabunt!
O quot corda calentium deorum
De te vulnera delicata discent!
O quot pectora principum magistris
Fient melle negotium sagittis!
Nam quæ non poteris per arma ferri,
Cui matris sinus atque utrumque sidus
Magnorum patet officina amorum?
Hinc sumas licet, O puella princeps,
Quantacunque opus est tibi pharetra.
Centum sume Cupidines ab uno
Matris lumine, Gratiasque centum,

Et centum Veneres: adhuc manebunt
Centum mille Cupidines; manebunt
Tercentum Veneresque Gratiæque
Puro fonte superstites per ævum.

IN SENERISSIMÆ REGINÆ PARTUM HIEMALEM.

SERTA puer: quis nunc flores non præbeat hortus?
  Texe mihi facili pollice serta, puer.
Quid tu nescio quos narras mihi; stulte, Decembres
  Quid mihi cum nivibus? da mihi serta, puer.
Nix? et hiems? non est nostras quid tale per oras;
  Non est: vel si sit, non tamen esse potest.
Ver agitur: quæcunque trucem dat larva Decembrem,
  Quid fera cunque fremant frigora, ver agitur.
Nonne vides quali se palmite regia vitis
  Prodit, et in sacris quæ sedet uva jugis?
Tam lætis quæ bruma solet ridere racemis?
  Quas hiemis pingit purpura tanta genas?
O Maria! O divum soboles, genitrixque deorum!
  Siccine nostra tuos tempora ludus erunt?
Siccine tu cum vere tuo nihil horrida brumæ
  Sidera, nil madidos sola morare notos?
Siccine sub media poterunt tua surgere bruma,
  Atque suas solum lilia nosse nives?
Ergo vel invitis nivibus, frendentibus Austris,

Nostra novis poterunt regna tumere rosis?
O bona turbatrix anni, quæ limite noto
Tempora sub signis non sinis ire suis!
O pia prædatrix hiemis, quæ tristia mundi
Murmura tam dulci sub ditione tenes!
Perge precor nostris vim pulchram ferre Calendis:
Perge precor menses sic numerare tuos.
Perge intempestiva atque importuna videri;
Inque uteri titulos sic rape cuncta tui.
Sit nobis sit sæpe hiemes sic cernere nostras
Exhæredatas floribus ire tuis.
Sæpe sit has vernas hiemes Maiosque Decembres,
Has per te roseas sæpe videre nives.
Altera gens varium per sidera computet annum,
Atque suos ducant per vaga signa dies.
Nos deceat nimiis tantum permittere nimbis?
Tempora tam tetricas ferre Britanna vices?
Quin nostrum tibi nos omnem donabimus annum:
In partus omnem expende, Maria, tuos.
Sit tuus ille uterus nostri bonus arbiter anni:
Tempus et in titulos transeat omne tuos.
Namque alia indueret tam dulcia nomina mensis?
Aut qua tam posset candidus ire toga?
Hanc laurum Junus sibi vertice vellet utroque;
Hanc sibi vel tota Chloride Maius emet.
Tota suam, vere expulso, respublica florum
Reginam cuperent te, sobolemve tuam.
O bona sors anni, cum cuncti ex ordine menses
Hic mihi Carolides, hic Marianus erit!

NATALIS DUCIS EBORACENSIS.

ET vero jam tempus erat tibi, maxima Mater,
  Dulcibus his oculis accelerare diem:
Tempus erat, ne qua tibi basia blanda vacarent;
  Sarcina ne collo sit minus apta tuo.
Scilicet ille tuus, timor et spes ille suorum,
  Quo primum es felix pignore facta parens,
Ille ferox iras jam nunc meditatur et enses
  Jam patris magis est, jam magis ille suus.
Indolis O stimulos! vix dum illi transiit infans;
  Jamque sibi impatiens arripit ille virum.
Improbus ille suis adeo negat ire sub annis:
  Jam nondum puer est, major et est puero.
Si quis in aulæis pictas animatus in iras
  Stat leo, quem docta cuspide lusit acus,
Hostis, io! est; neque enim ille alium dignabitur hostem;
  Nempe decet tantas non minor ira manus.
Tunc hasta gravis adversum furit; hasta bacillum est;
  Mox falsum vero vulnere pectus hiat.
Stat leo, ceu stupeat tali bene fixus ab hoste;
  Ceu quid in his oculis vel timeat vel amet,
Tam torvum, tam dulce micant: nescire fatetur
  Mars ne sub his oculis esset, an esset amor.
Quippe illic Mars est, sed qui bene possit amari;
  Est et amor certe, sed metuendus amor:
Talis amor, talis Mars est ibi cernere; qualis
  Seu puer hic esset, sive vir ille Deus.

Hic tibi jam scitus succedit in oscula fratris,
  Res, ecce! in lusus non operosa tuos.
Basia jam veniant tua quantacunque caterva;
  Jam quocunque tuus murmure ludat amor.
En! Tibi materies tenera et tractabilis hic est:
  Hic ad blanditias est tibi cera satis.
Salve infans, tot basiolis, molle argumentum,
  Maternis labiis dulce negotiolum,
O salve! Nam te nato, puer aure, natus
  Et Carolo et Mariæ tertius est oculus.

IN FACIEM AUGUSTISSIMI REGIS A MORBILLIS INTEGRAM.

MUSA redi: vocat alma parens Academia: noster
  En redit, ore suo noster Apollo redit.
Vultus adhuc suus, et vultu sua purpura tantum
  Vivit, et admixtas pergit amare nives.
Tune illas violare genas? tune illa profanis,
  Morbe ferox, tentas ire per ora notis?
Tu Phœbi faciem tentas, vanissime? Nostra
  Nec Phœbe maculas novit habere suas.
Ipsa sui vindex facies morbum indignatur;
  Ipsa sedet radiis O bene tuta suis:
Quippe illic Deus est, cœlumque et sanctius astrum;
  Quippe sub his totus ridet Apollo genis.
Quod facie Rex tutus erat, quod cætera tactus:
  Hinc hominem Rex est fassus, et inde Deum.

AD CAROLUM PRIMUM, REX REDUX.

ILLE redit, redit. Hoc populi bona murmura volvunt;
Publicus hoc, audin'? plausus ad astra refert:
Hoc omni sedet in vultu commune serenum;
Omnibus hinc una est lætitiæ facies.
Rex noster, lux nostra redit; redeuntis ad ora
Arridet totis Anglia læta genis:
Quisque suos oculos oculis accendit ab istis;
Atque novum sacro sumit ab ore diem.
Forte roges tanto quæ digna pericula plausu
Evadat Carolus, quæ mala, quosve metus:
Anne perrerati male fida volumina ponti
Ausa illum terris pene negare suis:
Hospitis an nimii rursus sibi conscia tellus
Vix bene speratum reddat Ibera caput.
Nil horum; nec enim male fida volumina ponti
Aut sacrum tellus vidit Ibera caput.
Verus amor tamen hæc sibi falsa pericula fingit:
Falsa peric'la solet fingere verus amor,
At Carolo qui falsa timet, nec vera timeret:
Vera peric'la solet temnere verus amor,
Illi falsa timens, sibi vera pericula temnens,
Non solum est fidus, sed quoque fortis amor.
Interea nostri satis ille est causa triumphi:
Et satis, ah! nostri causa doloris erat.

Causa doloris erat Carolus, sospes licet esset;
  Anglia quod saltem discere posset, abest.
Et satis est nostri Carolus nunc causa triumphi:
  Dicere quod saltem possumus, Ille redit.

AD PRINCIPEM NONDUM NATUM, REGINA GRAVIDA.

NASCERE nunc; O nunc! quid enim, puer alme, moraris?
  Nulla tibi dederit dulcior hora diem.
Ergone tot tardos, O lente! morabere menses?
  Rex redit, ipse veni, et dic bone, gratus ades.
Nam quid ave nostrum? quid nostri verba triumphi?
  Vagitu melius dixeris ista tuo.
At maneas tamen: et nobis nova causa triumphi:
  Sic demum fueris; nec nova causa tamen:
Nam, quoties Carolo novus aut nova nascitur infans,
  Revera toties Carolus ipse redit.

Reliqua desiderantur.

EPIGRAMMATA SACRA,

QUÆ SCRIPSIT GRÆCA ET LATINA.

LECTORI.

SALVE. Jamque vale. Quid enim quis pergeret ultra?
  Qua jocus et lusus non vocat, ire voles?
Scilicet hic, Lector, cur noster habebere, non est;
  Delitiis folio non faciente tuis.
Nam nec Acidalios halat mihi pagina rores;
  Nostra Cupidineæ nec favet aura faci.
Frustra hinc ille suis quicquam promiserit abi:
  Frustra hinc illa novo speret abire sinu.
Ille è materna melius sibi talia myrto;
  Illa jugis melius poscat ab Idaliis.
Quærat ibi suus in quo cespite surgat Adonis,
  Quæ melior teneris patria sit violis.
Illinc totius Floræ, verisque, suique
  Consilio, ille alas impleat, illa sinus.
Me mea (casta tamen, si sit rudis) herba coronet:
  Me mea (si rudis est, sit rudis) herba juvat.
Nulla meo Circæa tument tibi pocula versu:
  Dulcia, et in furias officiosa tuas.
Nulla latet Lethe, quam fraus tibi florea libat,

Quam rosa sub falsis dat male-fida genis.
Nulla verecundum mentitur mella venenum:
Captat ab insidiis linea nulla suis.
Et spleni, et jecori foliis bene parcitur istis.
Ah! male cum rebus staret utrumque meis!
Rara est quæ ridet; nulla est quæ pagina prurit:
Nulla salax, si quid nôrit habere salis.
Non nudæ Veneres: nec, si jocus, udus habetur:
Non nimium Bacchus noster Apollo fuit.
Nil cui quis putre sit detorquendus ocello;
Est nihil obliquo quod velit ore legi.
Hæc coram, atque oculis legeret Lucretia justis:
Iret et illæsis hinc pudor ipse genis.
Nam neque candidior voti venit aura pudici,
De matutina virgine thura ferens:
Cum vestis nive vincta sinus, nive tempora fulgens,
Dans nive flammeolis frigida jura comis,
Religiosa pedum sensim vestigia librans,
Ante aras tandem constitit; et tremuit.
Nec gravis ipsa suo sub numine castior halat
Quæ pia non puras summovet ara manus.
Tam Venus in nostro non est nimis aurea versu:
Tam non sunt pueri tela timenda Dei.
Sæpe puer dubias circum me moverat alas;
Jecit et incertus nostra sub ora faces.
Sæpe vel ipse sua calamum mihi blandus ab ala,
Vel matris cygno de meliore dedit.
Sæpe Dionææ pactus mihi serta coronæ;
Sæpe, mens vates tu, mihi dixit, eris.
I procul, I cum matre tua, puer improbe, dixi:
Non tibi cum numeris res erit ulla meis.

Tu Veronensi cum passere pulchrior ibis:
  Bilbilicisve queas comptius esse modis.
Ille tuos fingit quocunque sub agmine crines:
  Undique nequitiis par erit ille tuis.
Ille nimis (dixi) patet in tua prœlia campus:
  Heu nimis est vates et nimis ille tuus.
Gleba illa (ah! tua quam tamen urit adultera messis)
  Esset Idumæo germine quanta parens!
Quantus ibi et quantæ premeret puer ubera matris!
  Nec cœlos vultu dissimulante suos.
Ejus in isto oculi satis essent sidera versu;
  Sidereo matris quam bene tuta sinu!
Matris ut hic similes in collum mitteret ulnas,
  Inque sinus niveos pergeret, ore pari!
Utque genis pueri hæc æquis daret oscula labris!
  Et bene cognatis iret in ora rosis!
Quæ Mariæ tam larga meat, quam disceret illic
  Uvida sub pretio gemma tumere suo!
Staret ibi ante suum lacrymatrix Diva Magistrum:
  Seu levis aura volet, seu graves unda cadat;
Luminis hæc soboles, et proles pyxidis illa,
  Pulchrius unda cadat, suavius aura volet.
Quicquid in his sordet demum, luceret in illis.
  Improbe, nec satis est hunc tamen esse tuum?
Improbe cede puer: quid enim mea carmina mulces?
  Carmina de jaculis muta futura tuis.
Cede puer, qua te petulantis fræna puellæ;
  Turpia quæ revocant pensa procacis heræ;
Qua miseri male pulchra nitent mendacia limi;
  Qua cerussatæ, furta decora, genæ;
Qua mirere rosas, alieni sidera veris;

Quas nivis haud propriæ bruma redempta domat.
Cede puer (dixi et dico) cede improba mater:
Altera Cypris habet nos; habet alter Amor.
Scilicet hic Amor est. Hic est quoque mater Amoris.
Sed mater virgo. Sed neque cæcus Amor.
O puer! o Domine! o magnæ reverentia matris!
Alme tui stupor et religio gremii!
O Amor, innocuæ cui sunt pia jura pharetræ;
Nec nisi de casto corde sagitta calens!
Me, puer, o certa, quem figis, fige sagitta.
O tua de me sit facta pharetra levis!
Quodque illinc sitit et bibit, et bibit et sitit usque;
Usque meum sitiat pectus, et usque bibat.
Fige, puer, corda hæc. Seu spinis exiguus quis,
Seu clavi aut hastæ cuspide magnus ades;
Seu major cruce cum; seu maximus ipso
Te corda hæc figis denique. Fige puer.
O metam hanc tuus æternum inclamaverit arcus:
Stridat in hanc teli densior aura tui.
O tibi si jaculum ferat ala ferocior ullum,
Hanc habeat triti vulneris ire viam.
Quique tuæ populus cunque est, quæ turba, pharetræ;
Hic bene vulnificas nidus habebit aves.
O mihi sis bello semper tam sævus in isto!
Pectus in hoc nunquam mitior hostis eas.
Quippe ego quam jaceam pugna bene sparsus in illa!
Quam bene sic lacero pectore sanus ero!
Hæc mea vota. Mei sunt hæc quoque vota libelli.
Hæc tua sint Lector; si meus esse voles.
Si meus esse voles: meus ut sis, lumina (Lector)
Casta, sed o nimium non tibi sicca precor.

Nam tibi fac madidis meus ille occurrerit alis,
(Sanguine, seu lacryma diffluat ille sua:)
Stipite totus hians, clavisque reclusus, et hasta:
Fons tuus in fluvios desidiosus erit?
Si tibi sanguineo meus hic tener iverit amne,
Tune tuas illi, dure, negabis aquas?
Ah durus! quicunque meos, nisi siccus, amores
Nolit; et hic lacrymæ rem negat esse suæ.
Sæpe hic Magdalinas vel aquas vel amaverit undas;
Credo nec Assyrias mens tua malit opes.
Scilicet ille tuos ignis recalescet ad ignes;
Forsan et illa tuis unda natabit aquis.
Hic eris ad cunas, et odoros funere manes:
Hinc ignes nasci testis, et inde meos.
Hic mecum, et cum matre sua, mea gaudia quæres:
Maturus Procerum seu stupor esse velit;
Sive per antra sui lateat (tunc templa) sepulchri:
Tertia lux reducem (lenta sed illa) dabit.
Sint fidæ precor ah (dices) facilesque tenebræ;
Lux mea dum noctis (res nova!) poscit opem.
Denique charta meo quicquid mea dicat amori,
Illi quo metuat cunque, fleatve, modo,
Læta parum (dices) hæc, sed neque dulcia non sunt:
Certe et amor (dices) hujus amandus erat.

Si nimium hic promitti tibi videtur, Lector bone, pro eo cui satisfaciendo libellus iste futurus fuerit; scias me in istis non ad hæc modo spectare quæ hic habes, sed ea etiam quæ olim (hæc interim fovendo) habere poteris. Nolui enim (si hactenus deesse amicis meis non potui; flagitantibus a me, etiam cum dispendii sui periculo paterer eos experiri te in tantum favoremque tu inquam, fastidio tuo indulgere. Satis hic habes quod vel releges ad ferulam suam (neque enim maturiores sibi annos ex his aliqua vendicant) vel ut pignus plurium adultiorumque in sinu tuo reponas. Elige tibi ex his utrumvis. Me interim quod attinet, finis meus non fefellit. Maximum meæ ambitionis scopum jamdudum attigi: tunc nimirum cum qualecunque hoc meum pene infantis Musæ murmur ad aures istas non ingratum sonuit, quibus neque doctiores mihi de publico timere habeo, nec sperare clementiores; adeo ut de tuo jam plausu (dicam ingenue et breviter) neque securus sim ultra neque solicitus. Prius tui, quisquis es Lector, apud me reverentia prohibet; de cujus judicio omnia possum magna sperare: posterius illorum reverentia non sinit, de quorum perspicacitate maxima omnia non possum mihi non persuadere. Quanquam ô quam velim tanti me esse in quo patria mea morem istum suum deponere velit, genio suo tam non dignum; istum scilicet quo, suis omnibus fastiditis, ea exosculatur unice, quibus trajecisse Alpes et de transmarino esse, in pretium cessit! sed relictis hisce nimis improbæ spei votis, convertam me ad magistros Acygmanos; quos scio de novissimis meis verbis (quanquam neminem nominârim) iratos me reliquisse: bilem vero componant; et mihi se hoc debere (ambitioso juveni verbum tam magnum ignoscant) debere, inquam, fateantur: quod nimirum in tam nobili argumento, in quo neque ad fœtida de suis sanctis figmenta, neque ad putidas de nostris calumnias opus habeant confugere, de tenui hoc meo dederim illorum magnitudini unde emineat. Emineat vero; (serius dico). Sciant me semper habituros esse sub ea, quam mihi eorum lux major affuderit, umbra, placidissime acquiescentem.

EPIGRAMMATA SACRA.

Luc. xviii.

Pharisæus et Publicanus.

EN duo Templum adeunt (diversis mentibus ambo:)
Ille procul trepido lumine signat humum:
It gravis hic, et in alta ferox penetralia tendit.
Plus habet ille templi; plus habet ille Dei.

Ἄνδρες, ἴδου (ἑτεροισι νόοις) δύω ἱρον ἐσηλθον·
Τήλοθεν ὀῤῥωδεί κεινος ὁ φείκαλέος,

Αλλ' ὁ μὲν ως σοβαρὸς νηου μυχον ἐγγυς ἱκάνει·
Πλειον ὁ μὲν νηου, πλειον ὁ δ' εἶχε Θεοῦ·*

Matth. xxi. 7.

In Asinum Christi Victorem.

ILLE† suum didicit quondam objurgare magistrum:
Et quid ni discas tu celebrare tuum

* This Greek version is not in the edition
† Balaami asinus.

Mirum non minus est, te jam potuisse tacere
Illum quam fuerat tum potuisse loqui.

Luc. iv.

Dominus apud suos vilis.

EN consanguinei! patriis en exul in ori
Christus! et haud alibi tam peregrinus erat.

Qui socio demum pendebat sanguine latro,
O consanguineus quam fuit ille magis!

Joan. v.

Ad Bethesdæ piscinam positus.

QUIS novus hic refugis incumbit Tantalus undis,
Quem fallit toties tam fugitiva salus?

Unde hoc naufragium felix? medicæque procellæ?
Vitaque, tempestas quam pretiosa dedit?

Joan. xx.

Christus ad Thomam.

SÆVA fides! voluisse meos tractare dolores?
Crudeles digiti! sic didicisse Deum?

Vulnera, ne dubites, vis tangere nostra: sed eheu,
Vulnera, dum dubitas, tu graviora facis.

Matth. xvi. 25.

Quisquis perdiderit animam suam mea causa, inveniet eam.

I VITA; I, perdam: mihi mors tua, Christe, reperta est:
(Mors tua vita mea est; mors tibi, vita meæ)
Aut ego te abscondam Christi (mea vita) sepulchro.
Non adeo procul est tertius ille dies.

Joan. xx. 1.

Primò mane venit ad sepulchrum Magdalena.

TU matutinos prævertis, sancta, rubores,
Magdala; sed jam tum Sol tuus ortus erat.

Jamquè vetus merito vanos Sol non agit ortus,
Et tanto radios non putat esse suos.

Quippe aliquo (reor) ille, novus, jam nictat in astro,
Et se nocturna parvus habet facula.

Quam velit ô tantæ vel nuntius esse diei!
Atque novus Soli Lucifer ire novo!

Joan. vi.

Quinque panes ad quinque hominum millia.

EN mensæ faciles, redivivaque vulnere cœnæ,
Quæque indefessa provocat ora dape!

Aucta Ceres stupet arcana se crescere messe.
Denique quid restat? Pascitur ipse cibus.

ACT. VIII.

Æthiops lotus.

ILLE niger sacris exit (quam lautus!) ab undis:
Nec frustra Æthiopem nempe lavare fuit.
Mentem quam niveam piceæ cutis umbra fovebit!
Tam volet et nigros sancta Columba lares.

LUC. XVIII. 13.

Publicanus procul stans percutiebat pectus suum.

ECCE hic peccator tumidus petit advena templum:
Quodque audet solum, pectora mœsta ferit.
Fide miser; pulsaque fores has fortiter: illo
Invenies templo tu propiore Deum.

MARC. XII. 44.

Obolum viduæ.

GUTTA brevis nummi (vitæ patrona senilis)
Et digitis stillat non dubitantis anus;
Istis multa vagi spumant de gurgite census.
Isti abjecerunt scilicet; illa dedit.

Κερματίοιο βραχεια ῥανις, βιότοιο τ᾽ ἀφαυρῆς
Ἕρκος ἀποστάζει χειρος ἀπὸ τρομερας.

Τοις δε αναστιρτα πολυς ἀφρος ἀναιδεος ὀλβου,
Οἱ μεν ἀποῤῥιπτον. κεινα δεδωκε μονον.*

Luc. x. 30.

Maria vero assidens ad pedes ejus, audiebat eum.

ASPICE (namque novum est) ut ab hospite pendeat hospes!
Hinc ori parat, hoc sumit ab ore cibos.

Tune epulis adeo es (soror) officiosa juvandis,
Et sinis has (inquit) Martha, perire dapes?

Act. ii.

In Spiritus Sancti descensum.

FERTE sinus, o ferte: cadit vindemia cœli;
Sanctaque ab æthereis volvitur uva jugis.

Felices nimium, queis tam bona musta bibuntur;
In quorum gremium lucida pergit hiems!

En caput! en ut nectareo micat et micat astro!
Gaudet et in roseis viva corona comis!

Illis (o Superi! quis sic neget ebrius esse?)
Illis, ne titubent, dant sua vina faces.

* Not in the edition of 1634.

Luc. xv. 13

Congestis omnibus peregre profectus est.

DIC mihi, quo tantos properas, puer auree, nummos?
Quorsum festinæ conglomerantur opes?

Cur tibi tota vagos ructant patrimonia census?
Non poterunt siliquæ nempe minoris emi?

Act. xxi. 13.

Non solum vinciri sed et mori paratus sum.

NON modo vinc'la, sed et mortem tibi, Christe, subibo,
Paulus ait, docti callidus arte doli.

Diceret hoc aliter: Tibi non modo velle ligari,
Christe, sed et solvi* nempe paratus ero.

Act. xii. 23.

In Herodem Σκωληκοβρωτον.

ILLE Deus, Deus; hæc populi vox unica: tantum
(Vile genus) vermes credere velle negant.

At cito se miseri, cito nunc errasse fatentur;
Carnes degustant, Ambrosiamque putant.

* Phil. i. 23. τὴν ἐπιθυμίαν ἔχων εἰς τὸ ἀναλύσαι.

Matth. xiv.

Videns ventum magnum, timuit, et cum cœpisset demergi, clamavit, &c.

PETRE, cades, o, si dubitas: o fide: nec ipsum
(Petre) negat fidis æquor habere fidem.

Pondere pressa suo subsidunt cætera: solum
(Petre) tuæ mergit te levitatis onus.

Act. viii. 18.

Obtulit eis pecunias.

QUORSUM hos hic nummos profers? quorsum impie Simon?
Non ille hic Judas, sed tibi Petrus adest.

Vis emisse Deum? potius (precor) hoc age, Simon,
Si potes, ipse prius dæmona vende tuum.

Act. v. 15.

Umbra S. Petri medetur ægrotis.

CONVENIUNT alacres (sic, sic juvat ire sub umbras)
Atque umbras fieri (creditis?) umbra vetat.

O Petri umbra potens! quæ non miracula præstat?
Nunc quoque, Papa, tuum sustinet illa decas.

Marc. vii. 33. 36.

Tetigit linguam ejus, &c. . . . et loquebatur. . . . et præcepit illis ne cui dicerent: illi vero eo magis prædicabant.

CHRISTE, jubes muta ora loqui; muta ora loquuntur:
Sana tacere jubes ora; nec illa tacent.

Si digito tunc usus eras, muta ora resolvens;
Nonne opus est tota nunc tibi, Christe, manu?

Luc. x. 32.

Sacerdos quidam descendens eadem via, vidit et præteriit.

SPECTASNE (ah!) placidisque oculis mea vulnera tractas?
O dolor! ô nostris vulnera vulneribus!

Pax oris quam torva tui est! quam triste serenum!
Tranquillus miserum qui videt, ipse facit.

Luc. xvii.

Leprosi ingrati.

NUM linquunt Christum (ah morbus!) sanantur euntes:
Ipse etiam morbus sic medicina fuit.

At sani Christum (mens ah male-sana!) relinquunt:
Ipsa etiam morbus sic medicina fuit.

MATTH. VI. 34.

Ne soliciti estote in crastinum.

I MISER, inque tuas rape non tua tempora curas:
Et nondum natis perge perire malis.

Mî querulis satis una dies, satis angitur horis:
Una dies lacrymis mî satis uda suis.

Non mihi venturos vacat expectare dolores:
Nolo ego, nolo hodie crastinus esse miser.

MATTH. IX. 9.

A telonio Matthæus.

AH satis, ah nimis est: noli ultra ferre magistrum,
Et lucro domino turpia colla dare.

Jam fuge; jam (Matthæe) feri fuge regna tyranni:
Inque bonam felix i fugitive* crucem.

LUC. VII.

Viduæ filius e feretro matri redditur.

EN redeunt, lacrymasque breves nova gaudia pensant:
Bisque illa est, uno in pignore, facta parens.

Felix, quæ magis es nati per funera mater!
Amisisse, iterum cui peperisse fuit.

* Christi scilicet.

Matth. xviii.

Bonum intrare in cœlos cum uno oculo, &c.

UNO oculo? ah centum potius mihi, millia centum:
Nam quis ibi, in cœlo, quis satis Argus erit?
Aut si oculus mihi tantum unus conceditur, unus
Iste oculus fiam totus et omnis ego.

Luc. xiv.

Hydropicus sanatur.

IPSE suum pelagus, morboque immensus aquoso
Qui fuit, ut lætus nunc micat atque levis!
Quippe in vina iterum Christus (puto) transtulit undas;
Et nunc iste suis ebrius est ab aquis.

Luc. ii. 7.

Non erat iis in diversorio locus.

ILLI non locus est? Illum ergo pellitis? Illum?
Ille Deus, quem sic pellitis; ille Deus.
O furor! humani miracula sæva furoris!
Illi non locus est, quo sine nec locus est.

Luc. xvi.

In lacrymas Lazari spretas a Divite.

FELIX ô! lacrymis (ô Lazare) ditior istis,
Quam qui purpureas it gravis inter opes!
Illum cum rutili nova purpura vestiet ignis,
Ille tuas lacrymas quam volet esse suas!

Matth. xxvi. 65.

Indignatur Caiphas Christo se confitenti.

TU Christum, Christum quod non negat esse, lacessis:
Ipsius hoc crimen, quod fuit ipse, fuit.
Te ne Sacerdotem credam? Novus ille Sacerdos,
Per quem impune Deo non licet esse Deum.

Joan. xii. 37.

Cum tot signa edidisset, non credebunt in eum.

NON tibi, Christe, fidem tua tot miracula præstant;
(O verbi, ô dextræ dulcia regna tuæ!)
Non præstant? neque te post tot miracula credunt?
Mirac'lum, qui non credidit, ipse fuit.

MARC. I. 16.

Ad S. Andream piscatorem.

QUIPPE potes pulchre captare et fallere pisces!
Centum illic discis lubricus ire dolis.

Heus bone piscator! tendit sua retia Christus:
Artem inverte, et jam tu quoque disce capi.

JOAN. I. 23.

Ego sum Vox, &c.

VOX ego sum, dicis: tu vox es, sancte Joannes?
Si vox es, genitor cur tibi mutus erat?

Ista tui fuerant quam mira silentia patris!
Vocem non habuit tunc quoque cum genuit.

ACT. XII.

Vincula sponte decidunt.

QUI ferro Petrum cumulas, durissime custos,
A ferro disces mollior esse tuo.

Ecce fluit, nodisque suis evolvitur ultro:
I fatue, et vinc'lis vincula pone tuis.

In diem omnium Sanctorum.

REV. VII. 3.

Ne lædite terram, neque mare, neque arbores, quousque obsignaverimus servos Dei nostri in frontibus suis.

NUSQUAM immitis agat ventus sua murmura: nusquam
Sylva tremat, crispis sollicitata comis.

Æqua Thetis placide allabens ferat oscula Terræ;
Terra suos Thetidi pandat amica sinus:

Undique pax effusa piis volet aurea pennis,
Frons bona dum signo est quæque notata suo.

Ah quid in hoc opus est signis aliunde petendis?
Frons bona sat lacrymis quæque notata suis.

In die Conjurationis sulphureæ.

QUAM bene dispositis annus dat currere festis!
Post omnes Sanctos, omne scelus sequitur.

Deus sub utero Virginis.

ECCE tuus, Natura, pater! pater hic tuus, hic est:
Ille, uterus matris quem tenet, ille pater.

Pellibus exiguis arctatur Filius ingens,
Quem tu non totum (crede) nec ipsa capis.

Quanta uteri, Regina, tui reverentia tecum est,
Dum jacet hic, cœlo sub breviore, Deus!

Conscia divino gliscunt præcordia motu
(Nec vehit æthereos sanctior aura polos)

Quam bene sub tecto tibi concipiuntur eodem
Vota, et (vota cui concipienda) Deus!

Quod nubes alia, et tanti super atria cœli
Quærunt, invenient hoc tua vota domi.

O felix anima hæc, quæ tam sua gaudia tangit!
Sub conclave suo cui suus ignis adest.

Corpus amet (licet) illa suum, neque sidera malit:
Quod vinc'lum est aliis, hoc habet illa domum.

Sola jaces, neque sola; toro quocunque recumbis,
Illo estis positi tuque tuusque toro.

Immo ubi casta tuo posita es cum conjuge conjunx,
(Quod mirum magis est) es tuus ipsa torus.

Act. vii. 16.

Ad Judæos mactatores Stephani.

FRUSTRA illum increpitant, frustra vaga saxa: nec illi
Grandinis (heu sævæ!) dura procella nocet.

Ista potest tolerare; potest nescire: sed illi,
Quæ sunt in vestro pectore, saxa nocent.

Rev. i. 9.

D. Joannes in exilio.

EXUL, amor Christi est: Christum tamen invenit exul:
Et solitos illic invenit ille sinus.

Ah longo, æterno ah terras indicite nobis
Exilio, Christi si sinus exilium est.

Matth. ii.

Ad Infantes Martyres.

FUNDITE ridentes animas; effundite cœlo:
Discet ibi vestra (ô quam bene!) lingua loqui.

Nec vos lac vestrum et maternos quærite fontes:
Quæ vos expectat lactea tota via est.

Luc. ii.

Quærit Jesum suum beata Virgo.

AH, redeas miseræ, redeas (puer alme) parenti;
Ah, neque te cœlis tam cito redde tuis.

Cœlum nostra tuum fuerint ô brachia, si te
Nostra suum poterunt brachia ferre Deum.

Matth. viii.

Non sum dignus ut sub tecta mea venias.

IN tua tecta Deus veniet: tuus haud sinit illud
Et pudor, atque humili in pectore celsa fides.

Illum ergo accipies quoniam non accipis: ergo
In te jam veniet, non tua tecta, Deus.

Matth. xxvii. 12.

Christus accusatus nihil respondet.

NIL ait: o sanctæ pretiosa silentia linguæ!
Ponderis ô quanti res nihil illud erat!

Ille olim, verbum qui dixit, et omnia fecit,
Verbum non dicens omnia nunc reficit.

Luc. ii.

Nunc dimittis.

SPESNE meas tandem ergo mei tumere lacerti?
Ergo bibunt oculos lumina nostra tuos?

Ergo bibant: possintque novam sperare juventam:
O possint senii non meminisse sui!

Immo mihi potius mitem mors induat umbram
(Esse sub his oculis si tamen umbra potest)

Ah satis est. Ego te vidi (puer aure) vidi:
Nil post te, nisi te (Christe) videre volo.

Luc. viii.

Verbum inter spinas.

SÆPE Dei verbum sentes cadit inter; et atrum
Miscet spina procax (ah mala juncta!) latus.

Credo quidem: nam sic spinas ah scilicet inter
Ipse Deus verbum tu quoque (Christe) cadis.

Luc. xiv. 5.

Sabbatum Judaicum et Christianum.

RES eadem vario quantum distinguitur usu!
Nostra hominem servant sabbata; vestra bovem.

Observent igitur (pacto quid justius isto?)
Sabbata nostra homines, sabbata vestra boves.

Matth. x. 52.

Ad verbum Dei sanatur cæcus.

CHRISTE, locutus eras (o sacra licentia verbi!)
Jamque novus cæci fluxit in ora dies.

Jam credo, Nemo* est, sicut Tu, Christe, loquutus:
Auribus? immo oculis, Christe, loquutus eras.

* Joan. vii. 46.

MATTH. XII.

Onus meum leve est.

ESSE levis quicunque voles, onus accipe Christe:
Ala tuis humeris, non onus, illud erit.

Christi onus an quæris quam sit grave? scilicet audi,
Tam grave, ut ad summos te premat usque polos.

JOAN. VI.

Miraculum quinque panum.

ECCE vagi venit unda cibi; venit indole sacra
Fortis, et in dentes fertilis innumeros.

Quando erat invictæ tam sancta licentia cœnæ?
Illa famem populi poscit, et illa fidem.

JOAN. VIII. 52.

Nunc scimus te habere dæmonium.

AUT Deus, aut saltem dæmon tibi notior esset,
(Gens mala) quæ dicis dæmona habere Deum.

Ignorâsse Deum poteras, ô cæca; sed oro,
Et patrem poteras tam male nôsse tuum?

In beatæ Virginis verecundiam.

IN gremio, quæris, cur sic sua lumina Virgo
  Ponat? ubi melius poneret illa, precor?
O ubi, quam cœlo, melius sua lumina ponat?
  Despicit, at cœlum sic tamen illa videt.

In vulnera Dei pendentis.

O FRONTIS, lateris, manuumque pedumque cruores!
  O quæ purpureo flumina fonte patent!
In nostram (ut quondam) pes non valet ire salutem
  Sed natat; in fluviis (ah!) natat ille suis.
Fixa manus; dat, fixa: pios bona dextera rores
  Donat, et in donum solvitur ipsa suum.
O latus, ô torrens! quis enim torrentior exit
  Nilus, ubi pronis præcipitatur aquis?
Mille et mille simul cadit et cadit undique guttis
  Frons: viden' ut sævus purpuret ora pudor?
Spinæ hoc irriguæ florent crudeliter imbre,
  Inque novas sperant protinus ire rosas.
Quisque capillus it exiguo tener alveus amne,
  Hoc quasi de rubro rivulus oceano.
O nimium vivæ pretiosis amnibus undæ!
  Fons vitæ nunquam verior ille fuit.

Matth. ix. 11.

Quare cum Publicanis manducat Magister vester?

ERGO istis socium se peccatoribus addit?
  Ergo istis sacrum non negat ille latus?

Tu, Pharisæe, rogas Jesus cur fecerit istud?
  Næ dicam: Jesus, non Pharisæus, erat.

Matth. xxviii.

Ecce locus ubi jacuit Dominus.

IPSUM, ipsum (precor) o potius mihi (candide) monstra:
  Ipsi, ipsi, o lacrymis oro sit ire meis.

Si monstrare locum satis est, et dicere nobis,
  En, Maria, hic tuus en, hic jacuit Dominus;

Ipsa ulnas, monstrare meas, et dicere possum,
  En, Maria, hic tuus en, hic jacuit Dominus.

Φαιδιμε, μοὶ αυτον μαλλον μοι δεικνυθι αυτον.
  Αυτος μου, δεομαι, αυτος ἔχη δακρυα.

Εἰ δε τοπον μοι δεικνύναι ἅλις ἐστι, και εἰπειν
  Ὡ δε τεὸς Μαριαμ (ἤνιδε) κειτο ἄναξ.

Ἀγκοίνας μου δεικνυναι δυναμοι γε, και ειπειν
  Ὡ δε τεὸς Μαριαμ (ἤνιδε) κειτο ἄναξ.

Luc. xvii.

Leprosi ingrati.

LEX jubet ex hominum cœtu procul ire leprosos:
At mundi a Christo cur abiere procul?

Non abit, at sedes tantum mutavit in illis;
Et lepra, quæ fuerat corpore, mente sedet.

Sic igitur digna vice res variatur; et a se
Quam procul ante homines, nunc habuere Deum.

Joan. xx.

In cicatrices quas Christus habet in se adhuc superstites.

QUICQUID spina procax, vel stylo clavus acuto,
Quicquid purpurea scripserat hasta nota,

Vivit adhuc tecum: sed jam tua vulnera non sunt:
Non, sed vulneribus sunt medicina meis.

Act. v.

Æger implorat umbram D. Petri.

PETRE, tua lateam paulisper (Petre) sub umbra:
Sic mea me quærent fata, nec invenient.

Umbra dabit tua posse meum me cernere solem;
Et mea lux umbræ sic erit umbra tuæ.

Luc. xxiv. 39.

Quid turbati estis? Videte manus meas et pedes, quia ego ipse sum.

EN me, et signa mei, quondam mea vulnera! certe,
Vos nisi credetis, vulnera sunt et adhuc.

O nunc ergo fidem sanent mea vulnera vestram:
O mea nunc sanet vulnera vestra fides.

Act. xii.

In vincula Petro sponte delapsa, et apertas fores.

FERRI non meminit ferrum: se vincula Petro
Dissimulant: nescit carcer habere fores.

Quam bene liber erit, carcer quem liberat! ipsa
Vincula quem solvunt, quam bene tutus erit!

Act. xix. 12.

Deferebantur a corpore ejus sudaria, &c.

IMPERIOSA premunt morbos, et ferrea fati
Jura ligant, Pauli lintea tacta manu.

Unde hæc felicis laus est et gloria lini?
Hæc (reor) e Lachesis pensa fecere colo.

JOAN. XV.

Christus Vitis ad Vinitorem Patrem.

EN serpit tua, purpureo tua palmite vitis
Serpit, et (ah!) spretis it per humum foliis.

Tu viti succurre tuæ, mi Vinitor ingens:
Da fulcrum; fulcrum da mihi: quale? crucem.

ACT. XXVI. 28.

Pene persuades mihi ut fiam Christianus.

PENE? quid hoc pene est? Vicinia sæva salutis!
O quam tu malus es proximitate boni!

Ah! portu qui teste perit, bis naufragus ille est;
Hunc non tam pelagus, quam sua terra premit.

Quæ nobis spes vix absunt, crudelius absunt:
Pene sui felix, emphasis est miseri.

JOAN. III. 19.

Lux venit in mundum, sed dilexerunt homines magis tenebras quam lucem.

LUCE sua venit ecce Deus, mundoque refulget;
Pergit adhuc tenebras mundus amare suas.

At Stygiis igitur mundus damnabitur umbris:
Pergit adhuc tenebras mundus amare suas?

Luc. xvi.

Dives implorat guttam.

O MIHI si digito tremat et tremat unica summo
  Gutta! o si flammas mulceat una meas!

Currat opum quocunque volet levis unda mearum;
  Una mihi hæc detur gemmula, Dives ero.

Joan. iii. 4.

Quomodo potest homo gigni qui est senex?

DIC, Phœnix unde in nitidos novus emicat annos;
  Plaudit et elusos aurea penna rogos?

Quis colubrem dolus insinuat per secula retro,
  Et jubet emeritum luxuriare latus?

Cur rostro pereunte suam prædata senectam
  Torva ales, rapido plus legit ore diem?

Immo, sed adnixus præstat Lucina secundos?
  Natales seros unde senex habeat.

Ignoras, Pharisæe? sat est: jam credere disces:
  Dimidium fidei, qui bene nescit, habet.

Marc. xi. 13.

Arbor Christi jussu arescens.

ILLE jubet: procul ite mei, mea gloria, rami:
 Nulla vocet nostras amplius aura comas.

Ite; nec ô pigeat: nam vos neque fulminis ira,
 Nec trucis ala Noti verberat: ille jubet.

O vox! ô Zephyro vel sic quoque dulcior omni!
 Non possum Autumno nobiliore frui.

Luc. i. 12.

Zacharias minus credens.

INFANTES fore te patrem, res mira videtur;
 Infans interea factus es ipse pater.

Et dum promissi signum (nimis anxie) quæris,
 Jam nisi per signum quærere nulla potes.

Joan. iii.

In aquam baptismi Dominici.

FELIX ô, sacros cui sic licet ire per artus!
 Felix! dum lavat hunc, ipsa lavatur aqua.

Gutta quidem sacros quæcunque perambulat artus,
 Dum manet hic, gemma est; dum cadit hinc, lacryma.

Luc. xiii. 11.

Mulieri incurvatæ meditur Dominus, indignante Archisynagogo.

IN proprios replicata sinus quæ repserat, et jam
Dæmonis (infelix!) nil nisi nodus erat,
Solvitur ad digitum Domini: sed strictior illo
Unicus est nodus; cor, Pharisæe, tuum.

Matth. xxii. 46.

Neque ausus fuit quisquam ex illo die eum amplius interrogare.

CHRISTE, malas fraudes, Pharisaica retia, fallis:
Et miseros sacro discutis ore dolos.
Ergo tacent tandem, atque invitâ silentia servant:
Tam bene non aliter te potuere loqui.

Matth. xx. 20.

S. Joannes matri suæ.

O MIHI cur dextram, mater, cur, oro, sinistram
Poscis, ab officio mater iniqua tuo?
Nolo manum Christi dextram mihi, nolo sinistram:
Tam procul a sacro non libet esse sinu.

Matth. iv.

Si filius Dei es, dejice te.

NI se dejiciat Christus de vertice Templi,
Non credes quod sit Filius ille Dei.

At mox te humano de pectore dejicit: heus tu,
Non credes quod sit Filius ille Dei?

Luc. xix. 41.

Dominus flens ad Judæos.

DISCITE vos miseri, venientes discite flammas;
Nec facite ô lacrymas sic periisse meas.

Nec periisse tamen poterunt: mihi credite, vestras
Vel rèprimet flammas hæc aqua, vel faciet.

Luc. xviii. 11.

Nec velut hic Publicanus.

ISTUM? vile caput! quantum mihi gratulor, inquis,
Istum quod novi tam mihi dissimilem!

Vilis at iste abiit sacris acceptior aris:
I nunc, et jactes hunc tibi dissimilem.

Act. ix. 3.

In Saulum fulgore nimio excæcatum.

QUÆ lucis tenebræ? quæ nox est ista diei?
Nox nova, quam nimii luminis umbra facit!

An Saulus fuerit cæcus, vix dicere possum;
Hoc scio, quod captus lumine Saulus erat.

Luc. x. 23.

Beati oculi qui vident.

CUM Christus nostris ibat mitissimus oris,
Atque novum cæcos jussit habere diem,

Felices, oculos qui tunc habuere, vocantur?
Felices, et qui non habuere, voco.

Luc. vii. 15.

Filius e feretro matri redditur.

ERGONE tam subita potuit vice flebilis horror
In natalitia candidus ire toga?

Quos vidi, matris gemitus hos esse dolentis
Credideram; gemitus parturientis erant.

Matth. xi. 25.

In seculi sapientes.

ERGONE delitias facit, et sibi plaudit ab alto
  Stultitia, ut velit hac ambitione pati?

Difficilisne adeo facta est, et seria tandem?
  Ergo et in hanc etiam quis sapuisse potest?

Tantum erat, ut possit tibi doctior esse ruina?
  Tanti igitur cerebri res, periisse, fuit?

Nil opus ingenio; nihil hac opus arte furoris:
  Simplicius poteris scilicet esse miser.

Luc. iv. 29.

In Judæos Christum præcipitare conantes.

DICITE, quæ tanta est sceleris fiducia vestri?
  Quod nequiit dæmon, id voluisse scelus?

Quod nequiit dæmon scelus, id voluisse patrare!
  Hoc tentare ipsum dæmona (crede) fuit.

Rev. vii. 9.

In Draconem præcipitem.

I FRUSTRA truculente; tuas procul aurea ridert
  Astra minas, cœlò jam bene tuta suo.

Tune igitur cœlum super ire atque astra parabas?
  Ascensu tanto non opus ad barathrum.

LUC. II.

Beatæ Virgini credenti.

MIRARIS (quid enim faceres?) sed et hæc quoque credis:
Hæc uteri credis dulcia monstra tui.

En fidei, Regina, tuæ dignissima merces!
Fida Dei fueras filia; mater eris.

MARC. XII.

Licetne Cæsari censum dare?

POST tot Scribarum (Christe) in te prœlia, tandem
Ipse venit Cæsar: Cæsar in arma venit.

Pugnant terribiles non Cæsaris ense, sed ense
Cæsare: quin Cæsar vinceris ipse tamen.

Hoc quoque tu conscribe tuis, Auguste, triumphis.
Sic vinci dignus quis nisi Cæsar erat?

MATTH. IX.

In tibicines et turbam tumultuantem circa defunctam.

VANI, quid strepitis? nam, quamvis dormiat* illa,
Non tamen e somno est sic revocanda suo.

Expectat solos Christi sopor iste susurros:
Dormit enim; sed non omnibus illa tamen.

* Vers. 24. Non enim mortua est puella, sed dormit.

MATTH. VI. 19.

Piscatores vocati.

LUDITE jam pisces secura per æquora: pisces
Nos quoque (sed varia sub ratione) sumus.

Non potuisse capi, vobis spes una salutis:
Una salus nobis est, potuisse capi.

MARC. XII.

Date Cæsari.

CUNCTA Deo debentur: habet tamen et sua Cæsar;
Nec minus inde Deo est, si sua Cæsar habet.

Non minus inde Deo est, solio si cætera dantur
Cæsareo, Cæsar cum datur ipse Deo.

MATTH. XXI. 7.

Dominus asino vehitur.

ILLE igitur vilem te, te dignatur asellum,
O non vectura non bene digne tua?

Heu quibus haud pugnat Christi patientia monstris?
Hoc, quod sic fertur, hoc quoque ferre fuit.

Luc. xxi. 27.

Videbunt Filium hominis venientem in nube.

IMMO veni: aërios (ô Christe) accingere currus,
Inque triumphali nube coruscus ades.
Nubem quæris? erunt nostra (ah!) suspiria nubes:
Aut sol in nubem se dabit ipse tuam.

Joan. xx.

Nisi digitum immisero, &c.

IMPIUS ergo iterum clavos? iterum impius hastam?
Et totum digitus triste revolvet opus?
Tune igitur Christum (Thoma) quo vivere credas,
In Christum faceres (ah truculente!) mori?

Act. viii.

Ad Judæos mactatores S. Stephani.

QUID datis (ah miseri!) saxis nolentibus iras?
Quid nimis in tragicum præcipitatis opus?
In mortem Stephani se dant invita: sed illi
Occiso faciunt sponte sua tumulum.

Sancto Joanni, dilecto discipulo.

TU fruere; augustoque sinu caput abde (quod ô tum
Nollet in æterna se posuisse rosa)

Tu fruere: et sacro dum te sic pectore portat,
O sat erit tergo me potuisse vehi.

MATTH. II.

In lactentes Martyres.

VULNERA natorum qui vidit, et ubera matrum,
Per pueros fluviis (ah!) simul ire suis;

Sic pueros quisquis vidit, dubitavit, an illos
Lilia cœlorum diceret, anne rosas.

MATTH. I. 23.

Deus nobiscum.

NOBISCUM Deus est? vestrum hoc est (hei mihi!) vestrum:
Vobiscum Deus est, ô asini atque boves.

Nobiscum non est: nam nos domus aurea sumit:
Nobiscum Deus est, et jacet in stabulo?

Hoc igitur nostrum ut fiat (dulcissime Jesu)
Nos dandi stabulis, vel tibi danda domus.

Christus circumcisus ad Patrem.

HAS en primitias nostræ (Pater) accipe mortis
(Vitam ex quo sumpsi, vivere dedidici)

Ira (Pater) tua de pluvia gustaverit ista:
Olim ibit fluviis hoc latus omne suis.

Tunc sitiat licet et sitiat, bibet et bibet usque:
Tunc poterit toto fonte superba frui.

Nunc hastæ interea possit præludere culter:
Indolis in pœnas spes erit ista meæ.

In Epiphaniam Domini.

NON solita contenta dies face lucis Eoæ,
Ecce micat radiis cæsariata novis.

Persa sagax, propera: discurre per ardua regum
Tecta, per auratas marmoreasque domus:

Quære ô, quæ intepuit Reginæ purpura partu;
Principe vagitu quæ domus insonuit.

Audin' Persa sagax? Qui tanta negotia cœlo
Fecit, Bethlemiis vagiit in stabulis.

Luc. ii. 49.

Ecce quærebamus te, &c.

TE quæro misera, et quæro: tu nunc quoque tractas
Res Patris: Pater est unica cura tibi:

Quippe quod ad pœnas tantum et tot nomina mortis,
Ad luctum et lacrymas (hei mihi!) mater ego.

Joan. ii.

Aquæ in vinum versæ.

UNDE rubor vestris, et non sua purpura lymphis?
Quæ rosa mirantes tam nova mutat aquas?

Numen (convivæ) præsens agnoscite Numen:
Nympha pudica Deum vidit, et erubuit.

Matth. viii. 13.

Absenti Centurionis filio Dominus absens medetur.

QUAM tacitis inopina salus illabitur alis!
Alis, quas illi vox tua, Christe, dedit.

Quam longas vox ista manus habet! hæc medicina
Absens, et præsens hæc medicina fuit.

Marc. iv. 40.

Quid timidi estis.

TANQUAM illi insanus faceret sua fulmina ventus!
Tanquam illi scopulos nôrit habere fretum!

Vos vestri scopuli, vos estis ventus et unda:
Naufragium cum illo qui metuit, meruit.

Luc. ii.

Nunc dimittis.

ITE mei (quid enim ulterius, quid vultis?) ocelli:
Leniter obductis ite superciliis.

Immo et adhuc et adhuc, iterumque iterumque videte;
Accipite hæc totis lumina luminibus.

Jamque ite; et tutis ô vos bene claudite vallis:
Servate hæc totis lumina luminibus.

Primum est, quod potui te (Christe) videre: secundum,
Te viso, recta jam potuisse mori.

Matth. xiii. 24.

In segetem sacram.

ECCE suam implorat, demisso vertice, falcem:
Tu segeti falcem da (Pater alme) suam.

Tu falcem non das? messem tu (Christe) moraris?
Hoc ipsum falx est: hæc mora messis erit.

Luc. vii. 37.

Cœpit lacrymis rigare pedes ejus, et capillis extergebat.

UNDA sacras sordes lambit placidissima: flavæ
Lambit et hanc undam lucida flamma comæ.

Illa per has sordes it purior unda; simulque
Ille per has lucet purior ignis aqua.

Luc. xviii. 41.

Quid vis tibi faciam?

QUID volo (Christe) rogas? quippe ah volo, Christe, videre:
Quippe ad te (dulcis Christe) videre volo.

At video; fideique oculis te nunc quoque figo:
Est mihi, quæ nunquam est non oculata, fides.

Sed quamvis videam, tamen ah volo (Christe) videre:
Sed quoniam video (Christe) videre volo.

Matth. xv. 21.

Christus mulieri Canaaneæ difficilior.

UT pretium facias dono, donare recusas:
Usque rogat supplex, tutamen usque negas.

Hoc etiam donare fuit, donare negare.
Sæpe dedit, quisquis sæpe negata dedit.

Luc. II.

Beatus venter et ubera, &c.

ET quid si biberet Jesus vel ab ubere vestro?
Quid facit ad vestram, quod bibit ille, sitim?
Ubera mox sua et hic (ô quam non lactea!) pandet!
E nato mater tum bibet ipsa suo.

Joan. xv. 1.

In Christum vitem.

ULMUM vitis amat (quippe est et in arbore flamma,
Quam fovet in viridi pectore blandus amor:)
Illam ex arboribus cunctis tu (vitis) amasti,
Illam, quæcunque est, quæ crucis arbor erat.

Joan. xvi. 20.

Vos flebitis et lamentabimini.

ERGO mihi salvete mei, mea gaudia, luctus:
Quam charum (ô Deus) est hoc mihi flere meum!
Flerem, ni flerem: solus tu (dulcis Jesu)
Lætitiam donas tunc quoque quando negas.

JOAN. X.

In gregem Christi Pastoris.

O GREX, o nimium tanto Pastore beatus!
O ubi sunt tanto pascua digna grege?

Ne non digna forent tanto grege pascua, Christus
Ipse suo est Pastor, pascuum et ipse gregi.

In vulnera pendentis Domini.

SIVE oculos, sive ora vocem tua vulnera; certe
Undique sunt ora (heu!) undique sunt oculi.

Ecce ora! ô nimium roseis florentia labris!
Ecce oculi! sævis ah madidi lacrymis!

Magdala, quæ lacrymas solita es, quæ basia sacro
Ferre pedi, sacro de pede sume vices.

Ora pedi sua sunt, tua quo tibi basia reddat:
Quo reddat lacrymas scilicet est oculos.

MARC. II.

Paralyticus convalescens.

CHRISTUM, quod misero facilis peccata remittit,
Scribæ blasphemum dicere non dubitant.

Hoc scelus ut primum Paralyticus audiit: ira
Impatiens, lectum sustulit atque abiit.

JOAN. VIII. 59.

Tunc sustulerunt lapides.

SAXA? illi? quid tam fœdi voluere furores?
Quid sibi de saxis hi voluere suis?

Indolem, et antiqui agnosco vestigia patris:
Panem de saxis hi voluere suis.

In resurrectionem Domini.

NASCERIS, en! tecumque tuus (Rex auree) mundus,
Tecum* Virgineo nascitur e tumulo.

Tecum in natalis properat natura secundos,
Atque novam vitam te novus orbis habet.

Ex vita (Sol alme) tua vitam omnia sumunt:
Nil certe, nisi mors, cogitur inde mori.

At certe neque mors: nempe ut queat illa sepulchro
(Christe) tuo condi, mors volet ipsa mori.

MATTH. XXVIII. 17.

Aliqui vero dubitabant.

SCILICET et tellus dubitat,† tremebunda: sed ipsum hoc,
Quod tellus dubitat, vos dubitare vetat.

* Joan. 19. 41. Ἐν ᾧ οὐδέπω οὐδεὶς ἐτέθη.
† Vers. 2. Σεισμὸς ἐγένετο μέγας.

Ipsi custodes vobis, si quæritis, illud
  Hoc ipso dicunt,* dicere quod nequeunt.

JOAN. XX. 20.

In vulnerum vestigia quæ ostendit Dominus, ad firmandam suorum fidem.

HIS oculis (néc adhuc clausis coïere fenestris)
  Invigilans nobis est tuus usus amor.

His oculis nos cernit amor tuus: his et amorem
  (Christe) tuum gaudet cernere nostra fides.

LUC. VII. 19.

Mittit Joannes qui quærant a Christo, an is sit.

TU qui adeo impatiens properasti agnoscere Christum,
  Tunc cum claustra utere te tenuere tui,

Tu, quis sit Christus, rogitas? et quæris ab ipso?
  Hoc tibi vel mutus dicere quisque potest.

JOAN. XVIII. 10.

In Petrum auricidam.

QUANTUMCUNQUE ferox tuus hic (Petre) fulminat ensis,
  Tu tibi jam pugnas (o bone) non Domino.

Scilicet in miseram furis implacidissimus aurem,
  Perfidiæ testis ne queas esse tuæ.

* Vers. 4. 'Εσείσθησαν οἱ τηροῦντες, καὶ ἐγένοντο ὡσεὶ νεκροί.

MARC. III.

Manus arefacta sanatur.

FELIX! ergo tuæ spectas natalia dextræ,
Quæ modo spectanti flebile funus erat.
Quæ nec in externos modo dextera profuit usus,
Certe erit illa tuæ jam manus et fidei.

MATTH. XXVII. 24.

In Pontium male lautum.

ILLA manus lavat unda tuas, vanissime judex:
Ah tamen illa scelus non lavat unda tuum.
Nulla scelus lavet unda tuum: vel si lavet ulla,
O volet ex oculis illa venire tuis.

MATTH. XVII. 27.

In piscem dotatum.

TU piscem si, Christe, velis, venit ecce, suumque
Fert pretium: tanti est vel periisse tibi.
Christe, foro tibi non opus est; addicere nummos
Non opus est: ipsum se tibi piscis emet.

JOAN. XVI. 33.

Ego vici mundum.

TU contra mundum dux es meus, optime Jesu?
At tu (me miserum!) dux meus ipse jaces.

Si tu, dux meus, ipse jaces, spes ulla salutis?
Immo, ni jaceas tu, mihi nulla salus.

In ascensionem Domini.

VADIT (Io!) per aperta sui penetralia cœli:
It cœlo, et cœlum fundit ab ore novum.

Spargitur ante pedes, et toto sidere pronus
Jam propius Solis Sol bibit ora sui.

At fratri debere negans sua lumina Phœbe,
Aurea de Phœbe jam meliore redit.

Hos, de te victo, tu das (Pater) ipse triumphos:
Unde triumphares, quis satis alter erat?

In descensum Spiritus sancti.

JAM cœli circum tonuit fragor: arma, minasque
Turbida cum flammis mista ferebat hiems.

Exclamat Judæus atrox; Venit ecce nefandis,
Ecce venit meriti fulminis ira memor.

Verum ubi composito sedit fax blandior astro,
  Flammaque non læsas lambit amica comas;

Judæis, fulmen quia falsum apparuit esse,
  Hoc ipso verum nomine fulmen erat.

Οὐρανου ἐκ το πησε βρομος· πολεμου καὶ ἀπειλὰς
  Ἦγε τρεχων ἄνεμος συν φλογὶ σμιρδαλεη.

Αὖεν Ἰουδαιος· μιαρα στυγερων τα καρηνα
  Ἔφθασε της οργης το πρεπον ουρανίης.

Ἄλλα γαληναιω ὅτε κειναὶ ἥσυχον ἄστρω
  Φλεγμα, και ἀβλητους λειχε φιλον πλοναμους,

Εκθαμβει. ὅτι γαρ, κείνοίς οὐκ ἧεν ἀληθὴς,
  Νυν ετεον διοτι τῶδε κεραυνος ἔην.*

JOAN. III. 16.

Sic dilexit mundum Deus, ut Filium morti traduit.

AH nimis est, illum nostræ vel tradere vitæ:
  Guttula quod faceret, cur facit oceanus?

Unde et luxuriare potest, habet hinc mea vita:
  Ample et magnifice mors habet unde mori.

* Not in the edition of 1634.

LUC. XIV. 19.

Juga boum emi.

AD cœnam voco te (domini quod jussa volebant)
Tu mihi, nescis quos, dicis (inepte) boves.

Imo vale, nobis nec digne nec utilis hospes!
Cœna tuos (credo) malit habere boves.

ACT. XIV.

D. Paulum, verbo sanantem claudum, pro Mercurio Lystres adorant.

QUIS Tagus hic, quæ Pactoli nova volvitur unda?
Non hominis vox est hæc: Deus ille, Deus.

Salve, mortales nimium dignate penates!
Digna Deo soboles, digna tonante Deo!

O salve! quid enim (alme) tuos latuisse volebas?
Te dicit certe vel tua lingua Deum.

Laudem hanc haud miror: meruit facundus haberi,
Qui claudo promptos suasit habere pedes.

In S. Columbam ad Christi caput sedentem.

CUI sacra siderea volueris suspenditur ala?
Hunc nive plus niveum cui dabit illa pedem?

Christe, tuo capiti totis se destinat auris,
Qua ludit densæ blandior umbra comæ.

Illic arcano quid non tibi murmure narrat?
(Murmure mortales non imitante sonos)

Sola avis hæc nido hoc non est indigna cubare:
Solus nidus hic est hac bene dignus ave.

Πη ταχυεργος ἄγει πτερυγ' ἀστεροεσσαν ἐρετμός;
Ἢ τινι κεινα φερει την ποδα χιονενη;

Χριστε τεη κεφαλη πασαις πτερυγεσσιν ἐπείγει·
Πη σκια τοι δασιοις παιζε μαλα πλοκαμοις.

Ποία σοι ἀρρητω ψιθυρισματι κειν ἀγορευει;
Ἀρρητ', οὐκ ἠχης ἰσα μεν ἀνδρομενης.

Μουνα μεν ἡδ' ὅρνις καλιας ἐς ἄξια ταυτης·
Ἄξια δ' ὅρνιθος μουνα μεν ἡ καλια.*

Act. XII.

In fores Divi Petro sponte apertas.

QUID juvit clausisse fores (bone janitor) istas?
Et Petro claves jam liquet esse suas.

Dices, sponte patent: Petri ergo hoc scilicet ipsum
Est clavis, Petro clave quod haud opus est.

* Not in the edition of 1634.

LUC. XV. 12.

Murmurabant Pharisæi, dicentes, Recipit peccatores et comedit cum illis.

AH male, quisquis is est, pereat! qui scilicet istis
Convivam (sævus!) non sinit esse suum.

Istis cum Christus conviva adjungitur, istis
O non conviva est Christus, at ipse cibus.

MATTH. XV.

In trabem Pharisaicam.

CEDANT, quæ, rerum si quid tenue atque minutum est,
Posse acie certa figere, vitra dabunt.

Artis opus miræ! Pharisæo en optica trabs est,
Ipsum (vera loquor) quâ videt ille nihil.

JOAN. IX. 22.

Constituerunt ut si quis confiteretur eum esse Christum, synagoga moveretur.

INFELIX, Christum reus es quicunque colendi!
O reus infelix! quam tua culpa gravis!

Tu summis igitur, summis damnabere cœlis:
O reus infelix! quam tua pœna gravis!

MATTH. XX. 20.

De voto filiorum Zebedæi.

SIT tibi (Joannes) tibi sit (Jacobe) quod optas:
Sit tibi dextra manus; sit tibi læva manus.

Spero, alia in cœlo est, et non incommoda, sedes:
Si neque læva manus; si neque dextra manus.

Cœli hanc aut illam nolo mihi quærere partem;
O, cœlum, cœlum da (Pater alme) mihi.

JOAN. VI.

Ad hospites cœnæ miraculosæ quinque panum.

VESCERE pane tuo: sed et (hospes) vescere Christo:
Et panis pani scilicet ille tuo.

Tunc pane hoc Christi recte satur (hospes) abibis,
Panem ipsum Christum si magis esurias.

JOAN. XVI. 33.

De Christo contra mundum pugna.

TUNE, miser? tu (mundus ait) mea fulmina contra
Ferre manus, armis cum tibi nuda manus?

I lictor: manibusque audacibus injice vinc'la:
Injecit lictor vincula, et arma dedit.

Act. ix. 29.

Græci disputatores Divo Paulo mortem machinantur.

EUGE argumentum! sic disputat: euge sophista!
  Sic pugnum Logices stringere, sic decuit.
Hoc argumentum in causam quid (Græcule) dicit?
  Dicit, te in causam dicere posse nihil.

Luc. xxii. 26.

Qui maximus est inter vos, esto sicut qui minimus.

O BONE, discipulus Christe vis maximus esse?
  At vero fies hac ratione minor.
Hoc sanctæ ambitionis iter (mihi crede) tenendum est,
  Hæc ratio; Tu, ne sis minor, esse velis.

Luc. xix. 41.

VOBIS (Judæi) vobis hæc volvitur unda;
  Quæ vobis, quoniam spernitis, ignis erit.
Eia faces (Romane) faces! seges illa furoris,
  Non nisi ab his undis, ignea messis erit.

Matth. ii.

Christus in Ægypto.

HUNC tu (Nile) tuis majori flumine monstra:
Hunc (nimis ignotum) dic caput esse tibi.

Jam tibi (Nile) tumes: jam te quoque multus inunda:
Ipse tuæ jam sis lætitiæ fluvius.

Matth. ix.

In cæcos Christum confitentes, Pharisæos abnegantes.

NE mihi, tu (Pharisæe ferox) tua lumina jactes:
En cæcus! Christum cæcus at ille videt.

Tu (Pharisæe) nequis in Christo cernere Christum:
Ille videt cæcus; cæcus es ipse videns.

Matth. xvi. 24.

Si quis pone me veniet, tollat crucem et sequatur me.

ERGO sequor, sequor, en! quippe et mihi crux mea, Christe, est:
Parva quidem; sed quam non satis, ecce, rego.

Non rego? non parvam hanc? ideo neque parva putanda est.
Crux magna est, parvam non bene ferre crucem.

Luc. v. 28.

Relictis omnibus sequutus est eum.

QUAS Matthæus opes, ad Christi jussa, reliquit,
Tum primum vere cœpit habere suas.

Iste malarum est usus opum bonus, unicus iste;
Esse malas homini, quas bene perdat, opes.

Matth. xxv. 29.

Ædificatis sepulchra Prophetarum.

SANCTORUM in tumulis quid vult labor ille colendis?
Sanctorum mortem non sinit illa mori.

Vane, Prophetarum quot ponis saxa sepulchris,
Tot testes lapidum, queis periere, facis.

Marc. iii.

In manum aridam qua Christo mota est miseratio.

PRENDE (miser) Christum; et cum Christo prende salutem:
At manca est (dices) dextera: prende tamen.

Ipsum hoc, in Christum, manus est: hoc prendere Christum est,
Qua Christum prendas, non habuisse manum.

Ad D. Lucam medicum.

NULLA mihi (Luca) de te medicamina posco,
Ipse licet medicus sis, licet æger ego:
Quippe ego in exemplum fidei dum te mihi pono,
Tu, medice, ipse mihi es tu medicina mea.

Ουδεν, εγω, Λουκα, παρα σου μοι φαρμακον αἰτω,
Καν συ δ' ἰατρος ἐης, καν μεν ἐγω νοσερος.
'Αλλ' εν ὅσω παραδειγμα πελεις μοι πιστιος, αὐτος,
Αὐτος ἰατρος, ἐμοι γ' ἐστι ἀκεστοριη.

Luc. xiv. 4.

Hydropicus sanatus, Christum jam sitiens.

PELLITUR inde sitis; sed et hinc sitis altera surgit:
Hinc sitit ille magis, quo sitit inde minus.
Felix o, et mortem poterit qui temnere morbus!
Cui vitæ ex ipso fonte sititur aqua!

In cœtum cœlestem omnium Sanctorum.

FELICES animæ! quas cœlo debita virtus
Jam potuit vestris inseruisse polis.
Hoc dedit egregii non parcus sanguinis usus,
Spesque per obstantes expatiata vias.

O ver! o longæ semper seges aurea lucis!
Nocte nec alterna dimidiata dies!

O quæ palma manu ridet! quæ fronte corona!
O nix virgineæ non temeranda togæ!

Pacis inoccidnæ vos illic ora videtis:
Vos Agni dulcis lumina: vos—Quid ago?

MATTH. VIII. 13.

Christus absenti medetur.

VOX jam missa suas potuit jam tangere metas?
O superi! non hoc ire sed isse fuit.

Mirac'lum fuit ipsa salus (bene credere possis)
Ipsum, mirac'lum est, quando salutis iter.

JOAN. IX.

Cæcus natus.

FELIX, qui potuit tantæ post nubila noctis
(O dignum tanta nocte!) videre diem:

Felix ille oculus, felix utrinque putandus;
Quod videt, et primum quod videt ille Deum.

Matth. ix.

Et ridebant illum.

LUCTIBUS in tantis, Christum ridere vacabat?
Vanior iste fuit risus, an iste dolor?

Luctibus in tantis hic vester risus inepti,
(Credite mi) meruit maximus esse dolor.

Matth. xi. 25.

In sapientiam seculi.

NOLI altum sapere (hoc veteres voluere magistri)
Ne retrahat lassos alta ruina gradus.

Immo mihi dico, Noli sapuisse profundum:
Non ego ad infernum me sapuisse velim.

In stabulum ubi natus est Dominus.

ILLA domus stabulum? non est (Puer auree) non est:
Illa domus, quæ tu nasceris, est stabulum?

Illa domus toto domus est pulcherrima mundo;
Vix cœlo dici vult minor illa tuo.

Cernis ut illa suo passim domus ardeat auro?
Cernis ut effusis rideat illa rosis?

Sive aurum non est, nec quæ rosa rideat illic;
Ex oculis facile est esse probare tuis.

Οἶκος ὅδε ἐς αὐλη. ου μη. σεος οἶκος, Ἰησου,
Εν θ' ᾧ τυ τικτη αὔλιον ου πελεται.

Οἴκων μεν παντων μαλα δη καλλίστος ἐκεινος·
Οὐρανου οὐδε τεου μίκροτερος πελεται.

Ἤνιδε κείνο νεῳ δωμ' ἐμπυριζετο χρυσω,
Ἤνιδε κεινο νεοις δωμα ροδοισὶ γελα.

Ἦν ῥοδον οὐχὶ γελα, την οὐδε τε χρυσον ἐκειθεν·
Ἐκ σου δ' οφθαλμων εστιν ελεγχεμεναι.*

ACT. VIII.

S. Stephanus amicis suis, funus sibi curantibus.

NULLA (precor) busto surgant mihi marmora: bustum
Hæc mihi sint mortis conscia saxa meæ.

Sic nec opus fuerit, notet ut quis carmine bustum,
Pro Domino (dicens) occidit ille suo.

Hic mihi sit tumulus, quem mors dedit ipsa; meique
Ipse hic martyrii sit mihi martyrium.

In D. Joannem, quem Domitianus ferventi oleo (illæsum) indidit.

ILLUM (qui, toto currens vaga flammula mundo,
Non quidem Joannes, ipse sed audit amor)

Illum ignem extingui, bone Domitiane, laboras?
Hoc non est oleum, Domitiane, dare.

* Not in the edition of 1634.

In tenellos Martyres.

AH qui tam propero cecidit sic funere, vitæ
  Hoc habuit tantum, possit ut ille mori.

At cujus Deus est sic usus funere, mortis
  Hoc tantum, ut possit vivere semper, habet.

MATTH. IV. 24.

Attulerunt ei omnes male effectos, dæmoniacos, lunaticos—et sanavit eos.

COLLIGE te tibi (torve Draco) furiasque
    facesque,
  Quasque vocant pestes nox Erebusque suas:

Fac colubres jam tota suos tua vibret Erinnys;
  Collige, collige te fortiter, ut—pereas.

LUC. II.

Tuam ipsius animam pertransibit gladius.

QUANDO habeat gladium tua, Christe, tragœdia
    nullum,
  Quis fuerit gladius, virgo beata, tuus?

Namque nec ulla alias tibi sunt data vulnera, Virgo,
  Quam quæ a vulneribus sunt data, Christe, tuis.

Forsan quando senex jam caligantior esset,
Quod Simeon gladium credidit, hasta fuit.

Immo neque hasta fuit, neque clavus, sed neque spina:
Hei mihi, spina tamen, clavus, et hasta fuit.

Nam queiscunque malis tua, Christe, tragœdia crevit,
Omnia sunt gladius, virgo beata, tuus.

In sanguinem circumcisionis Domini. Ad convivas, quos hæc dies apud nos solennes habet.

HEUS conviva! bibin'? Maria hæc, Mariæque puellus,
Mittunt de prelo musta bibenda suo.

Una quidem est (toti quæ par tamen unica mundo)
Unica gutta, suo quæ tremit orbiculo.

O bibite hinc; quale aut quantum vos cunque bibistis,
(Credite mi) nil tam suave bibistis adhuc.

O bibite et bibite, et restat tamen usque bibendum:
Restat, quod poterit nulla domare sitis.

Scilicet hic, mensura sitis, mensura bibendi est:
Hæc quantum cupias vina bibisse, bibis.

Luc. ii.

Puer Jesus inter Doctores.

FALLITUR, ad mentum qui pendit quemque profundum,
Ceu possint læves nil sapuisse genæ.

Scilicet e barba male mensuratur Apollo;
Et bene cum capitis stat nive, mentis hiems.

Discat, et a tenero disci quoque posse magistro:
Canitiem capitis nec putet esse caput.

Joan. ii.

Ad Christum, de aqua in vinum versa.

SIGNA tuis tuus hostis habet contraria signis:
In vinum tristes tu mihi vertis aquas.

Ille autem e vino lacrymas et jurgia ducens,
Vina iterum in tristes (hei mihi!) mutat aquas.

Luc. ii.

Christus infans Patri sistitur in templo.

AGNUS eat, ludatque (licet) sub patre petulco;
Cumque sua longum conjuge turtur agat.

Conciliatorem nihil hic opus ire par agnum:
Nec tener ut volucris non sua fata ferat.

Hactenus exigua hæc, quasi munera, lusimus; hæc quæ
Multum excusanti sunt capienda manu.

Hoc donum est; de quo, toto tibi dicimus ore,
Sume Pater: meritis hoc tibi sume suis.

Donum hoc est, hoc est; quod scilicet audeat ipso
Esse Deo dignum: scilicet ipse Deus.

MATTH. VIII.

Leprosus Dominum implorans.

CREDO quod ista potes, velles modo: sed quia credo,
Christe, quod ista potes, credo quod ista voles.

Tu modo, tu faciles mihi, sol meus, exere vultus;
Non poterit radios nix mea ferre tuos.

MATTH. VIII.

Christus in tempestate.

QUOD fervet tanto circum te, Christe, tumultu,
Non hoc ira maris, Christe, sed ambitio est.

Hæc illa ambitio est, hoc tanto te rogat ore,
Possit ut ad monitus, Christe, tacere tuos.

Act. xvi. 21.

Annunciant ritus, quos non licet nobis suscipere, cum simus Romani.

HOC Cæsar tibi (Roma) tuus dedit, armaque? solis
Romanis igitur non licet esse piis?

Ah! melius, tragicis nullus tibi Cæsar in armis
Altus anhelanti detonuisset equo;

Nec domini volucris facies horrenda per orbem
Sueta tibi in signis torva venire tuis:

Quam miser ut staret de te tibi (Roma) triumphus,
Ut tanta fieris ambitione nihil.

Non tibi, sed sceleri vincis: proh laurea tristis!
Laurea, Cerbereis aptior umbra comis!

Tam turpi vix ipse pater diademate Pluto,
Vix sedet ipse suo tam niger in soliis.

De tot Cæsareis redit hoc tibi (Roma) triumphis:
Cæsaree, aut (quod idem est) egregie misera es.

Matth. iv.

Hic lapis fiat panis.

ET fuit: ille lapis (quidni sit dicere?) panis,
Christe, fuit: panis sed tuus ille fuit.

Quippe, Patris cum sic tulerit suprema voluntas,
Est panis, panem non habuisse, tuus.

Ἄρτος ἔην τοι δητ᾽ (εἶπειν θεμις εστιν) ἐκεινος
Χριστε τοι ἀρτος ἔην καὶ λιθος· αλλα τεος.

Ἣη οὔτως των πατρις ὀμη μεγαλου το θελημα
Ἄρτος ὀτ οὐκ ην τοι, Χριστε, τοι ἄρτος ἔην.*

MATTH. XV.

Mulier Canaanitis.

QUICQUID Amazoniis dedit olim fama puellis,
Credite: Amazoniam cernimus ecce fidem.

Fœmina, tam fortis fidei? jam credo fidem esse
Plus quam grammatice fœminei generis.

LUC. XI.

Deus, post expulsum Dæmonem mutum, maledicis Judæis os obturat.

UNA pene opera duplicem tibi Dæmone frangis:
Iste quidem Dæmon mutus; at ille loquax.

Scilicet in laudes (quæ non tibi laurea surgit?)
Non magis hic loquitur, quam tacet ille tuas.

* Not in the edition of 1634.

Joan. vi.

Dicebant, Vere hic est propheta.

POST tot quæ videant, tot quæ miracula tangant,
  Hæc et quæ gustent (Christe) dabas populo.
Jam Vates, Rex, et quicquid pia nomina possunt,
  Christus erat: vellem dicere, venter erat.
Namque his, quicquid erat Christus, de ventre repleto
  Omne illud vero nomine venter erat.

Joan. x. 22.

Christus ambulabat in porticu Salomonis, et hiems erat.

BRUMA fuit? non, non; ah non fuit, ore sub isto:
  Si fuit; haud anni, nec sua bruma fuit.
Bruma tibi vernis velit ire decentior horis,
  Per sibi non natas expatiata rosas.
At, tibi ne possit se tam bene bruma negare,
  Sola hæc, quam vibrat gens tua, grando* vetat.

Matth. xxviii.

Dederunt nummos militibus.

NE miles velit ista loqui, tu munera donas?
  Donas, quod possit, cum tacet ipse, loqui.
Quæ facis a quoquam, pretio suadente, taceri;
  Clarius, et dici turpius ista facis.

* Ver. 31. Sustulerunt lapides.

Beatæ Virgini

De salutatione Angelica.

XAIPE suum neque Cæsareus jam nuntiet ales;
Χαῖρε tuum penna candidiore venit.

Sed taceat, qui Χαῖρε tuum quoque nuntiat, ales;
Χαῖρε meum penna candidiore venit.

Quis dicat mihi Χαῖρε meum mage candidus autor,
Quam tibi quæ dicat candidus ille tuum?

Virgo, rogas, quid candidius quam candidus ille
Esse potest? Virgo, quæ rogat, esse potest.

Χαῖρε tuum (Virgo) donet tibi candidus ille;
Donas candidior tu mihi Χαῖρε meum.

Χαῖρε meum de Χαῖρε tuo quid differat, audi:
Ille tuum dicit, tu paris (ecce) meum.

Pontio lavante.

NON satis est cædes, nisi stuprum hoc insuper addas,
Et tam virginea sis violator aquæ?

Nympha quidem pura hæc et honesti filia fontis
Luget, adulterio jam temerata tuo.

Casta verecundo properat cum murmure gutta,
Nec satis in lacrymam se putat esse suam.

Desine tam nitidos stuprare (ah, desine) rores:
Aut dic, quæ miseras unda lavabit aquas.

In die passionis Dominicæ.

TAMNE ego sim tetricus? valeant jejunia: vinum
Est mihi dulce meo (nec pudet esse) cado.

Est mihi quod castis, neque prelum passa, racemis
Palmite virgineo protulit uva parens.

Hoc mihi (ter decies sat enim maturuit annis)
Tandem ecce e dolio præbibit hasta suo.

Jamque it; et o quanto calet actus aromate torrens!
Acer ut hinc aura divite currit odor!

Quæ rosa per cyathos volitat tam vina Falernos?
Massica quæ tanto sidere vina tremunt?

O ego nescibam; atque ecce est Vinum illud amoris:
Unde ego sim tantis, unde ego par cyathis.

Vincor: et o istis totus prope misceor auris:
Non ego sum tantis, non ego par cyathis.

Sed quid ego invicti metuo bona robora vini?
Ecce est, quæ validum diluit,* unda, merum.

In die Resurrectionis Dominicæ.

Venit ad sepulchrum Magdalena ferens aromata.

QUIN et tu quoque busta tui Phœnicis adora;
Tu quoque fer tristes (mens mea) delitias.

* Joan. xix. 34. Et continuo exivit sanguis et aqua.

Si nec aromata sunt, nec quod tibi fragrat amomum ;
(Qualis Magdalina est messis odora manu)

Est quod aromatibus præstat, quod præstat amomo:
Hæc tibi mollicula, hæc gemmea lacrymula.

Et lacryma est aliquid: neque frustra Magdala flevit:
Sentiit hæc, lacrymas non nihil esse suas.

His illa (et tunc cum Domini caput iret amomo)
Invidiam capitis fecerat esse pedes.

Nunc quoque cum sinus huic tanto sub aromate sudet,
Plus capit ex oculis, quo litet, illa suis.

Christe, decent lacrymæ: decet isto rore rigari
Vitæ hoc æternum mane, tuumque diem.

Luc. xxiv.

In cicatrices Domini adhuc superstites.

ARMA vidis; arcus, pharetramque, levesque sagittas,
Et quocunque fuit nomine miles Amor.

His fuit usus Amor: sed et hæc fuit ipse; suumque
Et jaculum, et jaculis ipse pharetra suis.

Nunc splendent tantum, et deterso pulvere belli
E memori pendent nomina magna tholo.

Tempus erit tamen, hæc iræ quando arma, pharetramque,
Et sobolem pharetræ spicula tradet Amor.

Heu! qua tunc anima, quo stabit conscia vultu,
Quum scelus agnoscet dextera quæque suum?

Improbe, quæ dederis, cernes ibi vulnera, miles,
Qua tibicunque tuus luserit arte furor.

Seu digito suadente tuo mala Laurus inibat
Temporibus; sacrum seu bibit hasta latus:

Sive tuo clavi sævum rubuere sub ictu;
Seu puduit jussis ire flagella tuis.

Improbe, quæ dederis, cernes ibi vulnera, miles:
Quod dederis vulnus, cernere, vulnus erit.

Plaga sui vindex clavosque rependet et hastam:
Quoque rependet, erit clavus et hasta sibi.

Quis tam terribiles, tam justas moverit iras?
Vulnera pugnabunt (Christe) vel ipsa tibi.

JOAN. XIV.

Pacem meam do vobis.

BELLA vocant: arma (o socii) nostra arma paremus
Atque enses: nostros scilicet (ah!) jugulos.

Cur ego bella paro, cum Christus det mihi pacem?
Quod Christus pacem dat mihi, bella paro.

Ille dedit (nam quis potuit dare certior autor?)
Ille dedit pacem: sed dedit ille suam.

ACT. IX.

In D. Paulum illuminatum simul et excæcatum.

QUÆ, Christe, ambigua hæc bifidi tibi gloria teli est,
Quod simul huic oculos abstulit, atque dedit?

Sancta dies animi, hac oculorum in nocte, latebat;
Te ut possit Paulus cernere, cæcus erat.

JOAN. XV.

Ego sum Via. Ad Judæos spretores Christi.

OSED nec calcanda tamen: pes improbe pergis?
Improbe pes, ergo hoc cœli erat ire viam?

Ah pereat (Judæe ferox) pes improbus ille,
Qui cœli tritam sic facit esse viam.

MATTH. II.

In nocturnum et hiemale iter infantis Domini.

ERGO viatores teneros, cum Prole Parentem,
Nox habet hos, queis est digna nec ulla dies?

Nam quid ad hæc Pueri vel labra, genasve Parentis?
Heu quid ad hæc facient oscula, nox et hiems?

Lilia ad hæc facerent, faceret rosa; quicquid et halat
Æterna Zephyrus qui tepet in viola.

Hi meruere, quibus vel nox sit nulla; vel ulla
  Si sit, eat nostra purius illa die.

Ecce sed hos quoque nox et hiems clausere tenellos:
  Et quis scit, quid nox, quid meditetur hiems?

Ah ne quid meditetur hiems sævire per Austros!
  Quæque solet nigros nox mala ferre metus!

Ah ne noctis eat currus non mollibus Euris!
  Aspera ne tetricos nuntiet aura Notos!

Heu quot habent tenebræ, quot vera pericula secum!
  Quot noctem dominum, quantaque monstra colunt!

Quot vaga quæ falsis veniunt ludibria formis!
  Trux oculus! Stygio concolor ala Deo!

Seu veris ea, sive vagis stant monstra figuris;
  Virginei satis est hinc, satis inde metus.

Ergo veni; totoque veni resonantior arcu,
  (Cynthia) prægnantem clange procul pharetram.

Monstra vel ista, vel illa, tuis sint meta sagittis:
  Nec fratris jaculum certior aura vehat.

Ergo veni totoque veni, flagrantior ore,
  Dignaque Apollineas sustinuisse vices.

Scis bene quid deceat Phœbi lucere sororem:
  Ex his, si nescis, (Cynthia) disce genis.

O tua, in his, quanto lampas formosior iret!
  Nox suam, ab his, quanto malit habere diem!

Quantum ageret tacitos hæc luna modestior ignes!
  Atque verecundis sobria staret equis!

Luna, tuæ non est rosa tam pudibunda diei:
  Nec tam Virgineo fax tua flore tremit.

Ergo veni; sed et astra, tuas age (Cynthia) turmas:
  Illa oculos pueri, quos imitentur, habent.

Hinc oculo, hinc astro: at parili face nictat utrumque;
  Ætheris os, atque os æthereum Pueri.

Aspice, quam bene res utriusque deceret utrumque!
  Quam bene in alternas mutua regna manus!

Ille oculus cœli hoc si staret in æthere frontis;
  Sive astrum hoc pueri; fronte sub æetherea.

Si Pueri hoc astrum æetherea sub fronte micaret,
  Credat et hunc oculum non minus esse suum.

Ille oculus cœli, hoc si staret in æthere frontis,
  Non minus in cœlis se putet esse suis.

Tam pulchras variare vices cum fronte Puelli,
  Cumque Puelli oculis, æther et astra queant.

Astra quidem vellent; vellent æterna pacisci
  Fœdera mutatæ sedis inire vicem.

Æther et ipse (licet numero tam dispare) vellet
  Mutatis oculis tam bona pacta dari.

Quippe iret cœlum quanto melioribus astris,
  Astra sua hos oculos si modo habere queat!

Quippe astra in cœlo quantum meliore micarent,
  Si frontem hanc possint cœlum habuisse suum.

Æther et astra velint: frustra velit æther, et astra:
  Ecce negat Pueri frons, oculique negant.

Ah neget illa, negent illi: nam quem æthera mallent
  Isti oculi? aut frons hæc quæ magis astra velit?

Quid si aliquod blanda face lene renideat astrum?
  Lactea si cœli terque quaterque via est?

Blandior hic oculus, roseo hoc qui ridet in ore;
  Lactea frons hæc est terque quaterque magis.

Ergo negent, cœlumque suum sua sidera servent:
  Sidera de cœlis non bene danda suis.

Ergo negant: seque ecce sua sub nube recondunt,
  Sub tenera occidui nube supercilii:

Nec claudi contenta sui munimine cœli,
  Quærunt in gremio Matris ubi lateant.

Non nisi sic tactis ubi nix tepet illa pruinis,
  Castaque non gelido frigore vernat hiems.

Scilicet ista dies tam pulchro vespere tingi
  Dignus; et hos soles sic decet occidere.

Claudat purpureus qui claudit vesper Olympum;
  Puniceo placeas tu tibi (Phœbe) toro;

Dum tibi lascivam Thetis auget adultera noctem,
  Pone per Hesperias strata pudenda rosas.

Illas nempe rosas, quas conscia purpura pinxit;
Culpa pudorque suus queis dedit esse rosas.

Hos soles, niveæ noctes, castumque cubile,
Quod purum sternet per mare virgo Thetis;

Hos, sancti flores; hos, tam sincera decebant
Lilia; quæque sibi non rubuere rosæ.

Hos, decuit sinus hic; ubi toto sidere proni
Ecce lavant sese lacteo in oceano.

Atque lavent: tandemque suo se mane resolvant,
Ipsa dies ex hoc ut bibat ore diem.

JOAN. XVI. 26.

Non dico, me rogaturum Patrem pro vobis.

AH tamen Ipse roga: tibi scilicet ille roganti
Esse nequit durus, nec solet esse, Pater.

Ille suos omni facie te figit amores;
Inque tuos toto effunditur ore sinus.

Quippe, tuos spectans oculos, se spectat in illis;
Inque tuo (Jesu) se fovet ipse sinu.

Ex te metitur sese, et sua numina discit:
Inde repercussus redditur ipse sibi.

Ille tibi se, te ille sibi par nectit utrinque:
Tam tuus est, ut nec sit magis ille suus.

Ergo roga: Ipse roga: tibi scilicet ille roganti
Esse nequit durus, nec solet esse, Pater.

Illum ut ego rogitem? Hoc (eheu) non ore rogandum;
Ore satis puras non faciente preces.

Illum ego si rogitem, quis scit quibus ille procellis
Surgat, et in miserum hoc quæ tonet ira caput?

Isto etiam forsan veniet mihi fulmen ab ore:
(Sæpe isto certe fulmen ab ore venit.)

Ille una irati forsan me cuspide verbi,
Una me metu figet, et interii:

Non ego, non rogitem: mihi scilicet ille roganti
Durior esse potest, et solet esse, Pater.

Immo rogabo: nec ore meo tamen: immo rogabo
Ore meo (Jesu) scilicet ore tuo.

In die Ascensionis Dominicæ.

USQUE etiam nostros Te (Christe) tenemus amores?
Heu cœli quantam hinc invidiam patimur!

Invidiam patiamur: habent sua sidera cœli;
Quæque comunt tremulas crispa tot ora faces;

Phœbenque et Phœbum, et tot pictæ vellera nubis;
Vellera, quæ rosea Sol variavit acu.

Quantum erat, ut sinerent hac una nos face ferri?
Una sit hic: sunt (et sint) ibi mille faces.

Nil agimus: nam tu quia non ascendis ad illum,
  Æther* descendit (Christe) vel ipse tibi.†

Νυν ἔτι ἡμετερον σε, Χριστε, ἔχομεν τ᾽ ἔρωτα;
  Οὐρανου οὐν ὁσον τε φθονον ὡς ἐχομεν·

Αλλα ἐχομεν. ἐχει ἐα μεν τα δ᾽ ἀγαλματα αἴθης·
  Ἄστρατε, καὶ φοιβον, και καλα των νεφελων.

Ὅσσον ἔτην, ἡμιν ὄφρ᾽ εἴη ἐν τοδε ἄστρον;
  Ἄστρον ἐν ἡμιν ἡ· εἰσί τοι ἄστρ᾽ ἑκατον.

Παντα ματην. ὁτι Χριστε συ ουκ ἀναβαίνες, ες αὐτον,
  Αὐτος μεν κατεβη οὐρανος εις σε τεος.

Luc. xviii.

Cæcus implorat Christum.

IMPROBA turba tace. Mihi tam mea vota propinquant,
  Et linguam de me vis tacuisse meam?

Tunc ego tunc taceam, mihi cum meus ille loquetur:
  Si nescis, oculos vox habet ista meos.

O noctis miserere meæ, miserere; per illam
  In te quæ primo riserit ore, diem.

O noctis miserere meæ, miserere; per illam
  Quæ, nisi te videat, nox velit esse, diem.

O noctis miserere meæ, miserere; per illam
  In te quam fidei nox habet ipsa, diem.

* Act. I. Nubes susceptum eum abstulit.

† Here the edition of 1634 ends. The Greek Version of this Epigram and all that follow are printed for the first time in that of 1670.

Hæc animi tam clara dies rogat illam oculorum :
  Illam, oro, dederis ; hanc mihi ne rapias.

Νυκτ' ἐλεησον ἐμην. ἐλεησον. ναι τοι ἐκεινο
  Χριστε ἐμου ἡμαρ, νυξ ὀδ' ἐμειο ἐχει.

Οφθαλμων μεν ἐκεινο, Θεος, δεεται τοδε γνωμης.
  Μη μοι τουτ' αἴρης, δος μοι ἐκεινο φαος.

Luc. xv. 4.

Quis ex vobis si habeat centum oves, et perdiderit unam ex illis, &c.

O UT ego angelicis fiam bona gaudia turmis !
  Me quoque solicito quære per arva gradu.

Mille tibi tutis ludunt in montibus agni,
  Quos potes haud dubia dicere voce tuos.

Unus ego erravi quo me meus error agebat,
  Unus ego fuerim gaudia plura tibi.

Gaudia non faciunt, quæ nec fecere timorem ;
  Et plus quæ donant ipsa peric'la, placent.

Horum, quos retines, fuerit tibi latior usus.
  De me, quem recipis, dulcior usus erit.

Εἷς μεν ἐγω, ἥ μου πλανη παρηγεν, ἄλημι·
  Εἷς δε τοι σως ἐσομαὶ γηθοσεναι πλεονες.

'Αμνος ὁ μη ποίων φοβον, οὐ ποιει δε τε χαρμα.
  Μειζων των μεν, ἐμου χρεια δε γλυκυ τερη.

Herodi D. Jacobum obtruncanti.

NESCIS Jacobus quantum hunc tibi debeat ictum,
Quæque tua in sacrum sæviit ira caput.

Scilicet ipso illi donasti hoc ense coronam,
Quo sacrum absciderás scilicet ense caput.

Abscissum pensare caput quæ possit abunde,
Sola hæc tam sæva et sacra corona fuit.

Ἓν μεν, Ιακωβε, κεφαλην τοι ξιφος ἀπηρεν,
Ἓν τοδε και στεφανον ξιφος ἐδωκε τεον.

Μουνον ἀμειβεσθαί κεφαλην, Ιακωβε, δυναίτο
Κείνος ὁδ' ὡς καλος, μαρτυριου στεφανος.

MATTH. XX. 34.

Cæci receptis oculis Christum sequuntur.

ECCE manu imposita Christus nova sidera ponit.
Sectantur patriam sidera fide manum.

Hæc manus his, credo, cœlum est. Hæc scilicet astra
Suspicor esse olim quæ geret ille manu.*

Χειρ ἐπίβαλλομενη Χριστου επίβαλλεν ὀπωπῶν
Ἄστρα. ὀπηδευει κεινα γε χειρὶ Θεου.

Χειρ αὐτη τουτοις πελεν ουρανος. αστρα γαρ οἶμαι,
Ἓν χερὶ ταυτ' οἴσει Χριστος ἐπείτα ἐη.

* Rev. I. 16.

Luc. xix. 4.

Zachæus in sycomoro.

QUID te, quid jactas alienis fructibus, arbor?
Quid tibi cum foliis non (sycomore) tuis?

Quippe istic ramo qui jam tibi nutat ab alto,
Mox e divina vite racemus erit.

Τι ππ᾽ ἐπικομπαζεις κενεον; ξεινω δε τε καρπω,
Και φυλλοις σεμνη μη, συκομωρε, τεοις;

Καί γαρ ὀδ᾽ ἐκκρημνης σου νυν μετεωρος ἀπ᾽ ἔρνους,
᾽Αμπελου ὁ κλαδων ἔσσεται οὐρανίου.

FINIS.

CHISWICK PRESS:—C. WHITTINGHAM, TOOKS COURT,
CHANCERY LANE.

Ingram Content Group UK Ltd.
Milton Keynes UK
UKHW020816120323
418334UK00004BA/233

9 780341 780908